Voice of Empathy:

A History of Franciscan Media in the United States

Voice of Empathy:
A History of Franciscan Media in the United States

Raymond Haberski Jr.

Academy of American Franciscan History
Oceanside, California
2018

Library of Congress Cataloging-in-Publication Data

Names: Haberski, Raymond J., 1968– author.
Title: Voice of empathy : a history of Franciscan media in the United States / Raymond Haberski Jr.
Description: Oceanside : Academy of American Franciscan History, 2018. | Series: United States Franciscan History Project
Identifiers: LCCN 2017055471| ISBN 0883822660 (hardcover : alk. paper) | ISBN 0883822652 (pbk.)
Subjects: LCSH: Franciscans--Missions. | Franciscans—United States—History. | Franciscan Media (Organization)—History. | Catholic Church—Publishing—United States. | Catholic literature—Publishing—United States—History.
Classification: LCC BV2280 .H1555 2018 | DDC 261.5/250882713073—dc23
LC record available at https://lccn.loc.gov/2017055471

FOR MY MOTHER

A woman born into the Catholic Church
whose enduring example of empathy
reflects the spirit and hope of St. Francis.

Preface

Franciscans have long been part of the American experience arriving with the earliest explorers in the so-called New World in the late fifteenth century. They played an integral role in the development of colonial Latin America, and much has been written about them; less has been written about Franciscans in the nineteenth and twentieth centuries in the United States. Our new series, the *United States Franciscan History Project*, seeks to address this lacuna. The Franciscan family is a diverse one including but not limited to Friars Minor, Capuchins, Conventuals, Third Order Regular, Poor Clares, Franciscan orders of women religious, and Secular Franciscans. Each group has played a role in the unfolding story of the Franciscans in the United States.

Our second volume by Raymond Haberski, *Voice of Empathy: A History of Franciscan Media in the United States*, examines the development and impact of Franciscan media on the United States. Franciscan print media emerged in the late nineteenth century to assist and promote the Third Order or Secular Franciscans. These early efforts soon developed into magazines of general interest such as the *St. Anthonys Messenger* and the *Franciscan Herald and Forum*, which addressed the needs and concerns of ordinary Catholics. Haberski argues that Franciscan media offered a "voice of empathy" to the many laymen and women trying to navigate a complex world and remain true to their faith in the midst of the "messiness" of life. Women particularly made use of this media. Franciscan media engaged the larger culture as well publishing a diversity of magazines that addressed social, spiritual, educational, and ecclesial issues with viewpoints ranging from conservative to liberal. As the media world developed, so did Franciscan media, delving into the world of radio and television, producing award winning shows such as *The Hour of St. Francis*. Throughout its history, Franciscan media reflected and attempted to fashion the U.S. culture of which it was a part, articulating the transformative vision of St. Francis of Assisi for the modern world, and embodying for many U.S. Catholics a much-needed "voice of empathy."

Our series will explore other elements of Franciscan life in the United States as well: Franciscan parish life, U.S. Franciscan missions to China and Latin America, Franciscan education, and Franciscan charity and social justice. Our hope is to make this little-known history accessible to scholars and students and to integrate the history of Franciscans in the United States into the larger narrative of U.S. history.

—Jeffrey M. Burns
Director, Academy of American Franciscan History

Table of Contents

Introduction

In August 1959 near the apex of America's midcentury media boom, representatives of American Franciscan provinces met to assess the promise and problems with their media. The venue for the meeting was the Franciscan Educational Conference, held at St. Leonard Friary and seminary, a modernist structure outside of Dayton, Ohio. At this annual conference, intellectual leaders from different Franciscan communities in the United States gathered to discuss themes, such as "The Mind of Modern Man" (1958), "Nature: The Mirror of God" (1955), "The Youth Movement" (1938), and "Franciscan Education" (1929). Over the course of a weekend in 1959, American Franciscan leaders mulled over the topic "Communication and the Franciscan Message" or, how print and electronic media related to the American Franciscan experience. Father Brendan Mitchell, OFM, one of the first editors of the San Francisco-based magazine *The Way of St. Francis*, opened the conference by speaking directly to the power of media to reach Americans. When "we center our attention on that revolutionary process for transmitting information," he said, we need "to ask ourselves some questions about getting the Message of St. Francis through to the reading, listening, viewing public."[1] Mitchell offered a statistical snapshot of that public, noting that *St. Anthony Messenger* was the largest-circulation Franciscan magazine of the time, with a little over three hundred thousand subscribers, and estimated that the total readership of Franciscan periodicals numbered around 4 million (out of 35 million Catholics and 176 million Americans). Even though Franciscan provinces focused primarily on publications, Mitchell pointed out that the single greatest exponent of the Franciscan media was undoubtedly *The Hour of St. Francis*—the radio show produced in Los Angeles and broadcast to hundreds of stations across the country and overseas. And this was not the only radio show produced by Franciscans; on the opposite coast the friars of Graymoor produced *The Ave Maria Hour* in New York City.

The topic of media had particular urgency given that Pope Pius XII's encyclical letter *Miranda Prorsus* on motion pictures, radio, and television

---

1. Brendan Mitchell, "Franciscan Goals in Communications," in *Communications and the Franciscan Message: Reports of the Fortieth and Forty-First Annual Meeting of the Franciscan Educational Conference*, Washington, DC, 1959, 2, 3.

1

had been promulgated two years earlier, in 1957.[2] *Miranda Prorsus* was the second key Vatican statement on mass media. Twenty-one years earlier, Pope Pius XI's 1936 papal letter on movies, *Vigilanti Cura*, had alerted the Catholic faithful to the dangers of motion pictures and the need to support the censorial work of the Legion of Decency.[3] The Legion of Decency was a church-sponsored organization that rated movies and rallied popular distrust of Hollywood. By 1957, things had changed. Although the Legion of Decency still existed, its effectiveness had waned, as both Catholics and the motion picture industry increasingly disregarded the threats and power plays made by Catholic officials to boycott movies the Legion did not like.[4] Furthermore, the Vatican had moved away from a confrontational posture and toward one of leveraging the power of media.[5]

In *Miranda Prorsus* Pope Pius XII sought to encourage Church engagement with media because, he noted, the power of electronic communication held great promise as well as great peril: "These new possessions and new instruments which are within almost everyone's grasp, introduce a most powerful influence into men's minds, both because they can flood them with light, raise them to nobility, adorn them with beauty, and because they can disfigure them by dimming their lustre, dishonour them by a process of corruption, and make them subject to uncontrolled passions, according as the subjects presented to the senses in these shows are praiseworthy or reprehensible." This encyclical shifted the Church's emphasis from attacking mass media (especially motion pictures) to making it more amenable to Catholic teaching.[6]

In keeping with the spirit of the Pope's message, Mitchell asked the Franciscans gathered at the 1959 conference to make a frank assessment of their

2. Pope Pius XII, *Miranda prorsus* (Encyclical on motion pictures, radio, and television), September 8, 1957, accessed July 10, 2017, http://www.vatican.va/holy_father/pius_xii/encyclicals/documents/hf_p-xii_enc_08091957_miranda-prorsus_en.html.

3. Pope Pius XI, *Vigilanti cura* (Papal Letter on the motion picture), June 29, 1936, accessed July 10, 2017, http://w2.vatican.va/content/pius-xi/en/encyclicals/documents/hf_p-xi_enc_29061936_vigilanti-cura.html.

4. For the evolution of Catholic engagement in controlling movies and literature, see Frank Walsh, *Sin and Censorship: The Catholic Church and the Motion Picture Industry* (New Haven, CT: Yale University Press, 1996); Gregory D. Black, *The Catholic Crusade Against the Movies, 1940–1975* (Cambridge, UK: Cambridge University Press, 1997); Raymond J. Haberski Jr., *Freedom to Offend: How New York Remade Movie Culture* (Lexington: University Press of Kentucky, 2007); Laura Wittern-Keller and Raymond J. Haberski Jr., *The Miracle Case: Film Censorship and the Supreme Court* (Lawrence: University of Kansas Press, 2008); Una Cadegan, *All Good Books Are Catholic Books: Print Culture, Censorship, and Modernity in Twentieth Century America* (Ithaca, NY: Cornell University Press, 2013).

5. The literature on the American Catholic Church and motion pictures is extensive, but perhaps the best single volume on this relationship is Walsh, *Sin and Censorship*, especially 287–90.

6. Pope Pius XII, *Miranda prorsus*.

media, primarily print. And while poor circulation and weak financing plagued all Franciscan publishing, the key problem, according to Mitchell, was the message not the medium. "The content frequently lacks a challenge," he argued, "and too rarely comes to grips with real problems in a real world. . . . It discusses the issues of current materialism and secularism, for instance, on a theoretical level, but not often enough in the terms which the lay reader recognizes and with which he identifies himself. It attacks pornography and salacious books, but not bad art and incompetent literature. It addresses contemporary man as if he were either a saint, a woman [an incredibly gendered reference to core readership], or a dweller in some secluded religious community."[7] Mitchell added that an issue related to both content and circulation was the proliferation of Franciscan publications that operated like house organs and ended up either preaching to ever smaller segments of an already small reading public or putting each other out of business through competition. "Is it *Cicero pro domo* [that is, focused inward, toward home], or *Cicero pro republica* [that is, focused outward, toward America]?" he asked. In other words, "Are we to communicate to ourselves (and a house organ has this legitimate purpose) or are we to communicate the Franciscan Message to America?" The Franciscan periodical had functioned in the first half of the twentieth century as a device to raise money, raise awareness, and lift spirits among a fairly discrete group of readers. The next half of the century, Mitchell suggested, needed to address a mainstream audience that had been largely overlooked.[8]

To emphasize his point, Mitchell included comments from a small sample of readers who said Franciscan periodicals were "too preachy," "prissy," and "Mickey Mouse"—"their people are so perfect we are unable to identify ourselves with them." And to continue the gendered nature of such criticism, Mitchell noted that a reader disliked Franciscan periodicals because there was "not enough interest for men."[9] That observation provided interesting insight into the dynamics of Franciscan media culture. *St. Anthony Messenger* was a key example because of its large circulation and aspirations to be a general-interest magazine. It became significant because it appealed to women—the group most likely to read religious periodicals in general, as well as the group that had traditionally been the most devoted to the institutional Catholic Church. However, the perception of media prestige followed the argument that Catholic magazines should seek to shape opinion rather than appeal to the cultural and, frankly, spiritual aspects of Catholic life. It was a position that created a false dichotomy: evangelization of the heart against appeals to the mind.

---

7. Mitchell, "Franciscan Goals in Communications," 8.
8. Ibid., 6–7.
9. Ibid., 8.

Mitchell quoted James Arnold, who in 1959 was a young media scholar at Marquette University, regarding the potential power of religious media in the hands of other denominations. Arnold had written a review of a book on the history of the *Christian Science Monitor*, a newspaper with a circulation of 178,000—far below the massive combined circulation of many Catholic periodicals. Arnold used his review to point out that despite the circulation of Catholic periodicals, they had "not a shred of the *Monitor's* prestige." He pointedly observed that "while the *Monitor* has been a potent factor in reforming the American press and reaching opinion leaders throughout the world, Catholic newspapers have been busy chronicling church anniversaries and bazaars, sermons and football victories, and the comings and goings of smutty literature."[10] Reflecting on what he saw as Arnold's point, Mitchell argued that the alternative to typical Catholic messaging was "fruitful commentary on the spiritual values and moral problems of our culture."[11]

Mitchell's speech to his Franciscan brethren echoed a broader challenge to Catholic intellectual life offered by John Tracy Ellis in 1955. In his essay "American Catholics and the Intellectual Life," Ellis argued that although the Catholic Church and its faithful invested a great deal of money and effort educating its people—in schools and universities and through magazines and books—this system had not produced many intellectual leaders. Ellis suggested this lack of intellectual output was due to a general Catholic resistance toward engaging new trends in science, philosophy, and the arts, as well as an avoidance of self-criticism.[12] Historian Patrick Allitt notes that Ellis's essay constituted one star in a constellation of critiques that appeared in the 1950s as Catholics addressed "a new role for the laity, the rise of a self-conscious liberal Catholicism, and the emergence of a small, yet visible Catholic counterculture" (such as Thomas Merton and Dorothy Day).[13] In short, Franciscan media, like Catholic intellectual life in general, had much ground to cover.

Thus, Mitchell urged his colleagues to improve Franciscan media by developing professional standards across print and electronic communications. That meant creative and determined editors and well-trained and technologically savvy writers and producers. For a group of people whose mission had little to do with timely advances in mass media, the need to advance a religious message in an era drenched in advertising and political jockeying posed a very serious challenge. Mitchell addressed that apparent incongruence by ending

---

10. James Arnold, quoted in ibid.

11. Mitchell, "Franciscan Goals in Communications," 9.

12. John Tracy Ellis, "American Catholics and the Intellectual Life," *Thought* 30 (1955): 351-88.

13. Patrick Allitt, *Catholic Intellectuals and Conservative Politics in America, 1950–1985* (Ithaca, NY: Cornell University Press, 1993), 41.

his talk with a list of points for all communicators to rally around. First, he said, Franciscans had to avoid sounding "stuffy"; rather Franciscan media should relate to and respond to the "man in the street." Second, all media had to recognize and address the situations and dignity of all people: "He talks *to* every man and never *down* to anyone" (emphasis original). Third, inspired by Francis's demonstration of charity, Franciscans needed to avoid peddling controversy for its own sake. Finally, the message needed to avoid the kind of moralizing that covers up real problems with idealistic solutions; rather Mitchell called Franciscan media to offer revelation, to bring readers into the discovery of solutions.[14]

In another talk at the same conference in 1959, Father Victor Drees, OFM, an assistant editor at *St. Anthony Messenger*, made a similar point: that readers of Franciscan periodicals would have little interest in dense doctrinal discussions or even in extensive coverage of Third Order and lay Franciscan activities. He observed: "The great bulk of the readers have not completed high school . . . one-third of these readers have never attended a Catholic school and . . . over half have never attended a Catholic high school." Drees thought it better to stick to basic religious education and photographs.[15]

Mitchell offered one final suggestion to his counterparts: "Is it possible to pool manpower, money and outlets, now often pointlessly competitive, in order by a kind of national strategy to produce a Franciscan battery of communications powerful enough to be heard and competent enough to command attention?"[16] While Mitchell undoubtedly had the financial health of Franciscan media in mind, he also overlooked, it seems to me, a core mission of why Franciscans communicated with their public—to provide a voice of empathy. Although such a purpose might not sound distinguished on a masthead, it certainly captured the sensibility projected by editors, writers, and producers of Franciscan media throughout the first half of the twentieth century. Indeed, a signature of Franciscan media was a tension between writing with intellectual authority and encouraging an emotional connection to media that entered the houses of millions of Catholic Americans.

What made Franciscan media interesting was its lack of coherence: it had elements that were confessional and exploratory, traditional and modern, and apparently quite ordinary even if at times controversial. Thus, if one theme runs through this media from the late nineteenth century to the twenty-first, it is the way Franciscans communicated with their audiences through print, radio, and television engaging how Catholics lived their faith in all of its messi-

---

14. Ibid., 13–14.
15. Father Victor J. Drees, OFM, "Franciscan Magazines," in *Communications and the Franciscan Message*, 36–38.
16. Mitchell, "Franciscan Goals in Communications," 15.

ness. Franciscans chose, quite consciously, to use their media to evangelize to the heart; to prize empathy above all other virtues for their mission. Although Franciscan media certainly contained intellectual arguments (often echoing what could be found in other places) and appealed to Church doctrine, Franciscans attempted to influence their audience by meeting them where and how they lived.[17]

A key theme that emerged in Franciscan media was an emphasis on listening rather than judging. Catholics who wrote letters to their Franciscan interlocutors in magazines, for example, confessed to the difficulties of living as a Catholic but were rarely judged harshly for failing. After all, what seemed sinful to one generation of Catholic Americans hardly raised an eyebrow twenty years later. Moreover, as historian Leslie Woodcock Tentler notes, Catholics often felt limited by the options available to them for unloading their troubles. "The sacrament of penance had typically been experienced as burdensome—a necessary dose of spiritual medicine, but medicine all the same."[18] Franciscan media provided an alternative place to discuss issues that Catholics raised with their confessors. But rather than castigate the faithful, magazines offered guidance through exchanges of letters and essays on topics relevant most often to women, the group most burdened by church dictates as well as the primary audience for Franciscan media.

Voice of Empathy uses the history of communicating Franciscan messages through print, radio, and television to investigate how Franciscans helped Americans negotiate their lives. This approach in turn offers a glimpse of Catholic culture as seen through such media. Thus I have tried at once to let trends visible in Franciscan media guide my understanding of this particular culture, while also being sensitive to the cultures of the American Church and the nation that influenced Franciscan media. Moreover, taking a cue from religious scholar Robert Orsi, I study how Catholic magazines show us an "everyday literary culture of American Catholicism"[19]; in this case, a Franciscan culture in the United States.

Much of what was published in Catholic magazines throughout the twentieth century targeted women and dealt with the realm of life over which editors and publishers assumed that women held sway: the family. While the story

17. For more on changes to the lived experience of Catholic confessionals, see James M. O'Toole, "In the Court of Conscience: American Catholics and Confession, 1900–1975," in *Habits of Devotion: Catholic Religious Practice in Twentieth-Century America*, ed. James M. O'Toole (Ithaca, NY: Cornell University Press, 2004), 147–49.

18. Leslie Woodcock Tentler, "Souls and Bodies: The Birth Control Controversy and the Collapse of Confession," in *Crisis of Authority in Catholic Modernity*, eds. Michael J. Lacey and Francis Oakley (New York: Oxford University Press, 2011), 308.

19. Robert A. Orsi, *Thank You, St. Jude: Women's Devotion to the Patron Saint of Hopeless Causes* (New Haven, CT: Yale University Press, 1996), xvi.

of twentieth-century Catholic culture is not simply one about the changing dynamics of Catholic women, women subscribed to, read, wrote to, and eventually wrote for Catholic magazines. And because women could not claim roles in Church authority, the presence of women in Catholic literary culture sheds light on the changes in a broader Catholic culture.

In his fascinating portrait of Catholic women and their devotion to St. Jude, the patron saint of lost causes, Orsi reconstructs a culture of letter writing, devotionals, and experiences that women forged to manage everything from their romantic relationships to the economic hardship of the Great Depression. A key source for such insight was the letters written to magazines and to the national shrine to St. Jude on the south side of Chicago. The vast majority of such letters were from women. Orsi concludes that the letters reveal a great deal about the lives of the writers: "Anger and disappointment with Jude finds expression; deeply felt needs are voiced; the full range of devotional practices are described . . . and many ways in which women thought of Jude are apparent."[20]

One way to consider the significance of Franciscan media is to trace how Catholic women received guidance through Franciscan media. They read articles and essays from women writers in the *Franciscan Message* who pushed readers—who were also mostly women—to ruminate on issues from marriage and children to civil rights and poverty. Journals of a more conservative persuasion, such as *The Lamp*, also ran sections that responded to readers' questions. Much like such letter sections in *St. Anthony Messenger*, many of these inquiries came from women and discussed children and marriage. When Franciscans produced radio programs and shows for televion, these outlets too echoed the messiness of lived Catholicism. Again, most consumers of such programs were women, thus perhaps it was fitting that one of the most prolific writers for the popular radio program *The Hour of St. Francis* was Juanita Vaughn.

Through the latter part of the twentieth century and into the new century, Franciscan media moved toward evangelizing across electronic platforms—from radio, to television, to the Internet. Two Franciscans in particular have enjoyed unusual success with these media: Mother Angelica of the Annunciation, PCPA and Father Richard Rohr, OFM. Although they were far apart ideologically, both offered guidance in eras defined by the shift toward a lay-oriented Catholicism, and both were products of and helped shape the confessional culture that still permeates the United States. Founded in 1981 and broadcast from Our Lady of Angels Monastery in Irondale, Alabama, Mother Angelica's Eternal Word Television Network (EWTN) reportedly reaches millions of households the world over.[21] While the programming

---

20. Orsi, *Thank You, St. Jude*, xii–xiii.
21. Adam Bernstein, "EWTN to launch daily news program with 'Catholic Perspective' in D.C." *Washington Post*, June 2, 2013, accessed on August 12, 2017, https://

varies—as it must, to fill so much airtime—Mother Angelica once anchored a twice-weekly, hour-long call-in show that attracted thousands of viewers. Though exchanges with her studio audience and callers often gave Mother Angelica occasion for humor and yet another pronouncement about Mary, they also resembled those found in the Franciscan journals. She spoke directly with and to the people devoted to her guidance. Meanwhile, Rohr has focused on discussing men's spirituality and making apparent how personal morality has significance only if aligned with those most marginalized in society—just the kind of material often taken up by more liberal Franciscan media before Vatican II, especially in *The Hour of St. Francis.* Importantly, both Mother Angelica and Rohr have websites that pull in, organize, and assist their audiences in ways that extend the kind of immediacy and intimacy that are the hallmarks of Franciscan media.

This study of Franciscan media confirms Orsi's view that magazines and other media thrived as significant outlets "in which modern American Catholics not only discovered who they were but constituted themselves as well, and where voices of alarm and authority sought to direct, educate, and discipline the tastes and hopes of new generations of Catholic men and women."[22] Exploring the various media published by Franciscans allows us to glimpse public exchanges about moral issues that are both private and, in the case of the Church, institutional. Franciscan media existed at a cultural-intellectual axis, where, as media scholar Stewart Hoover argues, "We must stand with viewers and audiences and look back with them at the media sphere through their practices or reception, meaning construction, and exchange."[23] What follows in the rest of this book, then, are discussions of how Franciscan media engaged, challenged, and, at times, enabled a deeper understanding of being Catholic in America—serving the faithful as a voice of empathy.

---

www.washingtonpost.com/lifestyle/style/ewtn-to-launch-daily-news-program-with-catholic-perspective-in-dc/2013/06/02/45939b66-bf09-11e2-97d4-a479289a31f9_story.html?utm_term=.9f289eb02ea2.

22. Ibid., xvii.

23. Stewart M. Hoover, "The Culturalist Turn in Scholarship on Media and Religion," *Journal of Media and Religion* 1, no. 1 (2002): 29, 30.

Chapter 1:
Franciscan Media, American Modernity, and Catholic Identity

BEING AMERICAN *AND* CATHOLIC: FRANCISCAN MAGAZINES AND THE THIRD ORDER

The Franciscans began publishing periodicals, magazines, books, and booklets in the United States in the late nineteenth century to communicate the Church's position on a myriad of issues shaping American life. Under this intellectual and, in most cases, doctrinal umbrella, Franciscans sought to coummunicate directly with the laity: to speak to members of the Third Order (or tertiaries), to profile the missionary work of friars for the benefit of Catholic communities that supported them, and to raise money.[1] Among the most representative Franciscan publications of this period were the *St. Anthony Messenger* and the *Franciscan Herald*. Both started out as small magazines for communities around Cincinnati and Chicago, respectively, but grew relatively quickly into larger regional and even national periodicals. Both distinguished themselves by evolving over time into publications that showcased a signature Franciscan characteristic—a strong association with readers. And both magazines enjoyed success throughout the twentieth century, though only the *St. Anthony Messenger* survived past the 1970s. While both magazines appear later in this book as part of a discussion of general interest magaizines, their early years illustrate how Franciscan media counseled their audiences on balancing life as a Catholic and as an American.

The origins of *St. Anthony Messenger* lay in 1876 when the Franciscan community based at the St. Francis Friary in the Over-the-Rhine district of

---

1. Father Jack Clark Robinson explains that the Third Order of Franciscans, or Tertiaries, consists of "both men and women who have been inspired to live a spiritual and devotional life inspired by St. Francis of Assisi, while they continue to maintain their ties to 'the age' in which they live by holding down jobs, staying in their own homes, often also marrying and raising families." By 1921 an estimated seventy-five thousand Tertiaries who lived in the United States had created local fraternal organizations as well as groups of men or, as Robinson observes, "more often single and widowed women, who would live together for mutual support or to run hospitals, orphanages, and schools": Jack Clark Robinson, "Structural History of the Franciscan Family in the United States, 1840–2000" (unpublished manuscript, 2013), 65.

Cincinnati, Ohio, began publishing a German-language monthly called *Der Sendbote* (*The Messenger*). In 1892 the Cincinnati Franciscans introduced another journal, the *St. Franciscus Bote* (*St. Francis Messenger*) that morphed a year later into the English-language *St. Anthony's Messenger*. The latter two "messengers" came from the work of one priest, Father Ambrose Sanning, OFM. Sanning was the rector of the seminary of Cincinnati's St. Francis Friary who founded the *St. Anthony's Messenger* in 1893 (the name would be changed to *St. Anthony Messenger* in 1917) as "a messenger of love and a herald of peace."[2] The original magazine served as an important ministry of the friars of St. John the Baptist Province of Cincinnati, an independent American province born from the work of the Tyrolese friars who in 1844 migrated from their native Austria to the Ohio River valley to serve the growing Catholic population in the US Midwest. *St. Anthony's Messenger* went out to members of the Third Order of St. Francis and helped in the work of the Holy Family Association, founded in 1892 by Pope Leo XIII to promote the organization of Catholic families in parishes throughout the world. But the magazine was also a product of its region and era. The early history of *St. Anthony's Messenger* reflected the tensions between Catholics and their America.

The first issue appeared in June 1893, in the middle of one the most tumultuous periods in the United States' industrial age, and within a Midwestern city that included large immigrant communities of workers. According to Father Norman Perry, OFM, a distant successor to Sanning as editor of *St. Anthony Messenger*, the original intention behind the magazine was to serve as a touchstone for the families who spoke both German (their native language) and English and who were in the middle of the roiling labor disputes of the period. As "city life brought its own threats and difficulties for family life," Perry explained, Sanning and his fellow Franciscans sought to promote the ideals of the tertiaries and the Holy Family Association to fortify their congregants.[3] Cincinnati historian and lay Franciscan Daniel Hurley, in an essay for the hundredth anniversary of *St. Anthony Messenger*, writes that the transition from earlier non–English-language publications in the 1870s to English-language magazines such as *St. Anthony Messenger* marked a transition in American Catholicism. Catholic communities were encouraged to participate in the building of their American towns and cities as well as to worship in churches watched over by Rome. Pope Leo XIII's landmark papal encyclical *Rerum novarum* in 1891 was inspired by this period of industrial

---

2. Father Norman Perry, "You've Come a Long Way St. Anthony Messenger" (essay for the hundredth anniversary of *St. Anthony Messenger*, 1985), St. Anthony Messenger Press archives, Cincinnati, OH.

3. Father Norman Perry, "100 Years of Reading Signs of the Times," *St. Anthony Messenger* 100 (June 1992): 50.

development in the western world and called for Catholic engagement with social issues by reiterating a concern for the poor who were the victims of industrialism. However, a central aspect of the encyclical was a strong defense of private property and an equally strong condemnation of socialism.[4] *St. Anthony's Messenger* reached out to immigrant communities, commenting on the plight and future of the working class, but stopped well short of advocating for anything that hinted at socialism.

The first issue of the magazine also included an enduring template: the cover was a brown woodcut of St. Anthony, and the contents included a poem, a monthly saint, articles and information for and about Franciscans, and thanksgivings, intentions, and a calendar of events.[5] That basic format and design characterized most issues through the 1920s. The core vision was also made clear in this first issue, as Hurley observes: "The central concern was . . . shedding the light of faith on 'the social question . . . the situation of the laboring class' posed by the emerging industrial society." Hurley notes that since most readers at the time earned wages as part of this industrial economy, the friars sought to offer religious guidance for working men. Industrial violence gripped America in the latter half of the nineteenth century, as protests from workers and their unions were met with guns, clubs, and even death at the direction of corporate and government leaders. As an alternative to public fear sparked by violent confrontations such as the Great Railroad Strike of 1877, the riot in Haymarket Square in 1886, and the Homestead Strike in 1892, Sanning told readers that the magazine "brandishes neither sword nor pistol like a Communist or Anarchist, for [it] has nothing in common with the use or rather abuse of bomb and dynamite. The *St. Anthony's Messenger*, advocates not revolution, slaughter or pillage. He is conservative, he announces and brings heaven's best boon—peace."[6]

According to Hurley the magazine consciously adopted an editorial policy that opposed radical politics and served as a mild-mannered check on capitalist excesses. In doing so *St. Anthony's Messenger* stayed within the mainstream of American Catholicism which, Hurley writes, "rejected the view of modern society shared by both 'de-Christianized capitalists' and atheistic socialists—

---

4. Pope Leo XIII, *Rerum novarum* (Encyclical on capital and labor), May 15, 1891, accessed July 15, 2017, http://w2.vatican.va/content/leo-xiii/en/encyclicals/documents/hf_l-xiii_enc_15051891_rerum-novarum.html. See also Michael P. Hornsby-Smith, *An Introduction to Catholic Social Thought* (Cambridge, UK: Cambridge University Press, 2006), 184.

5. Daniel Hurley, "St. Anthony Messenger: 100 Years of Good News," *St. Anthony Messenger* 100 (June 1992): 12.

6. Father Ambrose Sanning, quoted in ibid. For Catholic fear of violence, see the published edition of the 1952 dissertation of James E. Roohan, *American Catholics and the Social Question, 1865–1900* (New York: Arno Press, 1976).

that people are driven primarily by economic concerns, that social classes are a necessary part of modern society, and that class conflict is inevitable."[7] The labor movement's preoccupation with the well-being of those struggling to survive clearly resonated with Franciscan concerns about the poor. Moreover, as Hurley points out, "through the Third Order, the followers of Francis and Anthony also offered an organizational structure to implement meaningful reforms. *St. Anthony Messenger* frequently reminded readers that Pope Leo XIII himself regularly recommended the Third Order as an international counterweight to both Communism and Freemasonry."[8]

Around the same time, the *Franciscan Herald* emerged as an important Franciscan outlet for information on and for the Third Order. It began, though, as a small magazine known as the *Messenger of the Holy Childhood Church and School*, published by a Church-run boarding school for Native Americans in Harbor Springs, Michigan, by the Franciscan Fathers of the Holy Name Province in New York from 1895 to 1912 (the school itself remained open until 1983). By 1910 the magazine covered topics such as the International Eucharistic Congress of Montreal and what the editors viewed as political battles over the role of religion in public life. For example, one editoral entitled "How Europe Is Fighting Irreligion,"[9] warned readers of changes seen in France, including the removing of religious symbols, laws lifting the ban on working on Sundays, and the promotion of purely civil marriages.[10] The editors wrote that such moves proved "that modernism and the all-around attack on the Church and her domain" was "an evil crusade against all manner and form and principle of religion."[11] In another essay in the same issue, the editors pointed to a "Danger for Our Nation," which they explained, was the absence of religion from education—"an infidel school," they argued, "means infidel scholars; infidel scholars mean an infidel people." Interestingly, even though American Catholics had fought with their Protestant neighbors over the kind of religion taught to schoolchildren, on the issue of secularization, Catholic editors at the *Messenger of the Holy Childhood Church and School* had found an issue on which to ally.[12] The editors observed, "Scarcely a day passes but we hear earnest Protestants both clergy and laity,

7. Hurley, "St. Anthony Messenger," 14.

8. Ibid., 12.

9. "How Europe Is Fighting Irreligion," *Messenger of the Holy Childhood Church and School* 14 (January 19010): 245.

10. Brian Sudlow, *Catholic Literature and Secularisation in France and England, 1880–1914* (Manchester: Manchester University Press, 2011), 45–47.

11. "How Europe Is Fighting Irreligion," *Messenger of the Holy Childhood Church and School* 14 (January 1910): 245

12. On the issue of Catholic-Protestant debates over religion in schools, see John T. McGreevy, *Catholicism and American Freedom: A History* (New York: Norton, 2003), 122.

raising their voices against the school without religion."[13] On this issue, Catholics and Protestants would indeed raise their voices together (not in perfect harmony) for the rest of the century.

In December 1912 the *Messenger of the Holy Childhood Church and School* announced it would become the *Franciscan Herald* and be published in Teutopolis, Illinois, so that the faculty and students at St. Joseph's College in Teutopolis (a Franciscan Minor seminary) could help with the writing and editing. Beginning in January 1913 the *Franciscan Herald* promised—as editor Father Ferdinand Guen, OFM, stated—to "foster the spirit of St. Francis among the Tertiaries and to promote interest in the heroic labors of Franciscan missionaries."[14] The editors also explained that by moving the magazine to Illinois they would be able to produce a bigger, broader magazine and increase its circulation and distribution. Clearly though, the first purpose seemed squarely to be to "spread the Third Order by making it better known and loved, by reminding Tertiaries of their duties and by animating them to persevere in the noble calling." Noting the hope expressed by Popes Leo XIII and Pius X that tertiaries "everywhere should unite into brotherhoods," the *Franciscan Herald* sought to "bring isolated members of the Third Order in closer touch with one another by promoting unity of aims and interests." Undertaking its mission straight away, the magazine published a long essay on the relationship between the papacy and the Third Order and two essays on missionary work done by Franciscans.[15]

The editors made a strong appeal to "arouse and promote interest in Franciscan missions, and to keep its readers in touch with the labors of missionaries in our own and foreign countries." For missionaries "shed their blood for the faith they preached" and sacrificed "their health and life on the mission fields, amid untold labors and hardships." And while "every and all missionaries are heard to complain that not sufficient interest is shown their work by those of their own household . . . these followers of the Apostles ask no human praise or earthly remuneration." Yet the editors also asked for financial support—they needed money as well as prayers.[16]

From their somewhat humble origins as house organs for specific parishes, the *Franciscan Herald* and *St. Anthony Messenger* became sites for engaging American modernity, especially in regard to the role of women in modern families. They did this by broadening their subscriber base geographically and employing writers who addressed issues with implications for family life,

---

13. "Danger for Our Nation," *Messenger of the Holy Childhood Church and School* 14 (January 1910): 247.

14. "Greeting and Introduction," *Franciscan Herald* 1 (January 1913): 1.

15. "Greeting and Introduction," *Franciscan Herald* 1 (January 1913): 2–4.

16. "Greeting and Introduction," *Franciscan Herald* 1 (January 1913): 4.

Church doctrine, and American politics. By mixing discussions regarding Church doctrine with snapshots from Catholic life, these Franciscan magazines developed a way of addressing how Catholic families lived in America. Across dozens of issues published over decades, one can see a steady concern about how readers dealt with changes in their relationship to other faiths and the evolution of Catholic social status. At the center of the *Herald's* mission was an attempt to use tertiaries to advance Catholic family life. As Catholics who pledged to live by the example of St. Francis, tertiaries had the potential to energize Catholic social teaching if their energy were coordinated. In other words, by demonstrating how to make modern life work with Catholicism, other Catholics might better serve their church and communities. Looking back on this early history of the *Herald*, Father Mark Hegener observed that "in the very first issue in 1913 the young editor went after the Third Order. It was stagnant, disorganized, in a catacombs-condition. . . . There were no organized provinces. Fraternities existed but were not related to each other. . . . No bonds of unity. No organization." Hegener contended that it was the consistency and constancy of the work undertaken by the *Franciscan Herald* that contributed to the first Third Order National Convention in 1921. Shortly after that, in 1922, the prolific and tireless Father James Meyer, OFM, took over editorial duties, prodding "provinces to organize and to rally the federation of the Third Order provinces." Meyer edited the magazine for thirty-three of its first fifty years. Father Philip Marquard, OFM, served as manager of the journal for most of those years.[17] Together Meyer and Marquard helped shape how Franciscan media could be a site for discussions about living as a Catholic.

Father Marion Habig, OFM, recounted the early years of the *Franciscan Herald* by noting that its circulation in 1913 was 1,300; by 1922 it peaked at 152,000 subscribers, placing it among the leaders of Catholic magazines in the United States. Habig noted that around 1920 the magazine became "one of the best-known and most popular Catholic magazines in the country" as well as one of "the chief means for organizing the Third Order Secular of St. Francis in the United States on a national basis." The *Franciscan Herald* moved locations again in 1920, this time from Teutopolis, Illinois to Chicago, where it established its own imprint, the Franciscan Herald Press, much as the St. Anthony Guild had done. Meyer also moved to Chicago, though he continued to teach at St. Joseph's Seminary in Teutopolis until 1931. The rise in circulation occurred just as Meyer took over as editor in 1922. Over his long tenure as editor, the circulation fluctuated, and it even technically failed during the Depression. However in 1921 Meyer also helped start and

---

17. Mark Hegener, OFM, "After Fifty Years," *Franciscan Herald and Forum* 50 (January 1953): 3.

edit the *Third Order Forum* with Father Hilarion Durek, OFM. A magazine for Third Order directors, the *Third Order Forum* took off in 1922 as a quarterly, became a bimonthly in 1931, and finally became a monthly in 1938. It grew into the most recognizable organ for the Third Order and merged with the struggling *Herald* in 1940, creating the *Franciscan Herald and Forum.* Habig observed, "It is not an exaggeration to say that the shape of Third Order thought and of the Third Order movement in this country, during the three decades before 1955, was definitely taken from the editorials and many unsigned articles written by Father James [Meyer]."[18]

Meyer was the author of *The Social Ideals of St. Francis: Eight Lessons in Applied Christianity,* a 1938 book that gathered published work from both the *Herald* and the *Forum* that he had written in the wake of the fourth quinquennial congress of the Third Order of St. Francis held in Louisville, Kentucky in October 1936. He wanted these essays read as a call to action among tertiaries, to use the spirit of St. Francis as a way to counter the degrading effects of modern life on the human person. In the magazines he edited, Meyer had a fairly clear mission: to speak to and provide guidance to the American Third Order and those "directors among the non-Franciscan clergy" whose numbers had steadily climbed in the early 1920s. Both the *Third Order Forum* and the *Franciscan Herald* had played a role in integrating Franciscan evangelism across the tertiary community and among Catholic families. Meyer wrote as the new editor of the *Forum* in 1922: "The FORUM sets itself (we hope not too presumptuously) to encompass this wish [for inspiring tertiaries], not only by the aid it seeks to offer directors in their work, but by serving as a ground open to all who wish to enter, for the ventilation of questions and problems confronting the Third Order."[19] From the early editorials Meyer wrote in the *Forum*, it is easy to see how his legacy became synonymous with the Third Order movement. He intended to offer his audience of tertiaries a new magazine just for them with a name that showed its aspiration "to cover the entire sphere of Tertiary life and activity." "The presumptive purpose of the magazine," Meyer offered, was "to act as a common ground for the treatment of Tertiary matters readily suggests the name. As in the nature of a forum, opportunity shall be afforded to hear and to be heard, to give and to take, all in the spirit of brotherhood and of a common interest in a common cause."[20]

Meyer wrote in the first issue under his editorship: "Our aim is to furnish a magazine that will interest not only one, but every member of the family.

---

18. Marion A. Habig, OFM, "Herald for Half a Century," *Franciscan Herald and Forum* 50 (January 1953): 5–10.

19. James Meyer, OFM, "*Avete, Fratres!!,*" *The Third Order Forum* 1 (January 1922): 1–2.

20. Ibid., 2.

We wish to furnish a magazine that will be read with profit by all, no matter what interests they may have or what their individual vocations may be." In his first year the *Franciscan Herald* restored a section for women on the Christian home, expanded the magazine's length to forty-four pages, and aimed "to make each department still more entertaining," Meyer said. He also pointed out that the editorial page would continue to be the "most important page" of the magazine, with its influence already demonstrated through other magazines' great number of references to it. Central to the magazine's mission, though, was the intention to broaden popular understanding and participation in the work of the Third Order, including the Franciscan missions to Native American tribes. Meyer explained that the *Franciscan Herald* had been relaunched from the *Messenger of the Holy Childhood Church and School* in 1913 with an "express purpose of explaining the nature, scope, and advantages of this wonderful institution of St. Francis [and] to spread the devotion to St. Francis who is so aptly called 'The Saint of the whole world.'"[21]

Meyer contributed editorials that consistently promoted the work and character of the Third Order. In the July 1922 issue he wrote: "The Third Order, in its nature, scope and purpose, is essentially an organization that belongs to the entire Catholic Church and not only to the Franciscan Order." His hope for the *Franciscan Herald*, he said, was to promote it as a magazine that could capture the general-interest reader among Catholics and suggest that the Third Order represented one of the best ways to be an active Catholic. "Tertiaries," he explained, "will prove his [priest's] loyal supporters, the backbone of his parish, the men and women on whom he can depend for wholehearted and disinterested co-operation."[22] Meyer advanced a straightforward notion that Catholics needed a press that provided not only information about activities carried out in the name of their faith, but also reflections on Catholic living in a country that could seem somewhat hostile to the Catholic Church. While Meyer consistently linked Catholicism and Americana—including the Declaration of Independence and the general notion of religious freedom— he also exhibited a classic cultural conservatism, making the *Franciscan Herald* a bulwark against what he called "the godless press" and "the most formidable enemy of the Church," such as movies and indecent popular culture.[23]

One way Meyer pressed the importance and relevance of the Third Order was to keep Father Giles Strub, OFM, a staff member of the *Franciscan Herald* from 1914 through 1938, writing about tertiaries. Strub became a

21. James Meyer, OFM, "Franciscan Herald of 1922," *Franciscan Herald* 9 (December 1921): 420.

22. James Meyer, OFM, "The Third Order and the Secular Clergy," *Franciscan Herald* 10 (July 1922): 292.

23. James Meyer, OFM, "The Catholic Press and You," *Franciscan Herald* 10 (February 1922): 52.

long-term contributor to the magazine's mission by providing an outlet for the Third Order and by encouraging priests to promote the Third Order among their parishioners. For example, in the first issue Meyer edited, Strub wrote about incorporating young people into the Catholic Church through the Third Order as a way to save souls and the Church. "The Third Order of St. Francis," Strub wrote, "admitting as it does, children of fourteen years of age into its ranks, is eminently adapted to save them from themselves and from the ensnaring allurements of the world." According to Strub young people of this age "constantly" seek "models for imitation," so it would be of great benefit to the parishes if priests offered heroes such as St. Francis to young people before they became enthralled with Babe Ruth and entertainment stars.[24]

WOMEN, CATHOLICISM, AND AMERICAN MODERNITY IN THE *FRANCISCAN HERALD*

The *Franciscan Herald* took a fairly traditional position on women in American culture. Strub wrote an essay in May 1922 addressing the evident inequality between men and women written into the codes that governed the Third Order. In his column "Chats with Tertiaries," he recognized that while he hoped women would join the Third Order they would have to do so with a specific understanding: "Married women are not to be admitted without the knowledge of their husbands; if it is thought necessary to act otherwise, it should be done only on the motion of the priest who is the *judge of their conscience*" (emphasis mine). Strub apparently found the need to emphasize the church's authority over women because the United States had recently approved women's suffrage. Women, Straub argued, should follow the example of Mary and exhibit "holy reverence for those who are destined by the benign Creator to stimulate all that is highest and noblest in the heart of man by reproducing in themselves either the virginal or marital life of their august Sister, Mary, the Mother of God. . . . This high regard for womanhood that filled the heart of [the] Father, has been a characteristic mark of all his true sons of the First and Third Order." Straub did not provide similar instructions for men.[25]

Unlike women in the Catholic Church at large, though, those who wrote for and about women in the *Franciscan Herald* played a prominent role in the publication. The inclusion of women in Catholic media demonstrated one response that the Catholic Church made to the effects of modernity in Amer-

---

24. Father Giles Strub, OFM, Chats with Tertiaries, *Franciscan Herald* 10 (January 1922): 6.
25. Father Giles Strub, OFM, Chats with Tertiaries, *Franciscan Herald* 10 (May 1922): 198–99.

ica. Kathleen Sprows Cummings points out in her book *New Women of the Old Faith* that "by the early 1890s, the desire of Catholic writers to use their talents to defend the faith found concrete expression through the Apostolate of the Press, a loosely organized movement led by Walter Elliott, a Paulist priest." Cummings explains that members of the apostolate decided that to counter what they viewed as anti-Catholic untruths, Catholic writers needed to work through print media to "spread the 'Catholic truth.'" Many of these writers were women "who looked upon their work as a 'spiritual vocation.'"[26]

Catholic women rarely wrote for magazines in the United States during the nineteenth century, but early twentieth-century changes in the political and cultural status of women encouraged articles by Catholic women on living their faith in American society. Many articles played upon a tension between what these journals characterized as the "New Woman" versus the "Catholic Woman." Strub clearly referred to this tension in his May 1922 column on the role of women in the Third Order, and women who wrote for the *Franciscan Herald* directly addressed this tension as well. Cummings contends: "In addition to shoring up Catholic womanhood in the face of contemporary assaults against it, these examples were also used to articulate and defend a distinctive American Catholic identity."[27]

As a writer for the *Franciscan Herald*, Agnes Modesta offered what she considered an appropriate Catholic response to the modern woman. In 1922 she wrote about a lecture she had attended on "modern messages to modern women" that proved, according to her, the trite quality of lumping all women of any intelligence as modern and then dismissing the many who belonged to a medieval faith. She wondered about the "Ideal Modern Catholic Woman," and recalled something a friend of hers said: "But, my dear, there is no such thing as a modern Catholic woman. . . . The Church is essentially medieval and you Catholic women who adhere closely to your Church are not in the least modern. You have the viewpoint of the Dark Ages. You are—forgive me—most deliciously er—quaint!" In one sense this exchange captured for Modesta the predicament many Catholic women of the time found themselves in; and in another sense it exemplified a good deal of literature written by Catholic women in the early twentieth century. Catholic women writers like Modesta saw it as part of their purpose to shore up Catholic identity by portraying modernity as selfish and individualistic, especially when compared to the qualities she ascribed to Catholic women. Modesta explained at the time: "I am forced to concede that Catholic women are not wholly guiltless in the

26. Kathleen Sprows Cummings, *New Women of the Old Faith: Gender and American Catholicism in the Progressive Era* (Chapel Hill: University of North Carolina Press, 2009), 25.

27. Ibid., 27.

matter of permitting a fallacy [of Catholics as antimodern] to gain ground in the materialistic present-day society. . . . Many of us are content to let our sister moderns fondly believe that, if we show an ability to cope with the problems of the day, it is in spite of the Church rather than because of it."[28]

In a follow-up essay a few months later, Modesta raised what might be considered the consequence of being a modern Catholic woman: namely, the way one projects her religious commitment. Modesta decided that humility was among the most misunderstood virtues that Catholic women exhibited. In the popular mind, she explained, humility had become a condition to regret rather than a virtue to possess.

> The owner of that interloper which masquerades as humility, assures the world that she is an ugly creature, a thoroughly sinful creature, that she need never expect to become even moderately good and pleasing to God, as is Sister-So-and-So. She is not possessed of any of the graces and virtues that fall to the loss of Miss-Some-body-else across the way, and she is, in short, in a pretty bad way so far as her hope of reaching any eminence, either here or hereafter is concerned. But she is grateful none the less, for thank God, she is 'umble.

Rather than project an image of self-pity, Modesta encouraged Catholic women to become something different both to other Catholics as well as to non-Catholics. She suggested a counter-model: a Catholic woman who understands humility in the proper way as to be so "pleasant and agreeable" that "we should hardly note in her much that is different from the common run of human beings." Modesta remarked: "She makes use of her talents, whatever they may be, for the service of God and neighbor—and it is often surprising to those about her to discover how many gifts and graces she seems to have, once they know her well."[29]

If modernity made Catholic women feel inferior, advice from writers like Modesta seemed designed to make them feel self-conscious. Another writer similar to Modesta was Grace Keon who wrote a column called "In the Interest of Women." A fiction writer born about 1873 in New York City to Irish-American parents, Keon (a pseudonym for Mary Grace Wallace Doonan) wrote and published from 1904 into the 1940s in journals such as *Catholic World* and *Extension Magazine* and books such as *The Life on Earth of Our Blessed Lord, Told in Rhyme, Story, and Picture for Little Catholic Children* (1913); her novels included *Broken Paths* (1923), *The High Road* (1930), and

---

28. Agnes Modesta, "On Being a Modern Catholic Woman," *Franciscan Herald* 10 (February 1922): 56.

29. Agnes Modesta, "A Brief for True Humility," *Franciscan Herald* 10 (May 1922): 204.

Stars in My Heaven (1941).[30] Typical of the era, her essays in the *Franciscan Herald* often demonstrated a kind of piety designed to instruct her readers on how to live a Catholic life. For example, she wrote in response to a reader who asked how Keon felt about fancy rosaries: "Most decidedly you are a luxury-lover if you fish down into a thirty-dollar beaded bag for a nickel to put into the collection basket. You are indeed a luxury-lover if you put anything in God's world above your God."[31]

Throughout 1922 Keon wrote a series of essays that addressed what she called "danger signals." In her opening essay in February she walked readers through brief encounters with Catholic women that demonstrated a lack of humility. She used one exchange between two Catholic women after Mass to suggest that some women showed up at church to be seen rather than to pray. In another story she suggested that mothers traded on the success of their children—such as getting into a prestigious non-Catholic university—as a way to pass for something other than Catholic. The theme of skirting or even being embarrassed by one's Catholic identity was a recurring theme for Keon. She had two more archetypal characters chatter about a priest: "Wouldn't you think we could hear a different sermon once in a while? We get the same old stuff Sunday after Sunday! Catholic education! Catholic friends! Catholic husbands!" Keon remarked, "So they parted. Comments unnecessary." In other vignettes Keon addressed Catholics who begrudged the necessity of sending their kids to Catholic school and derided priests who passed judgment on popular films. But she concluded her "Danger Signals" essay with what she clearly considered the best of all archetypes, "Mrs. Ordinary Person." After dropping "her plain black beads into her plain black bag," Mrs. Ordinary Person met her son at the back of the church after he had seen one of the parish priests. The priest greeted them with what I imagine Keon thought every mother would hope to hear: "Well! Now you're reaping the reward of your many sacrifices. Your son will write O.F.M. after his name some day, please God!"[32]

This mother in Keon's story served as the vehicle for her most significant point—the danger signals created by modern life could be neutralized by simply living as a Catholic. Not surprisingly Keon introduced a priest in her story to deliver the final word: "You gave your children their full inheritance of a good Catholic education that their Catholic instincts might not be

---

30. See Terence E. Hanley, "Grace Keon (1873?)," *Tellers of Weird Tales: Artists & Writers in The Unique Magazine* (blog), April 9, 2014, accessed July 13, 2017, http://tellersofweirdtales.blogspot.com/2014/04/grace-keon-1873.html.

31. Grace Keon [Mary Grace Wallace Doonan], "Luxury-Lovers," In the Interest of Women, *Franciscan Herald* 10 (April 1922): 168.

32. Grace Keon, "Danger Signals," In the Interest of Women, *Franciscan Herald* 10 (February 1922): 121.

starved," the priest says. "Your other boy will be a fine Catholic physician before many years, and Marie's engagement to [a Catholic boy] means the beginning of a fine Catholic family." Even though the mother of the story admits she felt guilt for all her good fortune, her parish priest sets her straight, remarking that luck was not necessary when one chooses to live a Catholic life. What followed was a summary of an ideal Catholic mother: "Your bookcases were not too refined (I've heard the word!) to contain upon their shelves the works of good Catholic authors. Your tables held magazines indeed—not the current trash of the day—but many of the better class mixed with those published in the interest of our old Faith. You did not think that your children could only enjoy the 'higher life,' so-called, by associating with non-Catholics, that evil which leads to so many mixed marriages. No my Dear lady, if God has been good to you, you have helped Him to be so." The essay ended with the mother sighing, "I am only a very Ordinary Person, indeed"—to which the priest exclaims: "God bless all such Ordinary Persons, say I."[33]

Keon's columns in the *Franciscan Herald* were supposed to sound like a conversation that Catholics, and especially women, might have. Her follow-up essays dealt with negotiating the apparent conflicts between being Catholic and operating in an American culture that increasingly understood identity through consumption and material wealth. For example, in an essay titled "The Catholic Habit," Keon acknowledged the paradox many Catholic women faced: their children succeed in a society that was not Catholic and felt embarrassed by their Catholic upbringing. That latter point she emphasized in a story about a mother telling her teenage son that it would "hurt me very much" if he took a non-Catholic girl to a dance. "If I could leave you all the wealth of the world I would leave you nothing unless I pass on the Faith to you as it was passed on to me," she tells him. When asked if her discussion worked, the mother replied: "He had been brought up to look at things from a Catholic standpoint, so I don't see how he could refuse. He was too young to have any liking for the child—and I thought it a golden chance to impress on all his future the danger of associating with non-Catholics of the opposite sex."[34]

Keon's efforts to fortify her *Franciscan Herald* readers with Catholic pride met with some resistance. In an essay titled "On Being Narrow," Keon addressed her critics. She emphasized that her column was for "many mothers [who] are far away from town or city; many are raising families, and want to know how to do, oh, so many things that might seem trifling to others, but which are very big and real to them." Yet if Keon intended the column

---

33. Ibid., 122.
34. Grace Keon, "The Catholic Habit," In the Interest of Women, *Franciscan Herald* 10 (May 1922): 229.

as guidance, she also viewed it as a place to defend her faith against those who needed, in her view, a lesson in how to be faithful. For example, one reader wrote: "Aren't you afraid of being called a Catholic bigot? If a non-Catholic were to read [the May 1922 column titled] 'The Catholic Habit' which I have just finished, I'm afraid he'd say you were very close to that state." This was the kind of challenge Keon welcomed. She replied: "I am glad to avail myself of this opportunity to present the ideas of the thinking Catholic woman on the problems of the present day as they most vitally affect herself." In a style that was more stilted and formulaic than usual, Keon proclaimed her affinity for American values. "We are a Christian land," she declared, "as we make liberal allowance for, are tolerant of every man's worship of a Supreme Being. This is the sentiment—the attitude of Catholics. They aren't narrow or bigoted—and as Catholics we require from our neighbors—nay, we demand from them—the same tolerance we accord."[35] Not surprisingly Keon followed her emphatic support for American pluralism with a "but." She argued that making room for many faiths did not entail relegating Catholicism to a private act or admitting that it somehow fell afoul of modern America.

Keon warned against the timidity of Catholic women who failed to defend, at the very least, their obligation to bear the faith for their families and the community.[36] She insisted in another essay: "To demand everywhere for your beliefs the same consideration that you give to the belief of others is not selfishness, but a DUTY. To refuse to tolerate for a single instant the free and easy manner of the child who says, 'Oh, it's only mother!' is a NECESSITY."[37] She consistently responded to letters that questioned her tone. "I . . . know that these opinions may annoy some, who write that they do not agree with me. I suppose I am aggressively Catholic," she remarked. "One good little lady has called me that. But why shouldn't we be 'aggressively Catholic' when it is necessary?"[38] Indeed, one gets the impression that she felt quite responsible for the fate of her readers' families.[39]

What made Keon's column in the *Franciscan Herald* especially interesting was that unlike another section for women in the *Franciscan Herald* written

35. Grace Keon, "On Being Narrow," In the Interest of Women, *Franciscan Herald* 10 (May 1922): 267.

36. For a more public expression and defense of Catholicism, see Halsey, *American Innocence*, 6–7.

37. Grace Keon, "The Old and the New," In the Interest of Women, *Franciscan Herald* 10 (July 1922): 312.

38. Grace Keon, "Walking Warily," In the Interest of Women, *Franciscan Herald* 10 (August 1922): 361.

39. Grace Keon, "The Gifts of the Catholic Girl," In the Interest of Women, *Franciscan Herald* 10 (October 1922): 457.

publications. But this was a Catholic magazine with a responsibility to act on behalf of the church.

Thus a more official voice for readers appeared, primarily, in two columns in *St. Anthony Messenger*. The first, introduced in 1915, was "The Wise Man's Corner," written for thirty-two years by Father Norman Perry, OFM, who was also editor-in-chief of the magazine for eighteen of those years. The second, was the "Tertiary Den" maintained by a series of priests over the decades it existed. As the Wise Man, Norman Perry fielded questions regarding Catholic doctrine, dogma, and practice. The first such exchange in 1915 provided an indication of what would come: a writer wondered about the Church's policy on eating meat on Fridays. Perhaps not too surprisingly, the letter writer had obtained three different opinions, including one of a priest. Perry responded: "Your friend as well as the parish priest are not quite up-to-date. They still cling to laws of discipline which the late Holy Father [Pius X] suppressed. Catholics may eat meat on all holy days of obligation . . . if these chance fall on a Friday. You showed the proper Catholic spirit by abstaining under the circumstances."[44]

Perry numbered the letters to the Wise Man, and by December 1930 he began with number 2,597. He included a disclaimer that asked for the patience of his letter writers because they wrote in such volume that, he admitted, it might take him months to respond to questions. He also asked that writers send no more than three questions at a time. But it was also the nature of the questions as well as the volume that gave significance to the column. Thus the magazine named for St. Anthony of Padua, a Doctor of the Church, extended the tradition fostered by St. Anthony through direct interaction with the faithful. That is, rather than avoid difficult questions, *St. Anthony Messenger* invited them. The entries published by Perry stand among the most fascinating samples of Catholics struggling to live out their faith.

Obviously some questions were more difficult than others. For example, letter number 2,600 asked in the December 1930 issue: "If a person goes to Holy Communion on the First Friday of the month and leaves out Saturday, can he go to Communion on Sunday without going to Confession, provided he does not commit a sin?" Perry responded: "Yes, he may. Confession before receiving Holy Communion is prescribed only when one is in the state of mortal sin." But then consider this exchange from the same issue, in which another letter asked: "About eighteen years ago by a forced marriage I was united to a man who, being under the influence of alcohol most of the time, drove me and my baby from the house. Afterwards he left town and [re]married under an assumed name. Can I go to confession and receive Holy Com-

---

44. J.A., Cincinnati, letter, and Father Norman Perry, OFM, response, The Wise Man's Corner, quoted in Hurley, "St. Anthony Messenger," 14.

munion?" Perry counseled: "Certainly you can go to Confession. The priest will direct you in the course of action you are to follow." The range of other topics in just this December 1930 was remarkable: questions about God's knowledge of the time a person had on earth and whether the person determined his or her time of death; whether so-called real religion existed before Christ; how to properly address a priest in a letter; whether a married Protestant minister could become a married Catholic priest; whether it was a sin to go to a fortune teller; and why the pope has a three-cornered hat.[45]

What becomes clear from reading these different entries is that Perry could not have guessed what readers would ask and, moreover, he had to be nimble in crafting answers. Some of his responses fared better than others. In entry number 2,610, a reader asked a two-part question: "(a) If a person falls into mortal sin should he go to confession against his will, when he does not feel in a disposition to confess? (b) To make an act of perfect contrition, is it necessary to examine one's conscience?" Perry replied: "The Wise Man is amazed that a Catholic should ask such a question. Do you not know that mortal sin is the greatest evil that exists? Most certainly such a person should go to confession immediately. If he is not in the disposition to confess, then he should put himself into such a state of mind. . . . In order to make an act of perfect contrition it is not necessary to examine one's conscience." Perry's response was reminiscent of the truism that the Church does the thinking for the faithful and, in light of this reader's questions, also seemed to affirm the notion that Confession could absolve almost anybody of almost anything.[46]

Other exchanges were less abstract and more indicative of their moment. In June 1942 Perry labeled one question "Today's Big Problem" in a letter in which a young woman asked: "What do you think of young people marrying before leaving for the service?" Perry recommended waiting "until the boy sweetheart returns. He may not be the same lad when he returns as you know him now. . . . It pays to wait, young ladies. If your boy-friend is loyal, you'll meet him on his return with greater joy. War is hell, you know, and it plays hellish tricks with love."[47]

In a similar spirit, the magazine had "The Tertiary Den" (or simply "the Den"), anchored by the prolific Fulgence Meyer. If Perry dealt in the ambiguities and confusions of being faithful to Church doctrine, Meyer dealt with the complications of living as a Catholic. His column addressed a range of

---

45. Letter 2600, and Perry, response, The Wise Man's Corner, *St. Anthony Messenger* 38 (December 1930): 324. Letter 2568, and Perry, response, The Wise Man's Corner, *St. Anthony Messenger* 38 (December 1930): 324.

46. 2610, letter, and Perry, response, The Wise Man's Corner, *St. Anthony Messenger* 38 (December 1930), 325.

47. 3510, letter, and Perry, response, The Wise Man's Corner, *St. Anthony Messenger* 50 (June 1942): 105.

personal topics from sexual thoughts to marriage to religious life. In the early years of the section—from 1927 through 1938—Meyer was given at least six long columns over two pages to reprint heartwrenching as well as heartfelt letters from readers and then to add his own advice.

Meyer established a singular presence in twentieth-century Franciscan literary history. He was a well-regarded missionary priest who traveled primarily in the Midwest, the author of more than two dozen books and pamphlets on subjects ranging from sex education to religious retreats, and a contributor to *St. Anthony Messenger*. Meyer was born in Luxembourg and emigrated to the United States as a child, settling with his family in Cincinnati, Ohio. He entered the Franciscan order in 1892 and was ultimately sent to the College of St. Anthony (known as the Antonianum) in Rome where he was ordained a priest in 1900. Meyer excelled as a scholar, completing his theological training in Rome and earning the degree of *lector generalis*, which allowed him to teach theology in any Franciscan seminary in the world. He returned to the Midwest in 1901, teaching first at the Franciscan major seminary in Oldenburg, Indiana, and in 1916 becoming the rector of the school from which he had graduated: St. Francis Preparatory Seminary in Cincinnati. He then spent three years in Rome as a professor at the Antonianum and returned to the United States in 1919 as the commissary provincial of the Third Order of St. Francis. This station brought him into contact with thousands of Catholics in the Midwest and gave him a chance to preach missions and conduct retreats for men and women religious.[48]

Meyer's considerable experience as a counselor-priest inspired a remarkably prolific writing career. According to one report, by the time of his death his publications had generated more than five hundred thousand copies.[49] Among those many publications were a collection of small books intended to assist young people when navigating modern American mores.[50] Meyer offered his books as "plain talk" and "heart to heart chats" for boys and girls. In 1927 two volumes appeared, one, titled *Plain Talks on Marriage*, featured "frank and intimate talks on married life, its rights and duties, its virtues and sins, for people who are married, or who are about to be married."[51] A second,

---

48. "Death Claims Father Fulgence," *St. Anthony Messenger* 47 (January 1939): 17.
49. Ibid.
50. The literature on this period is extensive, but for explanations of both the perception and reality of challenges to traditional social mores, see Lynn Dumenil, *The Modern Temper: American Culture and Society in the 1920s* (New York: Hill and Wang, 1995); Stanley Coben, *Rebellion Against Victorianism: The Impulse for Cultural Change in 1920s America* (New York: Oxford University Press, 1991); and Paula S. Fass, *The Damned and the Beautiful: American Youth in the 1920s* (New York: Oxford University Press, 1977).
51. Fulgence Meyer, *Plain Talks on Marriage* (Cincinnati, OH: St. Francis Book Shop, 1927), cover insert.

titled *Youth's Pathfinder*, offered "heart to heart chats with Catholic young men and women on vocation, love, courtship and marriage." In this second volume, Meyer wrote in the foreword:

> This book is a sincere effort towards answering the eager, wistful and anxious query many of our Catholic young people of both sexes, who ask pleadingly as the youth Saul asked before the gates of Damascus: "Lord, what wilt Thou have me to do?" They ask this question frequently and variously. They ask it regarding their conduct towards God, towards their parents, and toward themselves. They ask it with reference to personal purity and virtue as well as to their choice and pursuit of a vocation in life. They ask it respecting their behavior on the way to the convent, in a life of virginity in the world, and in love and courtship on the road to marriage.[52]

Meyer's intentions, though, belied his tone.

In the pages of *St. Anthony Messenger*, Meyer often sounded empathic to the plight of the people who wrote him. In many of his advice books, he played the scold. For example, in *Youth's Pathfinder*, Meyer turned to St. Augustine to make a point about seeking gratification in the wrong things, namely "amusements of the world and the pleasures of the flesh."[53] Augustine, Meyer related, was "miserable from day to day until under the impulse of grace he turned to God." The moral of this story was not to imagine that life's difficulties made one stronger or taught important lessons, but to remind his young readers that "sacred and secular history of ancient and modern times are replete with instances of men and women in mature life deploring the follies and sins of their youth."[54] "Youth," Meyer declared, "is at the same time the most beautiful and the most dangerous period of life; it can be the most blessed, or the most fatal of seasons." For his intended audience of teenagers, Meyer clearly wanted to scare the devil out of them. He warned: "If in youth the traits of virtue and character are more promising, the germs of vice and evilmindedness are more deadly." Drawing on yet another metaphor, Meyer compared mistakes made in life to that of a railroad conductor who causes an accident—one accident can turn your life in to a train wreck.[55] Extending that metaphor, Meyer hoped to be the signal man, directing young people onto an ideal track for life.

In 1929 Meyer published two more books, one on the sex lives of young women, entitled *Helps to Purity*, and a second on the sex lives of young men,

---

52. Fulgence Meyer, *Youth's Pathfinder: Heart to Heart Chats with Catholic Young Men and Women* (Cincinnati, OH: St. Francis Book Shop, 1927), 1.
53. Meyer, *Youth's Pathfinder*, 6.
54. Ibid.
55. Ibid., 12, 13.

entitled *Safeguards of Chastity*. Taken together the books span a little less than two hundred pages, making them both accessible, and like *Youth's Pathfinders*, exercises in fear. And like his other books, they sold well: His publisher declared that "within the first month after their publication over 1,200 copies of each book were in circulation. This general demand shows the urgent need of sex books, written from the Catholic viewpoint, for . . . young people."[56]

Meyer's exhuberance for counseling youth in the dangers of living did not sit well with at least a few of his superiors. In the summer of 1928 Meyer sent his manuscripts on the sex lives of young men to Father Hugh Strand, OFM, Father Romuald Mollaun, OFM, and to a third priest, a Father Erwin; he sent his book on the sex lives of young women to three Sisters of Charity—Sister Maria Grattia, Sister Hildegarde, and Sister Cyril. Seeking their approval, Meyer instead received their rejection. Meyer first gave Father Hugh Strand, OFM, a copy of his book for boys. Strand replied with a single page report listing the problems he had with the book and concluded in no uncertain terms: "Drop the idea of this book and more so the one for girls. I feel you have not the correct attitude for such work. It does not befit you. It will do much more harm than good . . . [and] what little it conveys of sex knowledge is poorly given, the other material is covered by works already published by yourself." He concluded that publishing the book would harm Meyer's reputation and provide fodder for anti-Catholic groups.[57]

Two other letters from priests who read Meyer's manuscript also advised against publishing. Father Erwin, OFM, of St. Francis Seminary wrote to the Father Provincial of St. John the Baptist Provice in Cincinnati, Father Urban Freudt, OFM, that "I would not like to see a priest's name mentioned as the author" and that "St. Francis Bookshop should not be associated with such a publication." The problem, according to Father Erwin, was that Meyer made his points using descriptions that were so graphic that they might "become occasion of sacriligeous conversations."[58] Father Mollaun wrote to Meyer that after reading his manuscript carefully he concluded "Your approach to the subject to me seems very poor." Of particular concern to Mollaun was the way Meyer condemned things that the Church did not. For example, Meyer declared that various body parts would become "bad and sinful" if misused, something Mollaun dismissed. Mollaun also noted that "it is not true that the Church bars illegitimate children from the religious

56. "Popular Books on Vital Religious Topics by Franciscan Authors," March 15, 1949, in box DEC 159, folder "Writings," Fulgence Meyer Papers, Province of St. John the Baptist, 1615 Vine Street, Cincinnati, Ohio.

57. Father Hugh Straud to Fulgence Meyer, August 17, 1928, box DEC 159, folder "Letters, 1910–1951," Fulgence Meyer Papers.

58. Father Erwin to Father Urban Freudt, August 31, 1928, box DEC 159, folder "Letters, 1910–1951," Fulgence Meyer Papers.

state. . . . On the contrary solemn profession removes the irregularity arising from illegitimacy."[59] Collectively, the priests who critiqued Meyer's work found ultimate fault with his use of power—his books spoke to young people directly (and incorrectly, they argued) without regard for the authority of their parish priests who counseled them in the confessional or their parents who raised them at home.

Despite criticism from church officials, Meyer's books were published and sold well. And while Meyer dealt with similar issues in the Tertiary Den, there was a key difference between Meyer's books and this column: the column included stories told to Meyer, not by him. Nearly half the letters Meyer chose to reprint in "The Tertiary Den" had something to do with marriage, sex, relationships, or some other form of love. Almost all of the letters were from women. And nearly all of them sought advice on situations that illustrated a sense of being trapped between their life and the Church. A very brief and powerful illustration of this can be found in a letter from a woman, twenty-two years old, who in four very short paragraphs conveyed that she was a devout Catholic, had lost a child at six months old, and was getting a divorce because her husband drank and beat her. She wanted to know if there was a place she could "go and help and work for the poor; [to] stay there and live there almost as a Sister." Meyer acknowledged that her condition was "sad beyond words" and suggested that this woman could find a suitable place to do "God's work"—but he also suggested that God might not necessarily want or expect her to devote herself at such a young age to that course. Meyer recommended she speak to her pastor to procure the bishop's permission to gain a civil divorce and to seek guidance about her future.[60]

Another exchange in the "Den" suggested the significance of seeking advice outside the confessional. "I enjoy your column very much and am going to take a little of your time to tell you something that I can't tell anyone else but you and God," began a letter from Dixie M., a woman who identified herself as a young mother and a convert to Catholicism. In a letter of nearly six hundred words, Dixie M. asked for counsel from this Franciscan priest. Meyer obliged in a long response that ran another five hundred words, making the exchange a full page in the magazine.[61]

Dixie asked if she should stay with her abusive husband or leave with her two young boys. She felt trapped in the marriage because when her husband became angry—which she said was "very often"—he would demean her,

---

59. Father Romuald Mollaun to Meyer, October 25, 1928, box DEC 159, folder "Letters, 1910–1951," Fulgence Meyer Papers.

60. BA, letter, and Meyer, response, The Tertiary Den, *St. Anthony Messenger* 38 (November 1930), 273–74.

61. Dixie M. [pseud.], letter, and Fulgence Meyer, response, The Tertiary Den, *St. Anthony Messenger* 38 (November 1930): 273.

yelling, "I just married you out of sympathy and am only keeping you for a hired girl." Dixie explained that before she married, she had fallen "into sin, very sorrowful sin." When she was twenty, she met this man who would become her husband and told him about this past. Now as a mother of two young boys in an apartment that also housed her husband's father, and in a building where her husband's sister and two brothers also lived, Dixie had to endure her husband's tirades that were loud enough to be heard by his entire family and, more tragically, her two young sons. So she confessed, "I know that there isn't any such thing as a divorce for us but I wonder if it wouldn't be a good thing (I mean the best thing under the circumstances) to separate, so that my boys won't hear such things about me. I am so ashamed of myself and would not want them to grow up thinking that their mother is not a good woman, but a woman to be ashamed of." Dixie admitted, "Sometimes I wish I were dead, but I would hate to leave my little boys here all alone with their father." She concluded, "I haven't much faith in having a happy home with my husband and children, but I'm praying all the time for it and also for an increase of faith."[62]

Dixie M.'s confession, public and powerful, must have struck readers as it did the priests at the *Messenger*—as something that demanded reflection. Meyer's counsel, therefore, had to address the multiple contexts in which Dixie's letter existed: he was a Roman Catholic priest, she was a young American woman who lived under the rules of the Catholic Church; he was a Franciscan in the large St. John the Baptist Province in Cincinnati, she was a mother trapped in an apartment with an abusive husband; he was a missionary priest who traveled throughout the Midwest to run retreats, she was woman living in a liberal society that afforded her certain basic rights; he was a man with power and authority, she was woman subject to the misogyny of American life. What could Meyer say to Dixie in this public forum? "One would not hesitate to say that her husband is too cruel, heartless, and inhuman a man to stay with," Meyer began. "She should serve notice on him that if he ever outrages and insults her in the manner described she will take the children and leave him once for all time. No woman and mother is bound under any consideration to submit to such vile and offensive treatment." Meyer continued for four more long paragraphs, advising the women reading his column that he believed it "unwise for a girl before marriage or a wife after marriage to reveal her secret personal sins to her fiancé or husband." Of course, he added, women should generally avoid "every lapse against virtue." "A good, unspoiled, and unsoiled record is a girl's best earthly possession, whether she marries or not." And while Meyer made clear that Dixie deserved pity, he offered an observation that sounded familiar to many Catholic women of this

62. Ibid.

era: "The fact that she suffers what she does from her unworthy and unfeeling Catholic husband so humbly and penitently bespeaks a strong faith and a high spirit of sacrifice."[63] For Meyer and many Catholic priests of his era, treating a woman such as Dixie as a symbol of Catholicism's ethic of survival in the face of pain and hardship counted as high praise.

Dixie M.'s disclosure provided all readers a glimpse of the messiness and tragedies of life—especially a woman's life—in a Catholic community. And while Meyer was no liberal, he clearly wanted to craft a message for an audience that undoubtedly included many young women that was sensitive to the problems of Dixie's reality and faithful to the church's intention to impose order over that reality. In short, Meyer's response was itself a bit of mess. But grappling with such messiness was a fundamental mission of Franciscan media. Opening the pages of the magazine to the complexities of living as a Catholic often revealed the purpose of the church better than many of the practices that the faithful were taught to revere. Such an interpretation was not lost on critics of Franciscan media.

In January 1939 Father Severin Lamping, OFM—Meyer's colleague and his successor at the "Tertiary Den" following Meyer's death in November 1938—responded to a letter from a priest in St. Louis, Missouri, who wrote in to express his displeasure with the *Messenger*'s decision to air the problems of Catholic women. "It has been called to my attention by the local clergy and by people around this seminary to take notice of what is published in the *Tertiary Den*," the priest wrote to the *Messenger*. "The people here think it strange that this sort of thing gets into print and have asked me the purpose of it all. To tell the truth," he remarked, "I am at a loss for an explanation." The priest, not surprisingly, chose to focus his attack on what he claimed was the "material on sex" in the "Tertiary Den" column: "I fail to see that you have anything constructive in mind. The people are doubtful about letting their children read this matter." He continued along these lines, impugning the Catholic nature of the magazine and wondering whether this column was the right kind of sex education for Catholic youth. The priest was especially concerned with the publication of letters by young women—"these are delicate matters and should be answered privately," he advised. He did have good things to say generally about the *Messenger*, praising it for being better than the usual "pious publication" most often seen with the "missionary magazine."[64]

Lamping responded: "If *St. Anthony Messenger* is not to be simply a 'pious missionary magazine,' it is almost inevitable that matters be discussed, now and then, that are indelicate and inappropriate for childish ears." He acknowledged

---

63. Ibid.
64. Priest from St. Louis, letter, and Severin Lamping, response, The Tertiary Den, *St. Anthony Messenger* 46 (January 1939): 38–39.

that confessional letters did often appear in the mail but that publishing them often elicited positive letters of thanks. "Christ himself in giving us the parable of the Good Shepherd, tells how the latter leaves his flock of ninety-nine to seek the one sheep that is lost," Lamping preached. "I like to believe that the same search for the solitary individual who needs reformation, rather than ninety-nine who just need penance, finds exemplification in the *Tertiary Den.*"[65]

Although I could not find archives of the original letters sent to the *Messenger*, Meyer and Lamping often noted that the magazine received so many letters each week that the so-called Den Keepers could only respond to a fraction of them. And while Lamping adequately defended the rationale for the magazine's work, a short letter from another reader, reprinted alongside the St. Louis priest's letter suggested the significance of Franciscan media in the lives of Catholics. Rather than echo the priest's criticism of the "Tertiary Den," a young woman wrote to say that she too had been an "unfaithful Catholic." She confessed to having an affair with a married man—despite, she said, having "a fine home environment," "excellent training . . . in one of our leading Catholic universities," and the counsel of her brother, a Catholic priest. The affair (initiated by the married man) went on for nine months until she took her brother's advice and began to pray novenas to St. Joseph. In her letter she made clear that she found it very difficult to control her feelings and took great pains to avoid her lover. The moral of the story was that on the seventeenth day of prayers to St. Joseph, this young woman met a friend of her brother's, ended up marrying him nine months later, and with him had a son, named Joseph (of course). Lamping did not need to say much about this letter except to add a coda to his exchange with the St. Louis priest: "This letter should serve as a justification for my own remarks following the previous letter of criticism. 'Confessional' letters, however sordid they may at time appear, do accomplish good—perhaps more than we with our small and limited minds can adequately appreciate."[66]

Two months later, in the March 1939 issue of the *St. Anthony Messenger*, Lamping continued the discussion regarding the role of the "Tertiary Den" and of the magazine more generally as a counselor for all sorts of problems. Lamping explained in his column that the letters in the January 1939 issue that had caused controversy demonstrated that "it is too difficult to draw the exact boundary line as to how far one might go in this matter." Lamping acknowledged he would rather "safeguard the virtue of the 'little ones'" than court controversy; but he also suggested, "It seems too rigorous a viewpoint to maintain that every reference to moral lapses constitutes a danger to

---

65. Ibid., 39.
66. ALK, letter, and Severin Lamping, response, The Tertiary Den, *St. Anthony Messenger* 46 (January 1939): 38–39.

virtue." Lamping referred to St. Augustine and his "open and humble revelation of his past" as an example of seeing a confessional style as a Catholic
way of relating in a community.[67] When another letter writer chastised Lamping for not "knowing the difference between an honest penitent and a morbid
minded introvert," Lamping wondered, "Why is it that many Catholics are
shocked when offense against the sixth commandment are referred to and do
not react when grave sins against charity and justice are committed?"[68] At least
these letter writers had confessed to having problems. As yet another letter
writer remarked: "Truly, it was a confessional letter, but I for one have never
let a day go by without praying that God might grant this person the grace to
overcome sin and obtain forgiveness." To this Lamping replied: "This letter
is particularly gratifying because the writer mentions praying for a party in
need of prayer and grace."[69]

The use of the term "confessional" captured the character of the "Tertiary
Den." *St. Anthony Messenger* was not akin to the church confessional because
judgment was never the point, disclosure was. The exchanges in these
columns—"Tertiary Den" and to a lesser degree in the "Wise Man's
Corner"—carried value for the people directly involved and beyond that to
the readers of the magazine who looked for ways to resolve the demands of
their faith with the imperfections of their lives.

Not all letters were personal, tragic, and scandalous to reprint. Over the
years readers asked the Den keepers about joining the Third Order, going
into the priesthood, or becoming women religious, and many of these letters
seemed to be from young people under the age of thirty. Meyer and his fellow
friars answered hundreds of such letters, from young women as well as young
men, from readers of seemingly every socioeconomic class and ethnicity. To
the contemporary ear, the letters to Meyer and Lamping sound strikingly personal and heartfelt. But in an era in which weekly Confession remained a
common occurrence, and the parish priest was a confidant for large groups
of urban Catholics, the candid nature of the Den makes sense. What these
letters also suggest, though, are the limits of those parish priests. The editors
of *St. Anthony Messenger* created a magazine that demonstrated changes
among the laity and revealed the relationship Franciscans had with Catholics
in and out of the pews. The fact that many of the letters came from young
women in tragic circumstances who were—they often intimated—living in
tension with the Church posed an especially tricky situation for writers (priests

67. Lamping, Tertiary Den, *St. Anthony Messenger* 46 (March 1939): 54.
68. ABG, letter, and Lamping, response, The Tertirary Den, *St. Anthony Messenger* 46 (March 1939): 54.
69. BEG, letter, and Lamping, response, The Tertiary Den, *St. Anthony Messenger* 46 (March 1939): 54–55.

and lay people). But the letters also afforded opportunities to demonstrate empathy.

Priest-counselers in *St. Anthony Messenger* often projected a humility regarding the reality of life and the tragedies that, when they come, need to be confessed in a manner that gives a measure of liberation to those making the confession. Father Hyacinth Blocker, OFM, wrote an essay for *St. Anthony Messenger* that hinted at the condition that drove many letter writers to reach out to priests in the pages of a magazine. Catholics, women in particular, were so wracked with guilt about life that they trapped themselves in a cycle of so-called scrupulosity, or as Blocker wrote, "a condition of the mind in which one sees sin where there is no sin, or readily magnifies venial into mortal sin." Like Meyer, Blocker was a prolific writer. He began as an editor at *St. Anthony Messenger* in February 1937 at the age of thirty-two and published his first book of poetry in 1938. He wrote dozens of columns, essays, articles, and poems for many Catholic periodicals, including more than 350 pieces for *St. Anthony Messenger*. He also taught at Roger Bacon High School near Cincinnati, Ohio, and also like Meyer was active in the retreat movement.

In 1935 Blocker wrote that scrupulosity was a problem that vexed him and his fellow priests. He began his essay, entitled "Scrupulosity and Its Cure," by recounting a fictional young woman's descent into a gaunt shadow of her typically bubbly and "full-bodied" self. "Scrupulosity had eaten into her soul," he wrote. "Like other scrupulous persons, she saw sin everywhere. . . . Every temptation against purity became in her eyes a hideous, frightful, mortal sin." He observed that such a condition was not exclusive to women—men fell victim as well. Blocker compared the condition to a hypochondriac seeing sickness in everything that they do and encounter. And somewhat in line with the concerns found in the letters Meyer received, Blocker noted that "perhaps by far the greater number and most troublesome scruples center upon purity and sex." Like the Den Keepers, Blocker advised readers to have perspective: "The scrupulous persons imagine that they have committed the most grievous sins of thought or desire, of look or deed when very likely they have not sinned at all. The very fact that they worry so exceedingly is a clear indication that they did not, at least, want to sin willfully."[70]

The common feature that joined the letter writers to the Tertiary Den and the people Blocker identified was the apparent strained relationship Catholics had with their Church and, perhaps more specifically, with their parish priests. If those priests had failed, to some extent, to be competent confidants to letter writers, they also seemed inadequately equipped to deal with the intensity of Blocker's sufferers of scrupulosity. Either way, such letters to the *St. Anthony*

---

70. Hyacinth Blocker, "Scrupulosity and Its Cure," *St. Anthony Messenger* 43 (December 1935): 433.

Messenger demonstrated the occasionally pathological nature of Catholic attitudes toward sin and sexuality. Blocker observed that at least in regard to scrupulosity, the cause might be linked to "unnecessary gloomy and strict interpretation or religion and morality." The cure for this condition offered additional insight into its causes. Blocker observed that one obsessed with scrupulosity had to "humbly admit that he can no longer guide himself, [and] until he blindly accepts and eagerly accepts the advice of his confessor, he will never overcome his anxiety and worry." Rather than dwell mercilessly on the often imaginary mortal sins committed by admittedly troubled souls, Blocker advised "giving themselves the benefit of the doubt" for no amount of soul searching and conscience examining would reveal the kind of answer—some kind of ultimate truth—that the afflicted or their priests hoped for. Blocker seemed to urge all involved to get right with doubt. He wrote, bluntly, "They should pray sparingly and trust in the goodness of God than pray too much and indiscreetly and thus merely prolong their mental anguish." He closed his article by paraphrasing St. Francis de Sales: "It is better to trust too much to the goodness and mercy of God than not enough."[71]

CONCLUSION

Franciscan magazines grappled with their own power to channel the concerns of their readers through a medium that was originally for reporting on the Third Order and the teachings of the Church. Through such magazines one can glimpse the changing social character of the laity, and politics between the laity and Church officials. As American Catholics grappled with being part of a medieval Church in a modern democracy, they sought some guidance regarding their formation as "new" Catholics. And like many other Americans, Catholics in the United States negotiated changes in cultural norms throughout the early twentieth century—such as the appearance of the New Woman and new influences on the family—while they figured out what was and was not acceptable behavior within and, perhaps more significantly, outside the Catholic home. Not surprisingly, officials at various levels of the Church saw outreach to Catholics through print media as an increasingly significant part of their vocation. Among the most serious questions to follow from that recognition was how their vocation in media would effect their mission as Franciscans.

---

71. Ibid., 434.

Chapter 2:
The "Little Magazines" of Franciscan Publishing

I n his study of women's devotions to St. Jude, Robert Orsi notes that "by 1959 . . . the Catholic Press Association reported that there were 24,273,972 subscribers to 580 periodicals in the country." These magazines, he adds, "have until recently been overlooked as sources for the history of American Catholic culture, but in that medium popular theology was practiced with considerable fervor and verve, literally in response to current events as they unfolded."[1] Franciscan publications participated successfully in this culture and, not surprisingly, sought to build it up following World War II. The economic prosperity that allowed a growing number of Catholics to move into the American middle class also offered the potential revenue necessary to expand Franciscan media.[2] Such expansion held the promise, as Orsi suggests, of enriching theology—an area cultivated by Franciscans and their magazines, from the family or general magazines such as *St. Anthony Messenger* and *Franciscan Herald* to smaller magazines, which had subscription bases that were often driven by the personalities and politics of the editors. Thus from the 1940s to the early 1960s, the message from these various outlets expanded both in variety (from conservative to liberal) and in sheer numbers, supporting a golden age of Franicscan publishing.

In his address at the 1959 Franciscan Educational Conference on Franciscan communication, Father Mark Hegener, OFM, a rising star of Franciscan journalism as the editor of the *Franciscan Herald and Forum*, surveyed the great diversity of the Franciscan press with a critical eye. He noted that there were many serious presses, such as the Academy of American Franciscan History and the Franciscan Institute at St. Bonaventure University, as well as the larger presses: St. Anthony's Guild in Paterson, New Jersey, which stood as the largest Franciscan publisher in the world; the Franciscan Herald Press, which produced the journal Hegener edited; and the Catholic Information Society. Hegener observed that there were many foreign-language publishers

---

1. Orsi, *Thank You, St. Jude*, xvii.
2. Jay P. Dolan, *The American Catholic Experience: A History from Colonial Times to the Present* (New York: Doubleday, 1985), 381–82.

in the Franciscan fold, including Franciscan Publishers of Pulaski, Wisconsin; the Slovenian Franciscan Fathers of Lemont, Illinois, who published the journal *Ave Maria*; the Custody of St. Casmir for Lithuanians in America; the Croatian Franciscan Press in Chicago; the Slovak Franciscan Commissariat in Pittsburgh; and the Hungarian Franciscan Commissariat.[3]

But Hegener concluded that the diversity of Franciscan media posed a problem because all of this had developed without almost any coordination. He said, "approximately 150 assorted magazines, bulletins, college publications and seminary magazines" were issued by Franciscans in the United States. Taken together with those pieces of literature not counted because they were internal to a specific order, Hegener estimated "the Franciscan monthly output is about a half million copies of periodicals." Into that sea also drained the output of books from Franciscan presses. But if the problem with Franciscan magazines is that there were too many and they lacked intellectual weight, Franciscan books posed the opposite problem. Hegener contended, "We have not made books as available to our American Catholic and Franciscan audiences as we should"—and those books were written with a mythical Catholic in mind. Quoting a friend in the publishing business, Hegener pointed out: "The basis of the difficulty, both in word use and approach . . . lies in an over-flattering estimate of the interest and knowledge of the average Catholic lay person. . . . As a matter of fact, the 'average' Catholic reader is still to be caught; and where he has been caught he has to be held." According to Hegener the future of Franciscan publishing required understanding trends among the reading public—more people were reading more books, and many of those readers had an interest in Franciscanism. Yet, Hegener concluded, Franciscans had to face that they had "not succeeded in creating an audience and an authorship which would interpret the Franciscan ideal on more than the didactic level."[4]

Another issue that aggravated Franciscans about their media was the great number and diversity of publications. Father Victor Drees, OFM, the editor of *St. Anthony Messenger* after World War II, noted the spectrum of categories that characterized Franciscan offerings, including general-interest magazines, scholarly magazines, and those promoting missions, devotionals, and the Third Order. So in addition to these many publications competing with each other and often failing to find a sufficient audience to sustain production and distribution costs, Franciscan magazines also seemed to undermine the goal of a concerted message by producing too many different kinds of voices. Many of these magazines reflected positions taken by their editors—a position that

3. Mark Hegener, "Friars and the Apostolate of the Press," in *Communications and the Franciscan Message*, 18–22.
4. Ibid., 22, 28, 33.

changed over time and demonstrated a shift in how Franciscans related to Catholics living in America. At times the dueling imperatives of war (both hot and cold) and the Franciscan message created what sometimes looked like a split personality.

The mixture of Franciscan periodicals reflected the variety of American magazines in general and included what were called "little magazines." The phenomenon of little magazines in American culture traditionally refers to the period from 1915 through the 1930s when, as intellectual historian Charles Alexander explains, "publications came into being to propagate new theories of art and life and to publish writers whose work was too technically experimental to find an outlet in the established periodicals."[5] Little magazines have persisted since this early twentieth-century burst of modernist creativity, growing to serve communities interested in everything from literature to poetry to politics—from the graphic arts to religion. No matter what the themes of these periodicals or the communities they spoke to, little magazines typically have had idiosyncratic editorial voices. In contrast to the self-consciously family-oriented magazines, Franciscans also produced an alternative to secular little magazines that radiated the personality of their Catholic editors and often wrestled with and opposed modernist assumptions and tendencies. To editors such as Hegener or Drees, these periodicals might have appeared a disorganized mess; however to the historian they represent a cacophony of Catholic voices—lively because of their discord.

THE ANTHONIAN

Of the early Franciscan publications, perhaps the most self-consciously Franciscan were those published by the Holy Name Province—*The Anthonian* and *Friar*. Founded in 1926, *The Anthonian*—the official magazine of St. Anthony's Guild in Paterson, New Jersey—was the brainchild of the energetic Father John Forest Loviner, OFM, who founded the Guild to help Franciscan missions by training young men to become Franciscan priests. As director of St. Anthony's Guild, Loviner also had a regular column in every issue of *The Anthonian* for forty-seven years.[6] He was born in Columbus, Ohio in 1896 and died in New Jersey in 1970; in 1916 when he became a novice in the Holy Name Province in New York, he adopted his name from John Forest, an English martyr of the Reformation. He was ordained a priest in 1923,

---

5. Charles C. Alexander, *Here the Country Lies: Nationalism and the Arts in Twentieth Century America* (Bloomington: Indiana University Press, 1980), 31.

6. Joseph M. White, *"Peace and Good" in America: A History of the Holy Name Province Order of Franciscan Minor, 1850s to the Present* (New York: Holy Name Province, 2004), 156.

moved to Paterson the following year to start St. Anthony's Guild, and initially worked out of St. Bonaventure Monastery in Paterson. By 1926 the Guild had its own offices and began publishing *The Anthonian* as a quarterly, with a national circulation through a subscription of Guild members. Joseph White notes in his history of the Holy Name Province that "until changing its format in 1970, [*The Anthonian*] consisted of sixteen pages of essays, poems, and, for many years, a versatile column, 'Thoughts from the Cloister,' treating spirituality, practical living, and apologetics." White points out that the journal appealed to Third Order Franciscans and reached a circulation of two hundred thousand by 1930.[7]

While not necessarily small in circulation, the *Anthonian* projected the conservativism of its founder. Friars of the Holy Name Province contributed to and staffed the magazine, writing for both St. Anthony's Guild as well as the broader community of Third Order Franciscans. One of the most popular and lucrative ways the Guild helped the province was by creating and selling St. Anthony's Guild stamps with paintings of St. Anthony of Padua in his distinctive brown robes; the stamps were marketed for use on Christmas letters and packages.[8]

Father Felician A. Foy, OFM, noted in a retrospective essay on the St. Anthony's Guild, that in 1928 the Guild opened a print shop that grew into "one of the biggest producers of catechetical literature in the United States." In the 1930s the Guild also began publishing religious instruction material for the National Center of the Confraternity of Christian Doctrine, an account that it would continue for more than thirty years, producing "various editions of the Baltimore Catechism and a wide range of supplementary manuals designed for the Confraternity's comprehensive program for the religious instruction of Catholic children not attending Catholic schools." In 1939 Guild founder Loviner also pioneered the idea of a Catholic bookmobile, using buses that he had converted into mobile bookstores; over a decade of service they logged "nearly a million miles carrying books and religious articles from coast to coast" until the service ended in the late 1950s. Perhaps the largest project launched by the Guild was the publication of a translation of the *New American Bible*. From 1941 to 1945 the Guild released this modern translation of the New Testament selling over a million copies in five years. From 1952 through 1969, it helped produce the *New American Bible* in four volumes, an undertaking that dwarfed all other printing projects.[9]

Such success led Loviner to create St. Anthony's Guild Press, which from the 1930s through 2007 published a variety of products from Christmas cards

---

7. Ibid., 157.

8. Ibid., 157.

9. Felician A. Foy, "All in a Lifetime," *The Anthonian* 44, no. 4 (1970): 4–6.

to devotional booklets to works by several friars, including Father Valentine Long and Father Isidore O'Brien, editors of and contributors to *The Anthonian*. Writing on the occasion of Loviner's death in 1970, Father John Sylvester Ahearn, OFM, characterized the director as having "religious inspiration [that] was entirely uncomplicated, showing little evidence of the theological subtleties which so often creep into spiritual outlook and devotional life of one long trained in that subject." In other words Loviner had a conservative ecclesiastical outlook expressed through "permanent, bottomless devotion to the person and office of the Holy Father." Ahearn wrote of Loviner's credo: "Pontiff speaks, case closed."[10]

From its beginning *The Anthonian* was also shaped decidedly by Father Isidore O'Brien, who wrote many of the essays—some of which, such as "The Rosary," were later given new life as books. O'Brien was born in Braid, Ireland, on January 26, 1895; entered the Order of Friars Minor in the United States in August 1921; and professed his simple vows at St. Bonaventure's Monastery in Paterson, New Jersey, in September 1922. He studied philosophy and theology at St. Bonaventure University in upstate New York and was ordained a priest in June 1928. In 1931 he moved to St. Francis of Assisi Parish near Herald Square in Manhattan; in the early 1940s he served as a professor of sacred eloquence at St. Bonaventure University and a scriptor at Holy Name College Seminary at the Catholic University of America in Washington, D.C. O'Brien was a constant and consistently intelligent presence in the St. Anthony's Guild publishing operation, writing more than twenty pamphlets, dozens of essays for *The Anthonian*, and popular books, including *Mirror of Christ: Francis of Assisi* (1944) and *Peter and Paul, Apostles: An Account of the Early Years of the Church* (1950). Such output made O'Brien an intellectual force in Franciscan publishing and shaped the dynamic way he approached lived theology in his shorter essays for *The Anthonian*. He died in October 1953.[11]

O'Brien shared with Loviner a fundamental conservatism regarding basic devotion to the Church and faith in it. He also provided sophisticated explanations for the common person's faith in the Church.[12] For example, in an essay titled "I Am the Way," O'Brien took up the apparent conflict between reason and faith by addressing the idea that while "reason is one of the highest natural gifts," rational thought alone cannot comprehend God. To make his point he offered the Stoics as an example of men who "formulated a rational code of ethics which is humanly perfect. But the men who shaped the code did not

---

10. John Sylvester Ahearn, OFM, "The Father of 'Our Family,'" *The Anthonian* 44 (October 1970): 12–13.

11. "In Memoriam," *The Anthonian* 18 no. 1 (January 1954): n.p.

12. "In Memoriam," *The Anthonian* 18 (January 1954): n.p.

often follow it. For man needs more than mother wit to make up the difference between knowing what is right and doing what is right." A gap existed between the ability to understand what the world needs and how to use such knowledge to lead people to a higher truth worthy of their loyalties, O'Brien argued. In revelation—an experience that defies rational explanation—God's authority made clear the truth, O'Brien assured his readers: "He sent His Son to give us this message in our bewilderment: 'I am the Way, the Truth, and the Life. Follow Me.' Thus protected, it should be difficult for us to miss heaven."[13]

O'Brien's convictions about how to be faithful developed during a radical period of American politics and thought. From the 1920s to the end of World War II, many competing ideological systems, from pragmatism and liberalism to communism and scientism, offered Americans a variety of ways to make sense of rapidly changing social mores and the collapse of the American economy.[14] This was also a period of intense intellectual engagement by Catholics in the United States. William Halsey, a historian of Catholic thought, contends, "Having drawn for themselves the bleak outlines of an uncertain world . . . Catholics promptly set out to build their own world safe from disillusionment but wavering between the charms of innocence and the grip of paranoia."[15] Indeed, throughout a period racked by two world wars and a global Great Depression, O'Brien wrote a series of essays on miracles in the Gospels to explicate in almost empirical terms how the mysteries of faith provided a concrete moral program for society. Like his essay on reason and faith, O'Brien used essays on miracles to discuss how one might understand or comprehend the divinity of Christ. He also clearly used the idea of miracles as a way to describe the resources available to the faithful in a time of need.[16]

The tragic consequences of World War II gave many churches an opportunity to reflect on fundamental aspects of existence, and *The Anthonian* offered a series of reflections on how Catholic Church teachings could help people see their way through and beyond the war. O'Brien frequently asked his readers to reflect on the way in which the tragedy of war might deepen one's faith, thereby revealing a Catholic dimension of God's message. While Loviner spoke more directly to the experience of war on Americans: "As the

---

13. Isidore O'Brien, "I Am the Way," *The Anthonian* 16 (January 1942): 2, 4, 5.

14. See John Patrick Diggins, *Up from Communism* (New York: Columbia University Press, 1975); George Cotkin, *William James: Public Philosopher* (Urbana: University of Illinois Press, 1989); Daniel T. Rodgers, *Atlantic Crossings: Social Politics in the Progressive Age* (Cambridge: Harvard University Press, 1998); and Andrew Jewett, *Science, Democracy, and the American University: From the Civil War to the Cold War* (Cambridge, UK: Cambridge University Press, 2014).

15. William M. Halsey, *The Survival of American Innocence: Catholicism in an Era of Disillusionment, 1920–1940* (South Bend, IN: University of Notre Dame Press, 1980), 1.

16. Isidore O'Brien, "The Gospel Miracle: IX," *The Anthonian* 16 (January 1942): 8.

hardships and heartbreaks of this war are felt by our nation, we are coming to recognize that the pillars of that nation must be spiritual and not material."[17] That sentiment came to define the religious revival that followed the war, as Americans searched for a way to understand the double tragedies of economic depression and war. Robert Wuthnow, a sociologist of religion, explains that the moral atrocities of the war and the moral ambiguity of the atomic age encouraged some religious leaders "to argue for great moral crusades, confronting evil head-on; others, for quiet, sustained, individual contributions; still others, for various escapes, withdrawals, or idealistic alternatives." Overall, though, war elevated the role that religion and religious figures played in counseling Americans of all faiths.[18]

In a 1942 essay "The Dead Shall Live," O'Brien spoke to the way in which death depoliticized those who were fighting in the war: "These who are dying so young and in such multitudes are our spiritual kindred, no matter under what flag they fight. When a soldier falls anywhere on the vast battlefield," he counseled, "a brother of mine has fallen"—a remarkable statement in light of the passion unleashed by the war. O'Brien asked his readers to focus on the central Christian reality of the passage from death to resurrection: "Christ's own Resurrection, of course, gives proof and promise to all men's hopes for a future life. He came to earth to save mankind—not just one particular group of men, or one separate nation, but all." The message of ecumenism and hope in the midst of catastrophic hate and death addressed a concern that obsessed millions involved in the war: What was the fate of those who served? It was a question that occupied all those in the war, no matter on which side they fought, and no matter what faith they practiced. O'Brien suggested in the introduction to his essay that "[man] has always had a religion of some kind, and its central point has risen toward the conviction that his identity will continue beyond the grave." In his effort to give readers hope or comfort, O'Brien demonstrated in his work an expansive approach to lived theology that became a mainstay to *The Anthonian*.[19]

---

17. Father John Forest Loviner, Director's Page, *The Anthonian* 17 (July 1943): 14.

18. Robert Wuthnow, *The Restructuring of American Religion: Society and Faith Since World War II* (Princeton, NJ: Princeton University Press, 1988), 54. See also Mark Silk, *Spiritual Politics: Religion and American Since World War II* (New York: Simon and Schuster, 1988); David Ciepley, "The Thirties to the Fifties: Totalitarianism and the Second American Enlightenment," in *Prophecies of Godlessness: Predictions of America's Imminent Secularization, from the Puritans to the Present Day*, ed. Charles Matthews and Christopher McKnight Nichols (New York: Oxford University Press, 2008); Jason W. Stevens, *God-Fearing and Free: A Spiritual History of America's Cold War* (Cambridge: Harvard University Press, 2010); Raymond Haberski Jr., *God and War: American Civil Religion Since 1945* (New Brunswick, NJ: Rutgers University Press, 2012).

19. Father Isidore O'Brien, "The Dead Shall Live," *The Anthonian* 16, no. 2 (1942): 1, 2.

O'Brien used *The Anthonian* to address contemporary problems through essays that began with straightforward theological discussions but made their way toward conclusions with relevance to world affairs. For example, in April 1947 he wrote an essay entitled "Comparison and Contrasts" in which he pointed to an example with obvious profound ramifications: "Satan himself, the original sinner, was the first to suffer from making a comparison," O'Brien related: "He compared himself with God and followed up that proud and impious action by refusing to obey his Creator."[20] From this story O'Brien took readers through the Bible using comparisons and contrasts to suggest the danger lurking in pride even for those who believe they are currying God's special favor. Near the end of his essay O'Brien turned to his readers, with clear implications for the post-Nazi era:

> We do not mean, of course, to suggest that *all* comparisons tend toward evil, but only those—they are many and their evil fruit manifold—which lead to unreasonable dissatisfaction with true vocations in life, to discouragement in the face of trials and crosses, to ambitious changes which neither reason nor circumstances justify; and those others of larger scale which lead to religious and racial persecutions, witch-hunts and wars, to the establishment of color-lines and caste systems, to a silent acceptance (in days now happily ending, let us hope) of slum conditions, sweatshops, child labor and breadlines. It was comparison and contrasts which brought about such conditions as these—made by the holier-than-thous, the self-elected chosen peoples, the super-races, the smugly independent and the snobs.[21]

O'Brien earned a reputation as one of the intellectual guides for mid-century friars. White notes that O'Brien was among a small group assembled to "create a literary culture" among friars in the Holy Name Province. So his work in *The Anthonian* often served a double purpose of speaking to the laity as a priest and demonstrating to his younger charges how to write for their collective audience.[22] For example, for the January 1952 issue, O'Brien wrote an essay explaining the difference between dogmatic and moral theology: the former "tells us what to believe," and the latter "directs us how to live." His immediate reason for writing the essay was to point out that among the supernatural moral virtues, "prudence is defined as that supernatural moral virtue which enables us in all circumstances to form a right judgment by applying general principles to particular conclusions for a moral act." The rest of the essay explicated other moral virtues, specifically, justice, fortitude, and tem-

---

20. Father Isidore O'Brien, "Comparisons and Contrasts," *The Anthonian* 21, no. 2 (1947): 1.
21. Ibid., 5.
22. White, *Peace and Good*, 208.

perance. O'Brien often used his essays as extended sermons on themes readers might have heard but not fully understood, or perhaps had understood but been left wanting something more. Although often relatively brief—only five pages—his essays had a clarity and a biblical grounding that gave them theological weight. His voice was authoritative but not pedantic.[23]

Father Valentine Long, OFM, O'Brien's successor, wrote with a more politically conservative voice in an era defined in part by Catholics who prided themselves on their staunch anticommunism. Patrick Allitt points out that Catholic lay conservatives coming of age in the 1950s "generally [believed] that opposition to communism, foreign and domestic, was their most immediate vital task. . . . Many of them understood the contest with the Soviet Union not simply as a political standoff in which troops, aircraft, and industrial capacity and military resolve would be decisive. Rather, they believed the cold war must be seen as an eschatological struggle in which Christian Western Civilization, the preserve of truth and faith, confronted its demonic nemesis."[24] Long hoped to speak for the Catholic anti-communist position and to those Catholics he believed did not fully appreciate what was at stake in the Cold War.

Long was born in 1902 in Cumberland, Maryland and following graduation from St. Fidelis Seminary in Pennsylvania, was received into St. Bonaventure Friary in 1921. He was eventually ordained a priest in 1927. He studied at St. Bonaventure University, just as O'Brien had done, and earned degrees in theology and English literature. He taught at St. Joseph's Seraphic Seminary in Callicoon, New York, and also taught for over a decade at St. Bonaventure and for another twelve years at Siena College in Loudonville, New York, just outside Albany. Like O'Brien, Long wrote books—ten of them—and many pamphlets for St. Anthony's Guild.[25] With O'Brien's death in 1953, Long took on a larger role for *The Anthonian*.

In one of Long's first published essays, he passionately defended the Crusades as an example to contemporary Christians of the solidarity and force he believed necessary to combat communism. This analogy was not surprising, as many Catholic writers linked what they viewed as a heroic Catholic past to their contemporary American moment. The topic of this essay was the Battle of Muret, in which a crusade against the Cathar heresy had made devotion to the Blessed Mother a crucial factor in the defeat of troops loyal to the Cathars.

---

23. Father Isidore O'Brien, "Our Moral Compass," *The Anthonian* 26 (January 1952): 1.

24. Allitt, *Catholic Intellectuals*, 60.

25. "Valentine Long, OFM: 1902–1998," Franciscan Friars: Holy Name Province, accessed November 13, 2015, http://www.hnp.org/who-we-are/our-friars/deceased-friars/valentine-long.

Long viewed communism as the modern-day heresy and saw the visions at Fatima as the latest manifestation of Christianity's reliance on the Blessed Mother in its struggle to save civilization. More than merely representing a defeat of heresy, Long believed this modern-day parable also warned against weakness of faith: "What is it that gets into people from time to time to drive them to such collective madness; to goad large groups, even entire nations, into working against their own best interests—into opposing and annihilating the sanest and most beautiful elements in life? Why," Long pleaded, "should a folk of high culture of the Provencals, suddenly have found themselves destroying flowers, architecture, babies? . . . Or why, in our own day, should the intelligentsia have so largely fallen prey to the propaganda of a government which features brain-washing, slave labor, the concentration camp?" The charge of the present day, Long ordered, was to pray to the Immaculate Heart of Mary to "take a hand in our muddled affairs."[26]

Throughout the 1950s and early 1960s *The Anthonian* ran many devotional essays on the lives of saints and the Virgin Mary. Each piece typically included ways to improve one's practice of devotion while meditating on the imperatives for such devotion, considering both the present-day and biblical truth as explained by priests such as Long. His essays during this period reinforced a merging of social thought and religious observance. For example, in an essay entitled "Faith Makes Sense," he argued that modernist skepticism about faith should mean little to a truly faithful people because truth for them resides solely in the Church. "They somehow miss the logic that the Almighty who created the laws of nature," Long contended, "ought to be able to suspend or supersede them, if, and when, and as He sees fit."[27]

In a 1957 essay, "The Truth About Man," he wrote about the role of faith in the brutal Soviet crackdown of the 1956 uprising in Hungary. In the summer and fall of 1956, Hungarian students, intellectuals, and labor leaders had attempted to create a more democratic Hungary and to inject more autonomy within Hungarian international affairs. Hungarian agents of Soviet power concluded (as they had in other Eastern Bloc nations) that they needed direct Soviet intervention before they lost any more popular support. For a month in the fall of 1956, the Soviet Union sent tanks, soldiers, and KGB agents to suppress violently the democracy movement in Hungary.[28]

In his six-page essay "Truth About Man," published near the end of Hungarian resistance to the Soviet invasion, Long counseled his readers and friars on the need to retain hope. Reports from Hungary had painted a grim

---

26. Valentine Long, OFM, "Our Lady of Victory," *The Anthonian* 27 (April 1953): 3, 5, 8.

27. Valentine Long, "Faith Makes Sense," *The Anthonian* 29 (October 1955): 8–10.

28. Valentine Long, "The Truth About Man," *The Anthonian* 31 (April 1957): 1.

picture: "The savage slaughter of brave Hungary . . . her patriots shot down or loaded like cattle into boxcars to be shipped into a worse slavery, no pity shown to her women and children, while a horrified block of nations stand by, opening their arms to her pitiable refugees yet afraid to do more. . . ." "What doesn't meet the eye," Long asserted, "was the world, though so dreadfully more removed from our lost paradise than it ever had to be, is still watched over by the same Heavenly Father who made us in His image and has not forsaken the impaired image we have sadly become."[29] The event became a key flashpoint in the Cold War, sparking outrage among many Catholics in the United States who either had direct familial links to the Eastern Bloc countries or were already virulently anticommunist. For many Americans in Catholic parishes, Soviet repression of Hungarian "freedom fighters" (as they became known) symbolized all that was treacherous about the Soviet Union.

Like O'Brien, Long also sought to contribute to the lived theology of American Catholics. For example, Long reminded readers: "If fallen man feels sorry for himself, he is more of a tragedy than he has to be. His intelligence, however weakened, has not lost the power which lifts him to his supremacy over the beast; it can formulate philosophies, conceive sonatas, understand calculus. . . . Hasn't it, in the resources of its power, learnt to split the atom?" And yet Long's approach had a persistent circularity: faith always struck him as universally positive and left him vulnerable to an optimism that those who were faithful would ultimately prevail over their own worst tendencies because they had faith in God and that was good.[30]

Long's conservative tendencies took on a sharper edge following the Second Vatican Council—also called Vatican II, this meeting of Catholic bishops addressed relations between the church and the modern world from 1962 through 1965. The effects of the council generated vigorous debates among Catholics in the United States over changes to the mass, the expanding the role of the laity in church affairs, and a growing ecumenism within the Christian Church. Like some of his colleagues, Long felt alienated by some of the effects of Vatican II and embraced a conservatism in the postconciliar culture wars that followed. After his death, Long was remembered in a tribute written by ultraconservative Catholic writer James Likoudis in the reactionary newspaper *The Wanderer*. Likoudis reported that Long "was a good friend of Catholics United for the Faith [a conservative lay Catholic organization formed to interpret Vatican II for Catholics], and a frequent contributor to the pages of *The Wanderer*." Long's conservative bent took particular objection to what he viewed as "attacks on the Papacy," and his book *Upon This*

29. Ibid., 12.
30. Ibid., 5.

Rock, a 1982 work in apologetics, constituted, "a Thomistic antidote to the post-conciliar smog, which continues to circulate from today's dissenters," wrote Likoudis.[31]

Many of the positions Long developed in essays during the 1950s and 1960s, including his defense of Church dogma against so-called New Theologians and the failure of Catholic laity to be vigilant in their defense of the catechism, were reasserted in *Upon This Rock*. "To one who has studied the inanities of modern philosophy in the light of divine revelation," Long contended, "the present generation may be suffering quite as much from a mental breakdown as from a moral breakdown."[32] To an archconservative such as Likoudis, such statements made Long a hero.

The mission of the postwar *Anthonian* was, generally, to offer lay Catholics ways to live their Church's theology in a time that might seem both to challenge and need their faith. Gerald Dolan, OFM; Nicola Benson, a Franciscan tertiary; and John Sylvester Ahearn, OFM, contributed essays to that mission during this period that demonstrated a different, less conservative side of *The Anthonian*. In his October 1961 essay "You Are the Church," which Dolan subsequently developed into a book by the same title,[33] he began, "Wherever you may go in the world, the Catholic Church is there. Into whatever field of human activity one may enter, the influence of the Church is felt." He emphasized that the declaration Pope Pius XII made in 1946 to a gathering of new cardinals that "the Church cannot shut herself up, inactive, in the privacy of her churches" made clear the mandate that lay Catholics also had to heed. "You are the Church," Dolan exclaimed. "How can you, adult Christians, fulfill this commitment? How can you present a true image of the Church to those about you?" In the early 1960s the answer was to express one's Catholicism through prayer, personal holiness, and apostolic works.[34]

In another 1961 essay in *The Anthonian*, Benson offered St. Francis of Assisi as a more specific mentor for acting on one's faith. After establishing that modern America shared similarities with the era of material prosperity and "spiritual sterility" of Francis's time, Benson explained, "Lovers of St. Francis . . . should keep themselves in his spirit of loving joy in this matter [of our collective fallen state], and be on the lookout to scatter God's largesse when and where they can. Every good deed done in this spirit carries with it

---

31. James Likoudis, "Fr. Valentine Long, O.F.M.: A Belated Tribute to a Saintly Franciscan," *The Wanderer*, January 11, 2001, http://www.jameslikoudispage.com/Saints/frlong.htm, accessed on September 6, 2017.

32. Long quoted in Likoudis, "Fr. Valentine Long, O.F.M."

33. Gerald Dolan, *You Are the Church*, (St. Anthony's Guild Press, 1962).

34. Gerald M. Dolan, "You Are the Church," *The Anthonian* 35, no. 4 (1961): 16.

a measure of the love of Christ who inspires it, and by its kindness brings Him into the lives of others."[35]

By 1964 the tone with which such writers as Dolan and Benson spoke to the laity shifted from one that assumed popular obedience to the Church to one that addressed the waning relevance of it. Dolan asked, "Of what relevance is Christianity to us? What does Christianity mean today? When more than half of every tax dollar is spent on the development and production of armaments, how does one man, whose single vote does not seem to affect governmental policy, become a peacemaker?" His answer: "The Church must be thrust into the middle of modern civilization, even though society seems unable or unwilling to accept her teaching and, at times, ridicules the very fact of her existence." Once again, as in his earlier essay, Dolan pressed readers to be better, stronger, more fervent Catholics by emphasizing the liturgy and practicing the sacraments.[36]

Benson pushed an emphasis on practicing faith a bit further. He wanted readers to consider how faith taken seriously might place other obligations—especially material interests—in proper perspective. "We admire from a safe distance, those dedicated men and women who struggle to reclaim this twentieth century flotsam from the hungering waves of materialism, indifference, and crime. Yet," Benson wrote, "do we often face the fact that we ourselves, together with the vast majority of the human race past and present, are all, in regard to our loving Father in heaven . . . maladjusted children?" He chastised Americans, in particular, for failing to see how troubles in their world were moral in nature, not merely social or political, a failure that he said led them to blame their problems on groups—blacks and whites, Catholics and non-Catholics, capitalists and communists—rather than on the values of their community as a whole. Benson offered what he considered a more proper way: "Seen through the mind of Christ, these divisions mysteriously change; we come to realize that there is only one major division, that of believers and unbelievers. Inside all the former 'enemy' walls are those united to us by belief in and love of God—and those other who, because they have no belief, no love, and think they have no God, need all we have to give." Benson called this unity of believers a "spiritual front." And while he clearly advocated that this front could help unify Americans to do good, he also quite succinctly demonstrated the foundation for a political alliance among groups that in the latter half of twentieth-century America organized as much around the fact of being religious (in opposition to what they saw as secularization) as around their separate religious identities.[37]

---

35. Nicola Benson, "Easier for a Camel . . . ," *The Anthonian* 35, no. 4 (1961): 8, 13.
36. Dolan, "Because the Bread Is One," *The Anthonian* 38, no. 1 (1964): 5, 16.
37. Benson, "In the Cool of the Day," *The Anthonian* 38, no. 1 (1964): 6, 8, 12.

In addition to observing a division between the faithful and the secular, *The Anthonian* also addressed the postconciliar anxiety that accompanied changes in the Church, in its Mass, and in American society in general. Ahearn put it this way in 1968: "The most optimistic measurer of the Catholic mood today would have to confess that many Catholics are confused, pained, resentful, and in practical doubt about what to believe and whom to listen to. Everywhere, voices are being raised—to defend traditional teachings or lament their passing, to attach in one direction or another, to propound new, strange-sounding teachings."[38] Ahearn was born in 1921 in Salem, Massachusetts, and was ordained a priest in 1950. He served as a director of the print shop and an instructor at St. Bonaventure University in the 1950s and worked for St. Anthony's Guild and Sunday Publications from the late 1950s through the late 1970s.[39] Ahearn's essays in the *Anthonian* demonstrated how much the so-called little Franciscan magazines during the 1960s attempted to provide lay Catholics with guidance for how to live within a changing Church. In his essay "They Rule the Church of God," published in July 1968, he offered commentary on how to follow the teachings of Catholic officials and how to negotiate the fact that there were a set of people who did "rule the Church of God." In light of the re-assertion of Papal authority in *Humanae Vitae* over family life and childbearing, Ahearn reasoned that the "Church's moral competence" extended beyond matters that were strictly religious: "What would it profit us if the pope and bishops should preach Christ's words on the dignity of man, justice, mercy, marriage, but fail to guide us in particular instances involving, say, abortion, fair wages, racial equality, birth control, education of children, almsgiving, filial respect, patriotism, collective bargaining? Just such considerations are the object of the bishops' ordinary teaching prerogative."[40]

With the death of Father John Forest Loviner in 1970, the founder of St. Anthony's Guild and the director of its publications, a distinctly new tone emerged in the *Anthonian*. Father Salvatore Fink, OFM, the order's vocation director from 1952 to 1967, inaugurated two major changes as director of the *Anthonian*: the magazine focused each issue on a particular individual and incorporated more photo essays. To help craft the new format, Fink recruited his fellow friar, Fr. Boniface Hanley, OFM. Both Fink and Hanley, who, according to historian Joseph White, collaborated on seventy-two issues of the magazine that profiled "the lives and ministries of Catholics who had a

---

38. John Sylvester Ahearn, OFM, "They Rule the Church of God," *The Anthonian* 42, no. 3 (July 1968): 1.

39. "John Sylvester Ahern [sic], OFM: 1921–2005," Franciscan Friars: Holy Name Province, accessed November 14, 2015, http://www.hnp.org/who-we-are/our-friars/deceased-friars/john-s-ahern.

40. Ahearn, "They Rule the Church," 5.

major impact on people's lives."[41] Many of these profiles rang with a kind of heroic truth about people who had done extraordinary things during the Holocaust, as missionaries around the world, or by being exemplary Americans. While very few were Franciscans—all were Catholic, including Mother Mary Alphonsa (born Rose Hawthorne), Matt Talbot (the Dubliner), Father (now Blessed) Charles Eugène de Foucauld, Mother (now St.) Teresa of Calcutta (born Agnes Boyaxhiu), Father Andrew Quinn, St. Peter Claver, St. John Neumann, St. Maximilian Kolbe, Pierre Toussaint, and St. Teresa Benedicta of the Cross (born Edith Stein).

Fink was a self-taught photographer and a friar with, as Hanley remarked, "megatons of energy and talent."[42] Fink was born in 1916 in Buffalo, New York, and was ordained a priest in June 1944. He was quite famously and successfully a chaplain to a correctional facility for youth and the vocation director of Holy Name Province for seventeen years. He went on to direct St. Anthony's Guild from 1970 to 1988. Fink had honed his skills as a photographer during his stint as vocation director, taking pictures of the friars at work and play to encourage young men to join the order. He and Hanley not only edited dozens of issues of *The Anthonian* in the 1970s and 1980s, but also produced three books and numerous articles that coupled Fink's photographs with Hanley's writing.[43] Fink died in 1991. Hanley was a friar of Holy Name Province in New York City. He was born in 1924 in Brooklyn, and attended St. Joseph's Seraphic Seminary, the OFM seminary in Calicoon, New York. Hanley professed vows in 1946, was ordained in 1950, and received his master's degree in executive leadership from Columbia University in 1980.[44] Hanley not only helped change the format of *The Anthonian* but authored fourteen books. Before Hanley's death in 2010, he wrote a brief biography of Father Franz Stock, a World War II–era German priest and prison chaplain who is currently under consideration for canonization.

The transition toward a more biographical and historical approach to subjects could be detected throughout the essays in the earlier 1970s, such as Ahearn's essay "The Indestructible 'I,'" in which he wrote at length about finding oneself in both the uniqueness of the self and in the distinctiveness of heroic individuals. Not surprisingly Ahearn used St. Francis as the archetype who had been written about so thoroughly that his biography becomes something to worship, not his example of living out a practical life in a real time. "As we approach the saints for light and guidance," Ahearn observed, "we

---

41. White, *"Peace and Good in America."*
42. Boniface F. Hanley, OFM, "Megatons of Energy and Talent," *The Anthonian* 63 (Winter 1989): 3.
43. Ibid., 6–8.
44. Obituary of Boniface Hanley, *The Press of Atlantic City*, September 26, 2010.

need feel no compulsion to conform our practical thinking, our procedural decisions to theirs. Devotion to them does not entail a slavish imitation of their unique piety, their historically conditioned ideas. . . . What they bequeath us is the inspiration to develop for ourselves, in a manner consonant with our times, and our personalities, the qualities which bring one to holiness."[45] The magazine used the lives of St. Francis, other recognized Catholic saints, and contemporary figures with strong social justice credentials to provoke readers into thinking about the lives of such people as glimpses of what was possible in a Catholic life.

Beside changes to the format of the *Anthonian*, the tone of the magazine also grew less conservative. A signature indication of this shift was an essay in 1971 by Sally Cunneen titled "Is the Church Leaving *Me*?"[46] Cuneen and her husband, Joseph Cunneen, had begun editing an ecumenical Catholic journal called *Cross Currents* in 1950 in part to address the apparent lack of a straightforward intellectual journal in Catholic culture; it became a pioneering periodical of the ecumenical movement of the 1960s and 1970s. Catholic historian David O'Brien notes that the Cunneens "knew there were a lot of smart Catholics out there, some in, but most outside of, Catholic academic institutions, and they wanted to invite them into the worldwide flowering of Catholicism, first in the reflective assessment after World War II, then during the exciting explosions of Vatican II, then amid the awakening of fresh ideas and practices across the postconciliar and postcolonial global church."[47] In her essay for *The Anthonian* Cunneen addressed the typical laments about changes to the Mass and the apparent crises among priests and nuns (some leaving the Church altogether) in her discussion of how few Catholics at the time truly understood the Church's complex position in the world.

> What we have discovered is that the Church is a living organism, not a museum of tradition. In this understanding, well expressed in the [Second Vatican] Council's calling it "the people of God," we are able to comprehend both how everything we loved and were nourished by in our youth was good in its time . . . and why in a different world the Church must call upon its mysterious capacity for life and continuing growth if it is indeed to be true to the promise of Christ that he will be with us all days.[48]

---

45. John Sylvester Ahearn, "The Indestructible 'I,'" *The Anthonian* 44 (April 1970): 8.

46. Sally Cunneen, "Is the Church Leaving *Me*?," *The Anthonian* 45, no. 1 (1971): 19, 20.

47. David O'Brien, quoted in Jerry Filteau, "Cunneen, CrossCurrents Shaped US Catholicism for 50 Years," *National Catholic Reporter*, August 19, 2012, accessed November 15, 2015, http://ncronline.org/news/cunneen-crosscurrents-shaped-us-catholicism-50-years.

48. Cunneen, "Church Leaving *Me*?," 19, 20.

Another essay in the same issue by Sister Margaret Mary Modde, OSF, the national director of the Sister Formation Conference, posed a question similar to Cunneen's: "Are the sisters the same?" Modde provided a twist on the usual observation that because many nuns had begun to look different— that is, by no longer wearing a habit or living together in a cloister—they had become something different. Reflecting on the pioneering spirit that enlivened many women religious in American history, Modde asked her readers to give each nun a chance, as the Second Vatican Council recommended in *Guadium et spes*, to "discern the signs of the times, so that her free response will be made in accordance with them." She acknowledged, "It follows, then, that you will experience some changes and modifications that Sister will make in order to have her effective and affective presence felt in the Church and the world. Sister is a woman possessing the gifts peculiar to her role as helpmate—but she must be allowed to exercise them in her own unique way."[49]

From 1988 to the present, *The Anthonian* changed its design again, this time into a glossy publication, under a new editor, Father Kevin Mackin, OFM. The new magazine focuses more on contemporary Franciscans doing good in the world as a call for vocations. To mark that transition Mackin fittingly ran a special tribute to Hanley and Fink in the winter of 1989. The issue marked the close of an era and the end of a generation of priests who had witnessed great changes in the Church, and translated them through their work in *The Anthonian*.

FRIAR

Another publication from the Friars Minor of the Holy Name Province of New York began in January 1954 simply called *Friar*. In a bold editorial to introduce this new publication, the founding editor, Father Rudolph Harvey declared that the magazine would be a "clean current of living water" in a publishing world "brimming with froth and filth." Harvey made clear the blunt stance he would take on issues. By 1954 Catholics could choose from many different kinds of Catholic periodicals and even many kinds of Franciscan outlets. Yet the editor of *Friar* believed the "introduction of a new Catholic magazine [would stand as] a positive act of the highest patriotism in these days when disloyalty is found even in high places, because every Catholic organ of opinion has a divine mandate to expose the conspiracy existing abroad and at home, to extirpate the Christian ideals of Western civilization." While coupling religious devotion and patriotism was fairly conventional in

---

49. Sister Margaret Mary Modde, OSF, "Are Sisters the Same?," *The Anthonian* 45, no. 1 (1971): 17, 18.

the 1950s America, Harvey sought to distinguish *Friar* by placing anticommunism at the center of this Franciscan magazine.[50]

Throughout the Cold War, American Catholics had become notorious for their fixation on the threat of international communism. In his comprehensive history of American anticommunism, historian Richard Gid Powers writes: "Catholics took particular pride in their church's uncompromising anticommunism. American Catholics were told that the world Church had turned to America to protect Catholicism from communism."[51] American church leaders such as New York's Cardinal Francis Spellman and the Washington, D.C., foreign policy hawk Father Edmund Walsh crafted high-profile roles for themselves in the collaboration between the nation and the church.[52] The Catholic press was supposed to play its part by maintaining the tone of Catholic anticommunism for the laity.

Harvey agreed with that mission. He was a friar from St. Bonaventure Friary in Paterson who earned a doctorate in philosophy from Catholic University of America. The idea for *Friar* came from the prolific Isidore O'Brien, who as part of a literary committee of Holy Name Province suggested creating a new publication following the demise of *Franciscan*. According to White, O'Brien suggested that he might not have begun his own career in writing without that older magazine, so he believed that starting *Friar* would both develop the literary abilities of the friars as well as communicate a message. O'Brien died in 1953 just before the new publication launched, and thus Harvey stepped in as editor, a post he held for the next twenty-five years.[53]

White observes that the periodical had "a certain tension" during Harvey's tenure as editor. In addition to being editor of *Friar*, Harvey was a prolific and pointed contributor, yet his anticommunist "stridency increased in sharpness and bluntness through the years, in contrast to the more judicious contributions of others," as White puts it.[54] For example, Harvey openly supported US Senator Joseph McCarthy, whose red-baiting tactics terrorized many innocent Americans in public service. That position on McCarthy reflected deeper political pathologies that Harvey harbored about his era. In his first editorial, "For God and Country," Harvey declared his fidelity to George Washington and Abraham Lincoln and took issue with historians who questioned or sought

---

50. "Why Another Magazine," *Friar* 1 (January 1955): inside front cover.
51. Richard Gid Powers, *Not Without Honor: The History of American Anti-Communism* (New York: The Free Press, 1995), 251.
52. See John Cooney, *The American Pope: The Life and Times of Cardinal Spellman* (New York: Crown, 1984); and Patrick McNamara, *A Catholic Cold War: Edmund A. Walsh, SJ, and the Politics of American Anticommunism* (New York: Fordham University Press, 2005).
53. White, *Peace and Good*, 296.
54. Ibid., 297.

to debunk the sanctity of both presidents' legacies. "Only the width of the United States away, the barbarians are hammering again at the frontiers of civilization," Harvey warned. "Here at home their vanguard is tampering with the foundation-stones laid by Washington, Jefferson and Lincoln from the blueprint drawn by Aquinas and Bellarmine." He saw *Friar* playing a direct role in defending the nation from such enemies, for the "Catholic Press is the most patriotic press to be found anywhere on earth. . . . Founded for moral rather than commercial purposes, it is less exposed to the weaknesses of human nature. Its single dedication is to Truth."[55]

In a 1979 editorial as *Friar* neared the end of its run, Harvey addressed the age-old topic of Original Sin and its lost relevance. "Original sin is an unpopular subject," he noted, suggesting that "some of our mod theologians refuse to believe it at all, presumably because they did not originate it." Harvey ruminated on what progress had wrought, beside the decline of censorship and the expansion of freedom. "Are people in general more just and merciful, more modest and reverent, wiser or humbler or generally saner than in ages past? Have we better artists, sculptors or poets . . . ?" He commented on his rhetorical questions by returning to the idea that Original Sin kept humanity from rejoicing unconditionally in its progress. The danger, Harvey thought, lay in altering ancient truths to make them accord with the illusion that progress had created a new thing called modern man: "It is this non-entity that is used as a tailor's dummy for the patterning of so much of our social planning and even for some of our moral and liturgical evaluations."[56]

Over the lifecycle of *Friar*, Harvey's stridency defined the magazine's character. For example, the June 1954 issue defended movie censorship. In an essay called "Why Can't I See That Movie?" Damian Blaher, OFM, sought to counter what he considered a popular misconception: that censorship violates sacred American principles, such as liberty, and that Catholicism is behind such censorship. Conflating bigotry toward Catholicism with anticensorship in general, Blaher's essay appeared at an auspicious moment in the history of film censorship. Just two years earlier the US Supreme Court had handed down a ruling in the landmark case *Burstyn v. Wilson*, reversing a fifty-year-old precedent that allowed courts to treat motion pictures as nothing more than commercial products rather than as protected speech.[57] The movie that sparked this case was Roberto Rossellini's small 1948 film *Il Miracolo* (*The Miracle*), hotly and at times violently denounced by Catholic Church officials and laity in New York City. The Court's decision did not end censorship

---

55. Rudolf Harvey, "For God and Country," *Friar* 1 (January 1955): 6–7.
56. Rudolf Harvey, "The Blight at the Root," *Friar* 51 (May 1979): 3–5.
57. *Joseph Burstyn, Inc. v. Wilson*, 343 US 495 (1952), accessed July 20, 2017, https://www.law.cornell.edu/supremecourt/text/343/495.

entirely, but it did highlight the undue influence the Catholic Church exercised in the control of movie distribution and exhibition. Thus by 1954 control over the content of movies had begun to unravel, and independent producers in America and abroad began to contest the boundaries of popular taste for movies, much to the dismay of Franciscan journals like *Friar*.[58]

In "Why Can't I See That Movie?" Blaher presented instances of acceptable censorship, from illicit drugs to censorship of wartime letters, as evidence of an American understanding and willingness to tolerate censorship. Of course, he noted, many of these examples posed direct physical danger to people. But moral hazards were just as dangerous. "Without putting all the blame for moral delinquency or moral breakdowns on the movies," Blaher reasoned, "one can scarcely gainsay the fact that noxious reading and pernicious movies have a baneful influence." And so if any responsibility for these things could be connected to movies, then the state had a direct interest in restricting the public's exposure to them—lest Americans be damaged.[59] Blaher defended the instincts of the Legion of Decency to classify films for the protection of American souls and declared censorship in the name of such righteousness to be consistent with American freedom.

The debate over censorship in the United States took on special significance in New York City, the locus of *Friar*. New York long had the nation's most important movie culture because of its outsized influence in the financing of movies and the sheer number of moviegoers—the city could make or break films. The large Catholic population in New York also exerted influence that was disproportionate to the number of Catholics across the nation. In other words an essay like Blaher's in *Friar* affirmed that some Catholics were ready to defend their influence in movie culture, while it also illustrated an issue that divided Catholics. The fact that such essays seemed necessary hinted at the dissension within the Catholic population itself. That is, when priests feel the need to explain why parishioners should follow the Church's official line, things have already gone awry. Within a decade the Legion had lost its bite, and essays such as Blaher's would sound misguided.

Because the editors of *Friar* had consistently billed it as a family magazine, they tried to publish articles on topics relevant to the upbringing of children. Many of those pieces came from Father Alfred Martin, OFM, who was born in Dayton, Kentucky, in September 1896 and was ordained a priest in June 1921. From 1930 through 1935 Martin studied psychology at the Catholic University of America and then assumed the role as confessor and counselor at St. Francis of Assisi Church in midtown Manhattan from 1935 to 1944. After a brief stint in Florida, he returned to New York and began writing for

---

58. See Wittern-Keller and Haberski, *Miracle Case*.
59. Damian J. Blaher, "Why Can't I See That Movie," *Friar* 1 (June 1954): 12.

Friar, to which he contributed more than two hundred articles—many of which were rebundled and published as pamphlets.[60] He died in 1973.

A typical contribution from Martin dealt with the idea of "happiness in the home." Clearly employing his training in psychology, Martin addressed the issue of parenting through a classic dilemma: "why so many parents get such a small return in domestic joy for the labors and sacrifices they make for their children." He discussed his observations as a series of cautionary tales, or what he called "joy killers," which included tendencies such as exaggerating little mishaps, anticipating desired goals in ways that almost invariably leave parents disappointed, being ignorant of child development and normal behavior, and lastly failing to moderate what he generously called "parental passion," the outbursts (sometimes violent) of parents who are not only supposed to be in control but who do in fact control the house they keep. He made this last point quite clear: "Children who grow up in an atmosphere of emotional tantrums are scarred and handicapped by it for the rest of their lives. They generally become poor parents themselves and pass the curse on to their children." Interestingly, whereas Martin clearly used psychological research to offer advice to parents, he did not suggest that the Catholic Church or its schools were essential to the proper upbringing of children.[61]

White points out that Martin was the most prolific contributor to *Friar*. In addition to his incredible output for the magazine, he also published popular pamphlets with titles such as *Our Emotions and Our Moods* and *What Will I Do with My Life?* According to White, Martin's pamphlets sold so well he earned the distinction of being among "the most influential of the province's writers." By the mid-1960s, however, *Friar* had lost a good bit of its circulation, dropping to fewer than thirty-six thousand copies a year. By the late 1970s many magazines in the US encountered financial trouble from rising costs of publication. The *Friar* did not survive this crisis and ceased publication in 1973.[62]

THE VIEW: A CATHOLIC VIEW ON THE NEWS

Two other small magazines with ideologically conservative editors shared the greater New York City market with *The Anthonian* and *Friar*, and both engaged in the post–World War II debate over the role Catholics played in American culture. *The View: A Catholic View on the News* and *Padre: A Fran-*

---

60. "Alfred Martin, OFM, 1896–1973," Franciscan Friars: Holy Name Province, accessed November 16, 2015, http://www.hnp.org/who-we-are/our-friars/deceased-friars/alfred-martin.

61. Father Alfred Martin, OFM, "Happiness in the Home," *Friar* 24 (January 1966): 3, 10.

62. White, *Peace and Good*, 296–97.

ciscan Monthly of General Catholic Interest (discussed in the next section) held to a consistently conservative line on the Catholic interpretation and response to issues such as prayer in schools and popular culture.

The Capuchin Fathers in Yonkers, New York, had begun publishing a small magazine called *The Cowl* in 1937 as a house organ; by 1955 it grew into *The View: A Catholic View on the News*. Father Hugh Morley, OFM Cap, was editor of the magazine from its origins in the late 1930s through November 1962. A native New Yorker, he hailed from an old Irish neighborhood in East Harlem (across from the larger Irish neighborhood in the South Bronx) and joined the Capuchins during his high school years, attending the minor seminary of Mary Immaculate Seraphicate in Garrison, New York. He entered the order of Capuchins in 1928 and was ordained in 1935. He developed a strong love of journalism, going on to graduate from the Columbia University School of Journalism and becoming a fixture among the Catholic press for more than twenty-five years. In 1962 Morley was appointed the representative for the Catholic Press Union at the United Nations.

As an editor Morley emphasized the plight of Catholic education, fights over public funding for parochial schools, the dangers of big labor unions, and, of course, anticommunism.[63] In other words the magazine followed a rather standard line among New York City Catholics. The magazine also used sections with catchy titles such as "We Cheer" and "We Chide" to heap praise or scorn on a diverse collection of public officials and news items.

For example, R. Boyle, editor of this section in 1962, "cheered" former president Dwight Eisenhower for decrying popular American culture and entertainment. He also praised the Maryland Court of Appeals for deciding that "Bible reading and recitation of the Lord's Prayer in Baltimore public schools do not violate the U.S. Constitution." Boyle "chided" Frank Stanton, president of CBS, for "defending the exportation of any and every type of TV program overseas," including one episode of *The Defenders* that, according to Boyle, "advocated legalized abortion."[64]

Over time, the magazine increased its publication of news about the entertainment industry (television and movies especially) and journalism, while it continued to run small pieces about sports. In mid-1962 it also started a section digesting opinions from Catholic magazines on hot topics of the day, from school prayer to ecumenism.

Morley wrote from a classic conservative Catholic position—he disliked rapid change from any direction and had suspicions regarding those Catholics who

---

63. See "For the 4th 'R' $300,000,000 a Year: The Catholic School—Growth and Problems," *Catholic View* 19 (September 1955): 8–9. See also: McGreevy, *Catholicism and American Freedom*, 166–88.

64. R. Boyle, "We Cheer, We Chide," *The View*, 26, #6 (June 1962), 15-16.

appeared to have status in the secular press. For example, reflecting upon the debates stirred up by Catholic thinkers such as John Tracy Ellis and John Courtney Murray, Morley chided such men for being "as irritating as they are pompously negative."[65] In postwar American Catholic culture, Murray was the best-known and best-respected Catholic theologian, and Ellis was his counterpart among historians. Both had written influential essays critiquing the lack of sophistication among many Catholic cultural critics, not to mention Church officials and laity, for failing to engage with significant intellectual trends of the day. In 1955 Ellis published his landmark essay based on a talk he had given to the Catholic Commission on Intellectual and Cultural Affairs in which he observed, caustically, that American Catholics had yet to produce or contribute to American thought in a way proportional to their huge population and long history in the United States.[66] In 1956 Murray went one step farther in chiding Catholic officials and those who echoed their often antidemocratic-sounding dictates in his dissection of the Church's history with censorship. "A human society is inhumanly ruled when it is ruled only, or mostly, by fear," Murray argued. "Good laws are obeyed by the generality because they are good laws, they merit and receive the consent of the community, as valid legal expressions of the community's own convictions as to what is just and unjust, good or evil."[67]

In a 1961 essay criticizing both Ellis and Murray, Morley lumped them together as a group of "intellectuals" (his ironic quotation marks) who "bemoaned the same old lack of Catholic influence in the cultural and intellectual life of the United States." Alas, Morley argued that Catholic chauvinism rather than pessimism should have carried the day: "What is best in American life is Catholic at its core." He credited Catholics for inspiring the Declaration of Independence and for making apparent such "fundamental principles" as "individual liberty, human rights, respect for private property, the family as the basis of society and the dignity of man." Rather remarkably, Morley argued that American culture was both a product of what Catholics had given the United States and, at the same time, a debased culture run by Hollywood and big business. The contradiction simply meant, according to Morley, that Catholic intellectuals needed to focus on whatever was positive in American life, for that could be traced back to the Church, and denounce all that was negative, for Church principles could correct what ailed the nation.[68]

In general the tone of *The View* could seem a bit grouchy. When turning to women and news in two discrete sections, "Women *in* the News" and "Women

---

65. Morley, "Viewpoint," *The View*, 25, #3 (March 1961), 2.
66. Ellis, "American Catholics," 351–88.
67. John Courtney Murray, "Literature and Censorship," *Books on Trial*, June–July, 1956, 444.
68. Father Hugh Morley, "For Crying Out Loud!" *The View* 25 (March 1961): 2–3.

and the News," Doris Gray, editor of those sections, groused about "One-Worldism" (the theory that the United Nations had an obligation to draw people into a unified global government); the trend of teaching elementary-school children to speak a foreign language, such as Spanish or French; the fickleness of "youngsters huckstering everything" on television commercials; and new Parisian fashions that threatened to turn modern women back into "flappers."[69]

However, *The View* also helped reveal a difference between those Catholics who practiced a reactionary form of conservatism and those who were beginning to follow a more moderate line during the Cold War. Morley's April 1962 editorial about the political extremes in the nation appeared to make this distinction clear. Morley used the publication of Reverend John F. Cronin's booklet *Communism: Threat to Freedom* (1962) as way to address what he viewed as the dangers of the extremes in American politics—right as well as left. Although the booklet's title did not imply ambivalence toward communism, Cronin's basic argument was that as bad as communism was, anticommunism in the United States had grown so rabid in some cases (such as with the John Birch Society) that the reaction against communism threatened American freedom more than communism itself. Communism was indeed a threat, he argued, but it was an external threat to be dealt with by a strong military. Far from offering a defense of left-wing politics, Cronin did suggest that some shades of anticommunism had grown too dark for their own good.[70]

Morley's decision to feature Cronin's book generated some interesting letters. Mr. and Mrs. John J. Clarke of Woodhaven, New York wrote that his editorial on Cronin's book was "another of your subtle attacks on the right wing in this country." *The View*, they said, had committed an additional sin by reviewing the book differently than had other Catholic periodicals, such as *The Wanderer* and *The Tablet*. George F. Groves of Forest Hills, New York cried: "No doubt you agree with Father Cronin and his shameful utterances about a great American who died for his country. I mean the late Joseph McCarthy." Frank Maclus of Ardsley, New York, chided Morley for playing politics, something apparently a priest should not do, and argued that taking "this holy middle-of-the-road" position was antithetical to Christ's teachings.[71]

In the same issue *The View* published a letter from Mary Anderson of New York City denouncing the magazine for an editorial titled "Operation Equality." The editors (presumably Morley) had made it clear that the magazine supported intermarriage of blacks and whites and the social and political equality between blacks and whites.[72] *The View* also made clear that those who

69. Doris Gray, "Women and the News," *The View* 25 (March 1961): 22.
70. Father Hugh Morley, "Left, Right, and Center," *The View* 26 (April 1962), 2–3.
71. Letters, and Father Hugh Morley, responses, *The View* 26 (June 1962): 2–3.
72. Morley, "Operation Equality," *The View*, 26 (May 1962), 2.

did not accept integration would fall outside the Church's teaching and could be excommunicated. "Wonderful!" Anderson sarcastically exclaimed. "The Catholic Church is in politics." Morley noted below this letter: "The disobedient Catholic. When Pope Pius XI condemned the racism of Adolf Hitler, he was applying an everlasting doctrine of the Catholic Church."[73]

In 1962 Morley received an appointment to the United Nations and left the magazine. The last issue published with him as editor (September 1962) had an especially provocative cover: an image of a white-haired justice of the US Supreme Court sitting at a desk with a pair of scissors, looking over a book and cutting the word "God" out of it.[74] Standing behind him, hands clasped in obvious approval of this activity, was Satan. The cartoon captured the sentiment of Catholics who were enraged by the Court's ruling in *Engel v. Vitale* declaring it unconstitutional for the state to require students to recite a prayer in classrooms.[75] Given Morley's consistent position on religion in schools, and especially the role Catholic schools played in American education, it was an apt image with which to send him off.

PADRE: A FRANCISCAN MONTHLY OF GENERAL CATHOLIC INTEREST

Padre began publication in March 1950 as the journal of the Province of the Immaculate Conception in New York City. The first editor, Father Luke Ciampi, OFM, explained to readers that the magazine would not be about Franciscans but rather "be a mirror that reflects the Franciscan slant on life, liberty, and the pursuit of happiness. It is Franciscan preaching and teaching, applying the Word of God to everyday life." Once again, a Franciscan journal sought to be patriotic and Catholic—a combination necessary in the heyday of the Cold War, during which religion grew increasingly crucial to defending the nation from the scourge of communism. The friars chose the name *Padre* to emphasize the nature of Franciscans as priests of the people.[76]

Like the *View*, *Padre* addressed the usual Catholic issues. An editorial took issue with the Barden Bill, a 1949 measure in Congress to restrict federal funding to public schools exclusively. The issue of public funds for Catholic schools remained essential for *Padre*, as it did for many other Catholic journals at the time. Ciampi reiterated a skewed version of American educational history, lumping all private and parochial schools together against the public

---

73. Mary Anderson, letter to editor, and Father Hugh Morley, response, *The View* 26 (June 1962): 2.

74. *The View*, 26 (September 1962).

75. *Engel v. Vitale*, 370 US 421 (1962), accessed July 20, 2017, https://www.law.cornell.edu/supremecourt/text/370/421.

76. Luke Ciampi, "This 'n' That," *Padre* 1 (March 1950): 4.

system. He remarked, "Under a Supreme Court ruling God is put out of the classrooms of elementary and high schools . . . [and] those private and parochial schools which still dare adhere to the old traditional American Way of Life are penalized for it."[77]

In addition to the dangers of secularization, Ciampi also chastised Catholic families for allowing "printed poison" into their homes—a reference to comic books and cheap novels that caused an uproar among the guardians of traditional Catholic culture.[78] Historian Una Cadegan explains where such a sensibility fit in the church. "Regulation of reading and publication generated extensive companion literature," she writes, "intended both to explicate for Catholics the obligations the Church's law imposed on them and to construct a history and a rationale by which writers, scholars, and intellectuals could see themselves as both American and Catholic."[79] Ciampi made a case in the early issues of *Padre* that he and his writers acted as "the leaven of good Catholic reading," and he asked Catholics to subscribe to this or other Catholic publications to demonstrate that "you are a Catholic . . . in your thinking, speaking and acting."[80] Another way to understand Ciampi's approach was to view it, as historian Philip Gleason explains, as part of an outlook that filtered everything through a Catholic sensibility and identity. "The unifying impulse expressed itself in a variety of ways," Gleason writes, "in the comprehensiveness of Catholic teaching there was a 'Catholic viewpoint' on nearly everything; in the prizing of 'integral humanism' and curricular integration; in the concern for establishing and maintaining the correct order of relationships in every sphere (conjugal, familial, economic, etc.); and in the generalized conviction that the faith should make a difference in whatever one did."[81] Thus *Padre* sought to channel its readers toward mainstream Catholicism.

Like other Franciscan magazines *Padre* welcomed questions from readers that were quite thoughtful and often difficult. In December 1961 the magazine gave a priest named Father Raymond, OFM, STD, the opportunity to answer questions about why bad things happen to good people. Meditating on "why the good must suffer," Father Raymond explained: "Christ Himself tells us that the price of union with Him is suffering." Such suffering, he continued, is not an end in itself but a way for the "suffering Christian [to play] an intimate role with Christ in the redemption of man." While Father Raymond made a small gesture to personalize the pain of the letter writer, his

---

77. Ibid., 5.
78. Ibid., 5.
79. Cadegan, *All Good Books*, 125.
80. Ciampi, "A Catholic Hallmark," *Padre* 7 (February 1956): 48.
81. Philip Gleason, "Neoscholasticism as Preconciliar Ideology," *US Catholic Historian* 7, no. 4 (Fall 1988): 403–4.

point was that suffering cannot be mitigated by anything but the faith that has sustained Christians since the Crucifixion.[82]

Padre remained decidedly small in scale, printing the names of those for whom masses would be offered and other local news for the province. It ran a small section of cartoons and word games for children and it too succumbed to budget woes and stopped publication in the early 1970s.

THE WAY OF ST. FRANCIS

The Way grew out of a publication known as *The Western Tertiary* that began in 1938 and changed its name to *The Way of St. Francis* in 1944 and then simply *The Way* by 1962 and finally *Way/Catholic Viewpoints*.[83] At the center of this publication was Father Brendan Mitchell, a friar who cultivated a productive and long-term relationship between the Province of Santa Barbara, where the magazine was published, and the large and active Secular Franciscan Order (SFO) in the Province. Mitchell wrote editorials throughout the 1950s and early 1960s in a section that began each issue called "By the Way." In the July 1956 issue Mitchell offered a glimpse into the general editorial approach the magazine took. In a tone that projected informality and intimacy, Mitchell related, "The moment you read these words our minds have come into contact. . . . It's probably a thin thread, as meetings of the mind go. But pointedly person-to-person." He wondered, "Is it true that *Way* is probably the only magazine in which you notice who wrote what?" Did it matter if his readers noticed, Mitchell mused? Perhaps not, he concluded, because, no matter what, he and his writers were "committed to this personal kind of journalism. Stemming from the spirit of St. Francis, *The Way* couldn't be otherwise." This tone foregrounded Franciscan ideals, making *The Way* sound a bit different from its contemporaries. Mitchell stated, "While we want THE WAY's typography, layout, circulation, advertising, etc., to be thoroughly professional, we don't want its heart and spirit to be anything of the sort. We are engaged in communicating ideas—ideas distilled from the essence of Christianity in a Franciscan percolator." He offered his readers "a steaming cup of brew."[84]

It is difficult to assess whether *The Way*'s message distilled a Franciscan expression of Christianity better than other publications, though its positions on key issues suggest a significant difference. For example, in contrast to *Padre*, *The Way* also ran a short editorial on the responsibility to vote. In the

---

82. A.C.D. question, Fr. Raymond response, "Here's Your Answer," *Padre*, 12 (December 1961), 436.

83. For consistency, I will refer to the magazine by the name it is most often called, *The Way*.

84. Brendan Mitchell, By the Way, *The Way of St. Francis* 12 (July 1956): 3.

Padre piece on the 1960 election, Ciampi had noted the previous presidential election for its lackluster voter turnout.[85] In the November 1956 issue of *The Way*, Mitchell made the same observation about the 1952 election. Yet rather than play upon either the patriotic duty of citizens to vote or an outright appeal to a particular party and its candidate's ability to accord with a certain kind of Catholic worldview, Mitchell wondered if those who don't vote were simply discouraged by the distance they felt from so many things in life. He suggested, "Maybe this reluctant citizen can be reached if he is reminded that the act of voting is extremely personal—casting a vote is important to him." While showing concern for the ethical obligation of voting, Mitchell also illustrated the emphasis his magazine put on the social and personal as well as the political and doctrinal.[86] The soft personalism of *The Way* was a harbinger of the more extreme personalism that dominated 1960s culture that placed individuals in direct relation to nature and God.[87]

During the 1960s, a key person in the magazine's transition toward a more radical posture was Father Simon Scanlon, OFM, a Franciscan priest who worked at the magazine as assistant editor, then contributing editor, and finally by 1970 as editor. Scanlon was born in St. Louis in 1910, fought in World War II, joined the Franciscans in 1947, and was ordained a priest in 1954. Historian Jeffrey Burns points out that Scanlon emphasized social justice at the magazine, a position that grew out of his work with the poor in St. Boniface Parish in San Francisco, located in the Tenderloin District.[88]

At *The Way*, Scanlon and his fellow editors defended their interest in running articles and editorials on "the sore spots of our society" and "current controversial issues: capital punishment, peace marchers, atomic testing, medical care for the aged."[89] Despite objections from critics who viewed such material as secularism run amok, the editors proved unwilling to let the secular press monopolize discussion on political and social issues. Thus, as Burns observed, the magazine began running essays by Catholic liberal intellectuals: "Barbara Ward on ecumenism, Thomas Merton on the nuclear threat, Karl Rahner on free speech in the Catholic Church, and U.N. Secretary General U Thant on peace."[90]

Among the bellwether issues for Catholics was movie censorship, and *The Way* offered a new approach compared to other Catholic journals. Scanlon affirmed a new era in moviegoing for Catholics by publishing a pamphlet enti-

---

85. Ciampi, "All-American Jury."

86. Brendan Mitchell, By the Way, *The Way of St. Francis* 12 (November 1956): 3.

87. For the broader influence of personalism in American life, see James J. Farrell, *The Spirit of the Sixties: Making Postwar Radicalism* (New York: Routledge, 1997).

88. Jeffrey Burns, "Simon Scanlon, *The Way*, and Race," 2 (unpublished paper, American Catholic Historical Association Annual Meeting, January 8, 2016, Atlanta, GA).

89. As quoted in Burns, "Simon Scanlon, *The Way*, and Race," 2.

90. Ibid., 3.

tled *How to See a Film* written to accompany films being produced by the equally liberal Franciscan Communications in Los Angeles. Scanlon approached moviegoing as a visual art and assumed that his Catholic readers did too.[91]

In the September 1966 issue of *The Way*, Scanlon also contributed an essay that countered the historical role the Catholic Church had played in censoring and judging movies. Titled "Adults, Movies, and Censorship," Scanlon's essay had particular significance because it appeared a year after the Catholic Legion of Decency had officially changed both its name—to the National Catholic Office for Motion Pictures, or NCOMP—and its mission.[92] In 1966 Hollywood's in-house censorship regime, the Production Code Administration, disbanded because the body that governed it, the Motion Pictures Producers Association, had adopted a more lenient form of regulation that eventually became incorporated as the Code and Ratings Administration.[93] Thus by the time Scanlon made his observations about movie censorship to his readers, American movie culture as well as American Catholic culture was in a state of flux.

Echoing a line developed by other Catholic cultural critics, such as Walter Kerr and John Cogley,[94] Scanlon contended: "I believe that until now, with all its good will and all its hard work, the Legion has been a failure. . . . The Legion's noble ambitions at its founding, to raise the artistic level of motion pictures, has not been realized." Just as the NCOMP had shifted its mission in a more educational, rather than punitive, direction, so too did Scanlon see the need for Hollywood's censors to move toward a position that valued movies as art. To illustrate his point Scanlon remarked on the inane way both the Legion and the Production Code Administration had tried to lump films into categories based on truly uncharitable definitions of sex and violence—"to ask people to follow such categorization is to ask them to give up their intelligence and anesthetize their taste," he said. Scanlon pointed to Catholic film critics, including James Arnold at the *Davenport Messenger* and *St. Anthony Messenger*, Edward Fischer at *Ave Maria* (and author of *The Screen Arts*), John Fitzgerald in the *Our Sunday Visitor*, Philip Hartung at *Commonweal*, and Moira Walsh at *America* (and author of *Making Mature Moviegoers*). Scanlon also recommended that readers look at the film appreciation course produced by the *Hour of St. Francis* radio show's team, with a script and booklet by Edward Fischer.[95]

Scanlon was at his best writing on race. Burns observes that "underlying all his [Scanlon's] writings on race was the belief that at its core the race prob-

---

91. Simon Scanlon, *How to See a Film* (Los Angeles, OFM Productions, 1965).

92. Simon Scanlon, "Adults, Movies and Censorship," *The Way* 22 (September 1966); see also Mary L. McLaughlin, "A Study of the National Catholic Office for Motion Pictures" (PhD dissertation, University of Wisconsin, 1974), 90.

93. See Wittern-Keller and Haberski, *Miracle Case*, 164–69.

94. See Haberski, *Freedom to Offend*, 66, 89.

95. Scanlon, "Adults, Movies and Censorship," 22–24.

lem was a white problem, a problem the white community neither acknowl-edged nor accepted."[96] In a 1965 essay "The Big Black Anger," Scanlon took aim at Proposition 14, a popular referendum measure approved by California voters in 1964 that effectively reversed antidiscrimination laws in housing by giving property owners, such as landlords, final say regarding those to whom they sold or rented. Scanlon wrote in disgust: "The white citizens of California opted for special privilege and rejected decency, justice, Americanism, and moral fiber by an overwhelming majority."[97]

Scanlon also wrote a profile on Catholic layman John Howard Griffin, whose landmark book *Black Like Me* attempted to bring the feeling of racial segregation as close to whites as possible. Griffin undertook a very unusual experiment in radical empathy by darkening his skin and traveling through the American South in 1960. He documented his journey in a private journal and a published book that became a lightning rod for discussion on racism and ethnic appropriation in the mid-1960s.[98]

The Way addressed other hot-button issues as well. For example, in Novem-ber 1966 Scanlon ran two essays—one by Helen Tepraune and the other by the editor Father Francis Maynard, OFM—that reflected on the complicated relationship Catholics had with communism. In her essay "My Mother-In-Law Is a Bircher," Tepraune wrote about the John Birch Society in a way that con-trasted sharply with the heroic terms often used to describe anticommunism in other Catholic publications.[99] By the mid-1960s *The Way* found it possible to take on the extremes of anticommunism just as Scanlon had demonstrated there was an alternative to the anti-intellectualism of Catholic-sponsored censorship. The surprise in Tepraune's essay, though, was her description of being judged by her mother-in-law as someone utterly untrustworthy. In the pivotal passage of her story, Tepraune described her mother-in-law's reaction when confronted by a liberal. "'Don't say any more,' whispered the woman. 'No, you don't have

---

96. Burns, "Simon Scanlon," 7.
97. As quoted in Burns, Simon Scanlon, 7.
98. "John Howard Griffin," *The Way* 31 (March 1975): 2–17. Much has been written about Griffin, but for two essays that offer two different views of Griffin's life, see George Cotikin, *Morality's Muddy Waters: Ethical Quandaries in Modern America* (Philadelphia: University of Pennsylvania Press, 2010), 113–34; Justin D. Poché, "Catholic Like Me: The Conversions of John Howard Griffin," *US Catholic Historian* 32 (Spring 2014): 117–42.
99. Helen V. Tepraune, "My Mother-in-Law Is a Bircher," *The Way* 22 (November 1966): 18-25. The literature on domestic American anticommunism is immense, but a cross-section of that literature might include Fred Inglis, *The Cruel Peace: Everyday Life in the Cold War* (New York: Basic Books: 1991), especially part 1, "Waging the Cold War," and part 2, "The Balance of Terror"; Tom Engelhardt, *The End of Victory Culture: Cold War America and the Disillusioning of a Generation* (New York: Basic Books, 1995); Ellen Schrecker, *Many Are the Crimes: McCarthyism in America* (New York: Little, Brown & Company, 1998); Massa, *Catholics and American Culture*.

to say another word.' One hand came slowly up, a trembling finger pointed at me. 'You've revealed yourself. Now, we know you.'" Tepraune fled the house as if she had been exposed as an alien from Mars.[100]

"I found my mother-in-law's attitude (like that of her Bircher friends)," Tepraune wrote, "was characterized by a blind obedience to the dogmas, dictates and decrees of the John Birch Society and its publications and leaders."[101] California, according to a state commission investigating the society, was "the state most heavily infested with John Birchers."[102] Tepraune reviewed the ideological terrain of the group, remarking on the fanaticism of its *Blue Book*, which discussed political leaders and groups, and concluded that in this instance anticommunism had grown so dogmatic that its adherents had stopped thinking. To make sense of this ideological disjunction, Tepraune turned to theorists of postwar America, including David Reisman, William H. Whyte, and Betty Friedan. "Frustrated by their personal inadequacies and shortcomings, frustrated by their helplessness in a highly mechanized society which often doesn't seem to have time for them," Tepraune believed that, "these unhappy people displace their rage and hatred from its original focus (themselves) to a 'scapegoat,' which, in the case of the fanatic John Bircher, is the 'Communist Conspiracy.'"[103] Tepraune concluded that her mother-in-law and by extension all Birchers were basically mentally ill. While she did not suggest a cure, Terpaune agreed it was high time to stop enabling Catholics to claim anticommunism as always and under any circumstance a moral position.[104] She might also have been gently critiquing the Catholic position on church authority in general.

Francis Maynard, an editor at *The Way*, addressed another consequence of Catholic anticommunism, the Vietnam War. "For months now," Maynard wrote in 1966, "we have mentally agonized over what conclusion we should arrive at concerning the Vietnam War." He discussed the rationale for entering the war, the destruction of the war, and the stakes that seemed to draw America into the war. However, he concluded rather pointedly: "We do feel that the escalation of this conflict into a war of total scorched-earth destruction ought to cease." Softening that position a bit, Maynard did not claim to have ultimate answers to the problems that gave rise to the war, namely the intention of the communists in North Vietnam to take over the south. But he asked readers to consider with him and the magazine whether "the methods our country uses in its stated aims should be moral methods." As was often the case with Franciscan editors, Maynard hoped to entreat readers to consider

---

100. Tepraune, "My Mother-in-Law," 19.
101. Ibid., 19–20.
102. Ibid., 25.
103. Ibid., 22.
104. Ibid., 25.

the positions they held as things that they needed to live with and act on, not merely defend against a hostile outside world.[105]

Throughout the 1960s and into the 1970s, *The Way* was a voice for progressive Catholicism, demonstrated not only by the editorials by Maynard but also by contributions from writers such as Clayton C. Barbeau, Richard Gutzwiller, SJ, and Alice Ogle. Barbeau, who also served as an editor, had enjoyed a prominent reputation as a family therapist since the early 1960s but got his big break giving talks and writing a book on the subject of fatherhood. His first book, *The Head of the Family* (1961), was published by the well-regarded religious publisher Henry Regnery, establishing Barbeau nearly overnight as a lay Catholic expert on family life, parenting, and natural family planning. In *The Way* he often wrote a column called "For Wayfarers," in which he offered advice as a professional family therapist. He also wrote an episode on St. Thomas More for the popular television series *The Hour of St. Francis*, an episode that was filmed at Hearst Castle in California. Meanwhile Gutzwiller was a Jesuit theologian born in Zurich, Switzerland in 1896 who through his activities as a lecturer, spiritual counselor, and writer breathed new life into Swiss Catholicism. In the United States two books of his essays were translated and published in 1964: *The Parables of the Lord* and *Day by Day with St. Matthew's Gospel*.[106] And Alice Ogle contributed essays on racial and social justice to *The Way* as she had to other magazines, including the *Franciscan Herald and Forum*.

The Way also ran profiles of Thomas Merton, who wrote about racial issues in his "Letters to a White Liberal" (1964) causing a major stir.[107] The magazine covered issues such as hunger, poverty, racism, and lack of solidarity among Americans. And it reported on culture such as the San Francisco Film Festival, reviewed the premiere of the *Godfather*, and included poems and the award-winning cartoonist Joseph Noonan. Into the 1980s *The Way* tackled the difficult and controversial debates over nuclear weapons, American foreign policy in Latin America, and abortion. Throughout this period Scanlon held sway over the editorial page, acknowledging the mighty task of engaging, not dismissing, the prevailing assumptions and actions of both the religious left and right. Scanlon concluded: "We cannot build that Kingdom by writing off the extremes. By being smug, by withdrawing from the conflict, by indulging in self-pity, whining about being 'caught' in the middle. We can build it only by taking our stand with Christ, in the middle, from where we can reach out and embrace all extremes."[108]

---

105. Francis X. Maynard, OFM, "Vietnam War," *The Way* 22 (November 1966): 36–37.

106. "Gutzwiller, Richard," *Dictionnaire historique de la Suisse*, accessed November 21, 2015, http://www.hls-dhs-dss.ch/textes/d/D9858.php.

107. Clifford Stevens, "Thomas Merton: Prophet of Peace," *The Way* 31 (March 1975): 16–25.

108. Scanlon quoted in Burns, "Simon Scanlon," 10.

THE CORD

St. Bonaventure University has stood at the center of scholarship on Franciscanism in the United States for a long time. In November 1950, it launched a magazine called *The Cord* under the editorship of the remarkable Father Philotheus Boehner, OFM. In his first editorial, titled "*Pax Et Bonum*," (the traditional Franciscan greeting) Boehner made his case for a journal devoted to "traditional Franciscan Spirituality." While other journals certainly could claim to address a similar mission, Boehner had a very specific audience in mind. He wanted *The Cord* to educate women religious of the Franciscan orders. "There is a grave danger, especially among the women religious of our Order," Boehner argued, "that the essential spirit of Our Holy Father Francis may be lost sight of amid the superficial and sentimentally romantic concepts of Franciscanism so enthusiastically popularized today."[109]

Father Joseph Doino, OFM, writing in *Franciscan Studies*, the flagship journal of St. Bonaventure's Franciscan Institute, explains: "What prompted this new project was Boehner's burning concern regarding a romanticized or even sterile Franciscanism spawned by a superficial or indifferent attitude toward the rich tradition of Franciscan spirituality. Prophetically anticipating the *aggiornamento* of Vatican II, he had discerned already in the postwar years the value for the world of a revitalized commitment on the part of all Franciscan men and women." This was especially true for women who, Doino points out, "had been denied rightful access to the remarkable tradition of the Franciscan masters."[110]

The unique mission of *The Cord* was expressed in sections such as the monthly meditations on psalms and the Gospels (at first called "conferences") and Boehner's translation of St. Bonaventure's *Examination of Conscience*. According to Doino, among the most significant and distinctive features of the journal was Boehner's attention to the work of Bonaventure—his sermons and writings—"which appear from time to time in original English translation."[111] Moreover, as befitted a journal aimed at Franciscan women, many women wrote for the journal, as did lay Franciscans and members of Franciscan communities overseas.

In an editorial in the first issue Boehner welcomed readers and turned to the purpose of the journal, declaring, "It is hardly an exaggeration to say that the majority of Franciscan Sisterhoods in this country can hardly be distinguished, by their spirit, from other congregations." He characterized this spiritual deficit as a genuine crisis that threatened to generate a misguided con-

---

109. Father Philotheus Boehner, "*Pax Et Bonum*," *The Cord* 1 (November 1950): 1.
110. Joseph D. Doino, OFM, "The Cord," *Franciscan Studies* 51 (1991): 133.
111. Doino, OFM, "The Cord," 133.

ception of Franciscanism if the order did not invest in the intellectual education of its sisters. "The primary purpose of *The Cord* is to aid in effecting among us a deeper knowledge and more ardent love of the Franciscan way of life," he said. "It will restrict its material to Franciscan spirituality in its various forms and aspects and applications, and to such matters as are of particular concern and interest to the Franciscan family."[112]

Boehner's essay was a treatise of sorts on the "Franciscan Spirit," and used the first two pages to explain "what the Franciscan spirit is not." "Franciscanism is not a new doctrine or a new gospel," he declared. "Franciscanism is not essentially a life of penance, if by penance we understand self-inflicted corporal punishment and mortification," Boehner contended. "Franciscanism is not that charmingly natural, familiar, and wholly original attitude toward creatures that was so characteristic of Saint Francis." "Franciscanism, finally, is not that love of poverty and simplicity through which Francis, by means of his Order, effected the great social reform of his age." What, then, was Franciscanism? "Franciscanism, then, in its origin, was a true revolution, a movement back to the immediacy in which the Holy Gospel had been lived by the early Church. . . . In a word, Franciscanism is a religious youth movement with the Gospel as ideal."[113]

In the first issue Boehner also included a note thanking the mother superiors who had already subscribed their houses, as well as the anonymous donor who made the publication of the journal possible. He also thanked the Franciscan Educational Conference for providing financial help for the publication of the journal. It was, in short, a Franciscan family affair.[114]

Boehner became legendary for his extraordinary scholarship and tireless advocacy of Franciscan thought. He was born in 1901 in the Westphalian town of Lichtenau, Germany, and entered an academy run by Franciscans in part because he had problems at school—he beat up another boy. While still relatively young, he battled a terrible bout of tuberculosis but managed, while in the hospital, to translate a book about St. Bonaventure from French to German. He was ordained a priest in 1927 and in fairly short order was sent to Germany's most prestigious universities, in Munich and Muenster, to work on a doctorate in biology. During his studies he grew close to the German philosopher Peter Wurst and the French theologian and philosopher Eitenne Gilson, eventually working with the latter on a history of Christian philosophy and ultimately pursuing scholarship on William of Ockham that would animate the rest of his life.[115]

---

112. Boehner, "*Pax Et Bonum*," 2–3.
113. Boehner, "*Pax Et Bonum*," 3–6.
114. Boehner, "Message of the Editor," 38.
115. The Editors, "Father Philotheus Boehner, OFM," *The Cord* (1955), 209–10.

Boehner came to North America in 1939 to lecture on paleography at the invitation of the Pontifical Academy in Toronto. He decided to remain abroad, though, after the outbreak of World War II. His opposition to the Nazi regime had become known to German officials, and it had grown dangerous for him to return to his duties in Germany. His move to St. Bonaventure University came by an invitation from Father Thomas Plassman, OFM, the college's president, to lecture in Franciscan philosophy. It was the summer of 1940, and those lectures became the inspiration for the Franciscan Institute.[116]

Boehner's reputation in the United States grew from there—among his first students were Thomas Merton and Robert Lax. Boehner eventually collaborated with Ernest Moody of Columbia University on a multivolume critical edition of English Franciscan philosopher William of Ockham's *Opera non-politica*. With Plassman, Boehner revamped the scholarly journal *Franciscan Studies* to make it more rigorous, and then in 1950 he launched *The Cord* with Sister Mary Frances, SMIC, as an assistant editor.

His colleagues said that even though his personal lecture style was a bit difficult, because "he never mastered American speech," "there was such charm in his manner of presentation, such sureness and mastery of subject, such subtle humor in pointing out disconcerting facts, that his courses were always a delight to the students who were equal to him."[117]

For the first decade, at least, *The Cord* served Boehner's vision, publishing historical essays about Franciscans and Franciscan traditions. Boehner anchored the journal with a column titled "Examination of Conscience . . . According to Saint Bonaventure." Other sections were contributed by Franciscan priests, including Plassman's "Meditations in Preparation for Mass" and "Rule of the Third Order Regular" by Father Allan Wolter, OFM. The journal also became a kind of clearinghouse for courses and institutes run by Boehner for Third Orders at St. Bonaventure. And from the start, *The Cord* ran book reviews that served as a reading list for readers to consult.

The journal also fulfilled its commitment to Franciscan women. In January 1955, the editors called for biographical sketches of congregations of Franciscan sisters. The first profile they ran was of the Franciscan Sisters of Mary Immaculate who came from the Beguines in parts of western Europe in the fourteenth century. Their American chapter dated to the 1930s, when they were asked to send teachers for rural schools in Texas, New Mexico, and California. In subsequent issues Sister Jeannette Clare, OSF, contributed a series of essays on the founding of the sisters of the Third Order of St. Francis and the Franciscan Sisters of Calais. Throughout the late 1950s *The Cord* continued to run essays about different communities of Franciscan sisters. Judging

---

116. Ibid., 210.
117. Ibid., 211.

from what other Franciscan periodicals published, the accumulation of such accounts represented a unique opportunity to appreciate the expansive history of Franciscan women, and it offered a place for Franciscan sisters to publish essays—many on the orders they served, but also on topics related to the Third Order more generally. For example *The Cord* ran a special series titled "Crosses Over Nagasaki" written by Father Gerard Huber, OFM, and translated by Sister Mary Frances and Sister Mary Hildemar, SMIC, about Franciscan missions to Japan and the growth and persecution of Christianity in the sixteenth and seventh centuries.[118]

In 1955 Boehner died. Though an enormous loss in the Franciscan community, his established mission for *The Cord* continued. For a few years the journal shifted editorial duties around the Franciscan community, including moving the editorial offices to Holy Name College in Washington, D.C. for a short period in 1963. The editors added a note in the January issue of that year explaining that while the principle purpose for the journal would not change, they wanted to emphasize that *The Cord* would go on to focus on "doctrinal, rather than simply devotional or practical, presentation of Franciscanism." They also intended to continue to focus on the spirituality of Franciscanism and thus exclude "the strictly historical or social aspects of our heritage." As an extension of this idea, the editors proposed to "present a Franciscan view of spirituality rather than a view of Franciscan spirituality."[119]

The Cord also reflected broader currents in society and the interests of its diverse community. For example, in 1964 *The Cord* noted that in awarding the Third Order of St. Francis Peace Medal to Martin Luther King Jr., it became the first Catholic organization "to recognize formally the work of this courageous American."[120] In a strongly worded editorial that praised actions taken by Third Order laymen in the name of civil rights, the editors encouraged Catholics to get actively involved in protests, in keeping the peace, in boycotting businesses that practiced discrimination, and in contacting politicians and encouraging economic entities—such as unions and fair housing organizations—to help African Americans. Among the groups organizing for this purpose was the Action for Interracial Understanding (AIU), founded in 1961 by Third Order Franciscans who were active in civil rights struggles and who hoped to turn their activities into a broader movement among the tertiaries. According to William Wicks, SFO, the AIU had a brief existence from

---

118. Gerard Huber, OFM, "Crosses over Nagasaki," *The Cord* 9 (April- December, 1959): 140–46, 171–80, 219–24, 252–71; Gerard Huber, OFM, "Crosses over Nagasaki," *The Cord* 10 (January, April–August, November): 26–29, 86–92, 147–156, 172–180, 219–224, 252–256, 348–352.

119. Editorial, *The Cord* 13 (January 1963): 2–3.

120. "Racism—A Franciscan Response," *The Cord* 14 (January 1964), 27.

1961 through 1968 but was a part of similar initiatives by secular Franciscans to exercise more leadership over social justice.[121] *The Cord* continued to publish articles on civil rights, and Franciscan involvement in such movements continued throughout the 1960s.[122]

In 1964, as the third session of Vatican II convened, the journal took a short hiatus as it changed editors. When *The Cord* reappeared in 1965, it made slight modifications to its layout and introduced a new editor: Father Michael Meilach, OFM, a scholar of Christian doctrine who in addition to writing books such as *The Primacy of Christ in Doctrine and Life* (1966) and *From Order to Omega* (1967), wrote dozens of essays, reviews, and editorials for the journal from 1964 through 1986. In the April 1965 issue Meilach thanked readers for their patience as the journal began publishing once again. "One of the most difficult tasks we have faced," he explained, "is that of fulfilling the most specific needs possible for the most diverse segments of our readership as possible. Sisters, clerics, lay tertiaries, brothers, and priests: each group has its tastes and requirements, and each deserves consideration." The journal was also expanding its offerings, promising subjects "from speculative doctrinal theology, to biography, to concrete reports on the progress of *aggiornamento*."[123] *The Cord* also continued to run book reviews—sometimes as editorials, other times as stand-alone sections—that introduced readers to the scope of scholarship being done on Franciscanism and related areas.

For example, an essay entitled "Re-evaluating Franciscan Religious Life in a Changing World," written by Sister Lenora, OSF in 1964, received a prominent place in the journal and reflected the central role women religious played in shaping the content of the journal. Sister Lenora was a nun from the Mount St. Francis Province of the School Sisters of St. Francis in Illinois. She worked with the Young Christian Students movement and chaired the English department at Madonna High School in Aurora, Illinois. In her essay Sister Lenora sought to enliven the discussion about the role Franciscans played in the world by asking Franciscans to consider the tradition through which they engaged the world. "The task to re-evaluate Franciscan religious life poses problems not readily discernible on the surface for much goes under the label **Franciscan** that could just as well bear another name," she observed. "Are we evaluating **Franciscan** religious life or something that has posed for it?" Sister Lenora's roles as a teacher and writer provided the intellectual and

---

121. William Wicks, SFO, "A Brief History of the Secular Franciscan Order and Its Rules," National Formation Commission of the National Fraternity of the Secular Franciscan Order USA, accessed July 11, 2017, http://www.nafraformation.org/21%20-%20History%20of%20SFO%20&%20Rule%20-%20rev%207-25-2011.pdf.

122. "Racism—A Franciscan Response," *The Cord* 14 (January 1964): 27.

123. Father Michael Meilach, OFM, Editorial, *The Cord* 15 (April 1965): 83.

theological energy for her charge to other women religious. Her intention, it seems, was to pivot away from the parochial view of Franciscanism to one that challenged sisters to consider how they engaged a world they both worked in and had some responsibility over. She argued that "in developing an attitude toward changes in the world and the Church . . . it becomes imperative to take a long, hard look at the world of men, not failing to use all the natural disciplines at our disposal. . . . This means intense, intellectual discipline. The problems of our times with all the crosscurrents of complexity posit anything but naiveté. We have **to know** to be of use to man in the world today or we may do more harm than good."[124]

Meilach had a more basic problem: *The Cord* always had a relatively low circulation as well as rising production costs. To bring more attention to the journal and entice more subscribers, Meilach reached out to high profile religious writers to contribute essays. For example, Meilach wrote to Thomas Merton, famed author of *The Seven Storey Mountain*, to ask if he would write for *The Cord*. Merton responded positively and contributed a few essays to the journal in 1965 and 1966, including "The Climate of Mercy," in which Merton instructed readers: "There is but one center of all mercy, one merciful event, in which we receive mercy and give it, or give it and receive it. This event is the saving mystery of the Cross which alone enables us to enter into a true spiritual harmony with one another, seeing one another not only in natural fellowship but in the Spirit and mercy of Christ who emptied himself for us and became obedient even to death."[125] Mother Mary Francis, PCC, author of the mid-1950s best-selling book *A Right to Be Merry* [See below], also wrote for *The Cord*. Circulation totals for the journal were published regularly in the November issue each year from the 1967 through the early 1990s. In 1967 the journal had a circulation of 2,400, which represented its most prosperous period.[126]

One reason the journal generated interest came from the way Meilach engaged contemporary debates. Publishing essays by Merton might raise the profile of the journal, but Meilach's decision to tackle the growing divisions in the Church over interpretations and impressions of Vatican II also heightened readers' interests. For example, in the summer of 1967 Meilach attempted to dismiss popular distinctions between liberal and conservative positions on Church doctrine. "To attempt in either 'conservative' or 'liberal'

---

124. Sister Lenora, "Re-evaluating Franciscan Religious Life in a Changing World," *The Cord* 14 (November–December 1964): 261, 272 [emphasis in the original].

125. Thomas Merton, "The Climate of Mercy," *The Cord* 15 (April 1965): 89.

126. See the Thomas Merton papers at the Thomas Merton Center at Bellarmine University, accessed November 21, 2015, http://merton.org/Research/Correspondence/y1.aspx?id=1378.

fashion to separate the divine from the human in the Church is, ultimately, to deny that God has become man," he wrote. "It is, in crypto-docetist fashion, to see a *simpliste* answer to the problem of attaining a meaningful stance in the Church of the twentieth century."[127] Meilach ran a series of editorials and essays on Pierre Teilhard de Chardin, the French-born Jesuit who studied and taught geology and paleontology and whose work on intersecting evolutions of humans—spiritual as well as physiological—made him controversial to many in the Church. A few of the Jesuit's books were censured by the church during his lifetime and he was officially prevented from teaching in his native France.[128] The 1960s saw a renaissance of his reputation, and he became, along with debates over Vatican II, a flashpoint for the changes swirling around Catholic theology and social teaching.

In response to criticism that Meilach had an unhealthy interest in rebellious elements of the Church, a letter writer remarked: "We need change, and we are witnessing a lot of it already. But will your impatient tone help to consolidate and further this process of beneficial development?"[129] But of course such controversy only helped *The Cord* remain relevant.

The journal began 1970 with an issue demonstrating the paradox that befuddled Franciscan media: Should Franciscans be political or remain somewhat above the fray as spiritual guides? As a reply Meilach wrote an essay "Blessed Are the Peacemakers" in which he explained in an extended introduction, "As Francis concerned himself with a particular African conflict in his day, so I feel irresistibly impelled here to concern myself with the one in Viet Nam today. I earnestly hope that my concern, and all the expression I give it in the following pages, is a concern imposed and responded to in the name of God, of his Son Jesus Christ, and of Francis of Assisi."[130]

Throughout the 1980s and 1990s, the journal struggled with circulation numbers, though it continued to publish essays by leaders in Franciscan spirituality, including a rising star named Richard Rohr who became an extraordinarily popular Franciscan writer. In 2000 *The Cord* celebrated its fiftieth year in publication with a January issue that included an introductory editorial from Margaret Carney, OSF, who served as director of the Franciscan Institute until 2004 when she became president of St. Bonaventure University. The anniversary issue also included a long essay from Franciscan historian and

---

127. Father Michael Meilach, OFM, Editorial, *The Cord* 17 (July 1967): 195.
128. Scott Ventureya, "Challenging the Rehabilitation of Pierre Teilhard de Chardin," *Crisis Magazine: A Voice for the Faithful Catholic Laity* (January 20, 2015), http://www.crisismagazine.com/2015/challenging-rehabilitation-pierre-teilhard-de-chardin. Accessed July 5, 2017.
129. Letter to the editor, *The Cord* 17 (July 1967): 196.
130. Father Michael Meilach, OFM, "Blessed Are the Peacemakers," *The Cord* 20 (January 1970): 19.

priest Joseph Chinnici, OFM, based on a talk he gave to the international assembly of the Franciscan Sisters of Allegany in July 1996. The decision to showcase that essay for the first issue of the anniversary year made sense given the *Cord*'s relationship to women religious.[131]

In this essay, entitled "This Is What We Proclaim to You," Chinicci used the example of Evelyn Underhill, an Anglican spiritual writer from the late nineteenth and early twentieth centuries who, like many in the wake of the moral catastrophe of the First World War, found herself devastated by the dual loss of life and faith. Chinicci described how Underhill's spiritual rebirth began with her discovery of the Franciscan poet Father Jacopone da Todi and Underhill's fellowship with a Confraternity of the Spiritual Entente, who were—as Chinicci described them—a "small group of interdependent Christians founded by an Italian Franciscan sister." In Franciscan spirituality Underhill learned "to face the Christ Incarnate, a God not of pure spirit but a God who is powerful enough to dwell as a human being in misshaped institutions, in sinful and limited corners of life, in the experience of impossibility, in the small piece of bread, in human beings, in the poor, in imperfection, in her very self."[132]

Chinicci's reflection on Underhill's reawakening captured the spirit of *The Cord* over its fifty years as a journal that did more to bridge the gap between Franciscan men and women, and between Franciscan spirituality and Catholic theology, than almost any other periodical. Remarkably true to its original mission, *The Cord* (renamed *Franciscan Connections* in 2015) remains a singular source in print for a generous understanding of Franciscan spiritual thought, from poetry to theology to historical analysis.

IMMACULATA AND THE
FRANCISCAN DEVOTIONAL MAGAZINE

Devotional magazines, while smaller in number, also aimed to attract large audiences. However, unlike general-interest magazines, devotional magazines made specific appeals to Catholics. One group that fit this approach was the Militia of the Immaculata (MI) through its journal *Immaculata*, published by the Conventual Franciscan Friars in Kenosha, Wisconsin. The magazine has served as the official magazine of the Knights of the MI since 1949, and it carried forward the cause begun by Father Maximillian Kolbe in 1917. Founded by Kolbe and six other friars in the Conventual Franciscan seminary in Rome, the MI has, according to its official line, sought to bring "the world

---

131. Joseph Chinnici, "This Is What We Proclaim to You," *The Cord* 50 (January 2000): 3.
132. Ibid., 5.

to Christ through the consecration to the Virgin Mary."[133] Mary forms the central theological understanding for MIs, and for years the magazine ran hundreds of articles on everything from the Rosary to visions of Mary. Accordingly the editors devoted a great deal of space over the years to promote the centrality of Mary to Christianity and to attract adherents to venerating Mary. For example an entire issue in 1980 walked through "all the major appearances of the Blessed Virgin which have occurred during the past century and half."[134] The account began with Sister (now St.) Catherine Labouré's 1830 vision in Paris of Mary, the vision which provided the model for the Miraculous Medal, and proceeded through to the apparition of the Virgin of the Revelation, appearing in 1947 to Bruno Cornacchiola in Rome.

That last revelation of Mary fit nicely the appeal of the magazine. On April 12, 1947, Cornacchiola, an Italian railway worker, had a vision. Although an unlikely recipient of the Virgin Mary's blessing, he was a lapsed Catholic and a self-described "bad man," Cornacchiola was also the kind of person the church had often celebrated when converted. Frederick Dempsey, an editor of *Immaculata* in 1980, wrote: "Identifying in Bruno Cornacchiola something of all sinners, the Blessed Virgin said that in our moments of doubt and discouragement, a safe return to God is to be found in the Holy Gospel. . . . Therefore, the best remedy is to turn to the pure fountain of truth, the infallible teaching of the Catholic Church."[135]

Mary appeared in many issues of *Immaculata*, but Mary was not the only organizing force for *Immaculata*. Kolbe's own story framed the MI mission in heroic terms. In 1982 Pope John Paul II proclaimed Kolbe "a martyr of charity." The Polish Pope—himself now a saint—canonized the Polish priest who had perished in Auschwitz, the most notorious Nazi concentration camp in Poland.

St. Maximilian Kolbe was born Raymond Kolbe in 1894 in the Polish town of Zdunska-Wola, near Lodz. As a young man he joined the Conventual Franciscans, took the name Maximilian, and studied in Rome. He founded the MI in 1917 as a way to evangelize the world. He traveled throughout his native Poland and as far as Japan. He returned to Poland in 1936 and following the outbreak of war in 1939 operated a hospital and refugee center that accepted Jews. In February 1941 the Nazis arrested and imprisoned him and by May he was sent the death camp at Auschwitz. On August 14, 1941, a

---

133. "What Is the Militia of the Immaculata?," "Consecrating the World to Mary," special edition, *Immaculata* (n.d.): 15, available from Militia of the Immaculata, 7645 Libertyville, Illinois 60048.

134. Ibid.

135. Frederick R. Dempsey, "Virgin of the Revelation," *Immaculata* 31 (December 1980): 24.

camp guard killed him with an injection of carbolic acid. Kolbe died among prisoners who were sent to a starvation bunker after Nazi guards discovered that a prisoner had escaped from their section of the camp. When the guards sentenced these men to death by torture, Kolbe volunteered to go with them, to be with them until they perished, ultimately sacrificing himself by taking the place of another prisoner with a family. When the Nazi guards asked why he was willing to exchange his life for another man's, Kolbe reportedly declared, "I am a Catholic Priest."[136]

In one of Kolbe's addresses to his fellow friars in 1937 (reprinted in a special edition of *Immaculata*), the Polish priest emphasized the "we must will to be good." "The Sacred Scriptures say that a just man falls seven times daily. We fall more often than that," Kolbe preached. "But we must rise again and again. If anyone should say, 'Enough! I can do nothing more,' he would reveal his pride that prompts him to trust his own strength. Meanwhile our strength comes from God's grace. The Lord can permit us to fall so we might learn we are nothing."[137] Kolbe's dramatic and tragic story, beginning with his founding of MI and ending with his martyrdom in Auschwitz, gave intellectual and spiritual form to *Immaculata*. The MI promoted the magazine as one to which anyone who needed to be saved could turn and through which anyone, no matter what he or she had been previously, could find a path to salvation, through devotion to the Virgin Mary and in light of the heroic example of Kolbe.

Because devotion to the Blessed Mother was the organizing idea behind the magazine, it enlisted Mary's help for many different purposes, including as a way to "spring the trap" against communism during the Cold War. Not mincing words, one writer, Martin Herbert, argued in 1958: "She will crush thy head," because she "alone has destroyed all the heresies in the whole world." Not surprisingly Herbert also referred to the vision of Mary at Fatima, in which she promised the conversion of Russia.[138] More often though, the magazine ran essays on the necessity of devotion to Mary and different ways to practice such devotion. The "M.I. Roundtable" column also began in the same issue and became a fixture in the magazine, dispensing rationale to encourage the laity to pray to Mary. "It is she whom one should imitate and come close to," one "Roundtable" entry implored. "It is she who is put up as an example of imitation for all Militia members and all Christian souls. We,

---

136. Father Patrick Greenough, "Saint Maximilian and Auschwitz," "Consecrating the World To Mary," special issue, *Immaculata* (n.d.): 22,

137. Maximillian Kolbe, "Maximillian Speaks: 'We Must Will to Be Good,'" op. cit. *Immaculata* (n.d.): 27.

138. Martin Herbert, "'Consecrated' Communists, Consecrated Christians," *Immaculata* 9 (August 1958): 3.

particularly, who have consecrated ourselves to her properly, become more and more like unto her. Behold the peak of perfection in man."[139]

While *Immaculata* offered constant devotions to Mary, the magazine had other sections. Father Albert P. Roemer, director of the Brothers of St. Pius X, had a column called "Aiming for High Heaven." Typically he included local news from Marytown and the surrounding areas (commonly Milwaukee) and from missions in Japan and the Pacific Rim. Another regular feature was the over-the-top piety of Alberta Schumacher, who wrote stories about what she identified as women's issues. Schumacher wrote a story entitled "The New Teacher" for the September 1958 issue in which she used the contrivance of a fifth-grade class to catalog and critique the many problems of the modern American family. For example, the teacher in the story had herself been a product of a college education that "had not left her in the dark as to the problems of lost innocence." Though, Schumacher added, "Thank God for Mariology Club where she [the teacher] had learned also the cure." Schumacher pointed to a child with a "personality defect caused by pre-school years of complete aloneness" and another boy who stuttered from "emotional troubles" caused, the author implied, from a "gay mother who went 'partying' when she should be 'mothering.'" But the center of the story was a description of a girl with "knowing eyes, dark eyes that would be lovely but for their boldness." To save this child of "lost innocence" and others with lesser "ailments," Schumacher had her teacher turn to Mariology and the "True Devotion to the Blessed Virgin Mary." And in their devotion to Mary, the class, even the girl with the "lowered glance of shame," found ways to purify their hearts.[140]

Another feature for women was the column "Open Letter to Peggy" in which a priest, the pseudonymous Father Frank, would write about how the Church saw a particular issue and how women should follow the Church's dictates. For example, the "Open Letter to Peggy" column for September 1959 was about the rhythm method of birth control (the forerunner to the more nuanced modern method called natural family planning). Father Frank acknowledged that sex is a "delicate matter," and pronounced that for the Catholic Church the "ideal is a large family," he admitted that "still the Church does not say that a couple must have all the children physically possible." Father Frank explained systematically why Catholic women should embrace the rhythm method, with particular emphasis on the traditional Catholic argument for getting married. "If they enjoy the delights that go with married life," Father Frank asked rhetorically, "aren't they obliged, when

---

139. M.I. Roundtable, *Immaculata* 9 (August 1958): 9.
140. Alberta Schumacher, "The New Teacher," *Immaculata* 9 (September 1958): 15.

it is reasonably possible, to do their share in peopling earth and heaven?"[141] Historian Leslie Woodcock Tentler explains that "'rhythm' was a staple of Catholic experience into the 1960s. . . . Church teaching would hardly have been credible to the laity without it, not once the church had begun to enforce it vigorously. . . . Faith in rhythm [method] made it possible for a reforming elite among the clergy to embrace a more positive theology of marriage— something for which, in twentieth-century circumstances, a reliable mode of fertility control was obviously necessary."[142]

The approach the magazine's editors and writers took toward women might be summed up in a 1965 editorial entitled, "Putting Woman Back on the Pedestal." The editors argued that "today it is pretty well accepted fact that women do not receive the respect they did 50 years ago." The idea of equality with men, the editors contended, led women to "ape men" thus failing to complement and complete "what is lacking in the male." "To retain her inherent nobility and dignity," the editors suggested, "women must bring into social and public life the meekness, chasity, gentleness, modesty, dedication, and motherliness which men could admire."[143] Among the modifiers the magazine attached to women, the only one that was fully operational in practice was motherhood. In an article written by Eileen Farrell in the same issue as the editorial above, Farrell castigated other magazines and women writers who had drifted away from promoting "the famous three dimensions—home, husband, and children," in favor of encouraging women "to get out into the great world."[144] Farrell was the author of the book *To Be Or Not to Be: The Question of Parenthood*, in which she made the case that a woman's identity— her existence—formed through her devotion to childbearing and child-rearing.[145] Both her book and her essay in *Immaculata* took aim at widespread acceptance of family planning, something she argued had "facilitated the mass flight from motherhood." And so, she sharply criticized those women who contested what she identified as a "woman's primary function." But she also related the debate over women's identities to Protestantism and modernism. Farrell asserted that women who disagreed with her view were "the direct descendants of those who generations ago rejected the still higher meaning of spiritual motherhood as it is lived in the state of consecrated virginity. The

---

141. Father Frank [pseud.], Open Letter to Peggy, *Immaculata* 10 (September 1959): 5.

142. Tentler, "Souls and Bodies," 300.

143. Editorial, "Putting Woman Back on the Pedestal," *Immaculata*, 16 (January 1965), 1.

144. Eileen Farrell, "Feminity, Freedom, and Fulfillment," *Immaculata*, 16 (January 1965), 9.

145. Eileen Farrell, *To Be or Not To Be: The Question of Parenthood*, (Cleveland: Scepter Press, 1964).

flight from motherhood began with a flight from Mary and from the reality of spiritual maternity. It becomes complete," she concluded, "with modern woman's rejection of the cradle."[146] Farrell's essay was a stark rejoinder to material that appeared in other Catholic and Franciscan periodicals that reflected the complications of living as a Catholic in an era that afforded a woman certain rights as an individual. The magazine's editors liked Farrell's essay so much they ran an excerpt from it as an editoral in May 1972.[147]

By the mid-1960s, *Immaculata* ran articles on the developing world (Brazil, southeast Asia, and Africa), changes in the Mass in the wake of Vatican II, the war in Vietnam, and various revolutions around the world. Included in this latter category was the civil rights movement, which editors at *Immaculata* covered as a domestic revolution by African Americans. Throughout the 1960s and into the early 1970s, the editors took a consistently hard line on topics that would come to fall under the heading of culture wars, including contraception, pornography, abortion, legalization of marijuana, and women's liberation.[148] Such an approach seemed consistent with the central mission of the magazine, which was to treat the idea of women as part of the veneration of Mary.[149] And so editors ran pieces on the visions at Fatima and Lourdes (both very popular with readers) and even multiple stories (basically all the same) about George Washington's vision at Valley Forge in which a woman (described in angelic terms) showed him an image of a victorious America. And because the letters to the editor section in each issue offered little more than a page or two of praise for the magazine's positions, there is little way to know if all readers supported the magazine's drift.

Immaculata viewed itself as a bulwark against trends that forced the American Catholic Church in the sixties and seventies to debate issues that in earlier decades had rarely been open to deliberation. For instance, in the 1960s the editors started a section called "Straight Reporting," which reprinted articles and statements from newspapers and other sources with which the mag-

---

146. Farrell, "Feminity, Freedom, and Fulfillment," 10.
147. Eileen Farrell, "To Be a Woman Is to Be a Cradle," *Immaculata*, 23 (May 1972), 1.
148. See Brother Francis Mary, OFM, Conv., "Until the Slaughter Stops," *Immaculata*, 23 (March 1973), 26–7, 35; Brother Francis Mary, OFM, Conv., "Twenty-Five Years—Past and Future," *Immaculata*, 26 (May 1975), 3–4, 34; Brother Francis Mary, OFM, Covn., "A New Program that Combats Anti-Life Forces . . . With Prayer—Action," *Immaculata*, 27 (March 1976), 5–8, 29; Brother Charles Madden, OFM, Conv., "IWY Using Streamroller Tactics in Attempt to Destroy Family Life," *Immaculata*, 28 (September 1978), 10–11.
149. See Dr. C.X. Furtado, "The Dignity of Woman," *Immaculata*, 23 (May 1972), 3–4; Rev. Gerard Mackin, M.S.F., "Two Women," *Immaculata*, 23 (May 1972), 4, 6; Kathleen Sommers, "13 Children, Age 48, and Pregnant—By Choice," *Immaculata*, 33 (May 1982), 5–6, 8.

azine agreed. In May 1971 *Immaculata* readers could read an excerpt from the reactionary newspaper *The Wanderer* arguing that it was hypocritical for people to condemn the war in Vietnam but not speak out as bluntly on the issue of abortion—both of which involved killing. That same issue of *Immaculata* also included a report that Maryland had defeated the "liberalization of abortion law." In the June/July 1971 issue the editors reprinted a statement from the ultraconservative congressman John G. Schmitz, who argued for ramping up American nuclear capabilities to face down the Soviets. Just below that readers saw a negative review of the popular 1971 movie *Jesus Christ Superstar*.

The general tone of the magazine during the 1960s and 1970s came across as decidedly reactionary, as it argued that the Church stood as a particular kind of challenge to its people and should never accommodate positions that might sound secular or liberal. Thus the magazine often defended and critiqued Vatican II at the same time. It liked the way the Council made Mary central to the proceedings—beginning as it did on one feast day of Mary (the Feast of the Maternity of Mary) and ending on another feast day of Mary (the Immaculate Conception). But the editors did not like how Vatican II seemed to open the Church to new kinds of parenting or new ways to relate to traditions such as the veneration of Mary. The editors devoted the September 1972 issue to catechetics and opened with an editorial that declared: "Never before in the history of the Church in America were parents forced to take their children out of Catholic schools for fear they might lose their Faith."[150] And just a couple of issues before that, in June/July 1972, the editor known by the initials B. F. M. paid tribute to the recently deceased J. Edgar Hoover, FBI director from 1935 to his death, for being a "real American" by fighting organized crime, bringing order to a lawless time, hunting out suspected "Reds," keeping files on "popular Americans" even when he was "vilified" for doing so, and of course telling an interviewer "of the great importance he placed on religion and prayer in his life."[151] The conservative convert to Catholicism, James Likoudis, warned readers about the "onslaught of secular humanism" and its influence in American society."[152]

However troubled by contemporary American society *Immaculata* seemed to be, its finest moment was undoubtedly the beatification of Maximilian Kolbe in October 1971. Begun in the late 1960s, the beatification process was clearly the reason why the province published *Immaculata*. They ran many articles about Kolbe's prayers, his martyrdom, and his service to

---

150. Editorial, *Immaculata* 23 (September 1972): 1.
151. Brother Francis Mary [pseud.], editorial, *Immaculata* 23 (June–July 1972): 1.
152. James Likoudis, "The Onslaught of Secular Humanism," *Immaculata*, 28 (October 1977), 3.

those who prayed to him. Until the beatification of Kolbe, *Immaculata* printed a section about "the last days" of Kolbe, designed to emphasize his martyrdom on his last day in Auschwitz. Kolbe's example and his devotion to the Blessed Mother provided a singular presence in Franciscan media. Pope John Paul II canonized Kolbe as a martyr in 1981.

The magazine continued publishing into the twenty-first century, but issues became smaller in size and consistently lost money. In the Summer 2009 issue, Fr. Stephen McKinley, OFM, CONV, rector of the National Shrine of St. Maximilian Kobe, explained that while grateful for the contributions to the magazine, "we still haven't covered all the costs for each issue."[153] With the explosion of on-line media, though, most of the material produced and published by the Militia of the Immaculuata became available through its website.[154]

PADRES' TRAIL AND THE
FRANCISCAN MISSIONARY MAGAZINE

Among the most interesting missionary work recorded in Franciscan media was the work of Franciscan missionaries who ministered to the Navajo peoples across northeastern Arizona and northwestern New Mexico. The Franciscans who chose the Southwest distinguished themselves by becoming experts in the Navajo language as a way to develop a catechism for the people of that region. The friars from St. John the Baptist Province in Cincinnati founded St. Michael's Mission in Apache County, Arizona, and established St. Michael Press in 1909 to publish materials on missions to the Navajo in both English and the Navajo language.[155]

Cincinnati Franciscans ventured to the Southwest as both Catholic emissaries and competitors with the Protestant missionaries. In 1873 a lay man and veteran of the Civil War, Charles Ewing, became the first commissioner for the Bureau of Catholic Indian Missions. The impetus for this organization was a complicated fight in the latter part of the nineteenth century over how the US federal government would operate and relate to American Indian nations on reservations. During his presidency Ulysses S. Grant decided to offer Christian missionaries jurisdiction over tribal lands.[156] Through this policy Grant set in

---

153. Fr. Stephen McKinley, OFM, CONV, "Letter from the Editor," *Immaculata*, (Summer 2009), 1.

154. Please see: http://missionimmaculata.com

155. Ross Enochs, "The Franciscan Mission to the Navajos: Mission Method and Indigenous Religion, 1898–1940," *The Catholic Historical Review* 92, no. 1 (January 2006): 47.

156. Tim Lanigan, "A Voice for Catholic Indians: The Birth of the Bureau of Catholic Indian Missions," Black and Indian Mission Office, accessed July 10, 2017, http://blackandindianmission.org/aboutus/bcim.

motion a largely Protestant mission system for ministering to Native tribes. The Bureau of Catholic Indian Missions was created by the American Catholic hierarchy in Washington, D.C., to counter what they saw as unfair access both to missionary work and to the evangelization of Native peoples—some of whom were already Catholic. In 1901 the Society for the Preservation of the Faith Among Indian Children (later simply referred to as the Preservation Society) was established by the Bureau of Catholic Indian Missions in Washington, D.C. That society produced its first publication in 1902, called the *Indian Sentinel*. Like other outlets of this kind, the *Indian Sentinel* served as both a recorder of events and a call for donations. Woefully underfunded, the Bureau of Catholic Indian Missions became an umbrella organization under which other branches of missionary work attempted to secure financial stability. Among those was an organization founded in 1907 by Franciscan missions, the Society for the Preservation of the Faith among Indian Children also known as the Franciscan Branch of the Preservation Society.[157]

In 1913 Franciscan missions to the Southwest, primarily supported by the St. John the Baptist Province, established a journal to tell supporters about the work being done by priests, brothers, and sisters in the Southwest. That journal, *The Franciscan Missions of the Southwest*, ran from 1913 through 1922. It was reassembled in the 1930s as *Traveling the Padre's Trail: The Mission Travel Club* to chronicle the experiences of the Franciscans among the Native tribes of the Southwest. That iteration lasted into the early 1940s, when the magazine again changed its name slightly, becoming simply *Padres' Trail*. The distinguishing feature of all these publications from St. Michaels, Arizona, was the way they dealt with and dwelled on the Navajo Nation.

When the Franciscans began to publicize their work among the Navajo, the United States had not yet accepted Arizona as a state. Moreover, outright racism informed prevailing assumptions guiding national policy on relations with Native tribes. The Franciscans of the Southwest made clear their mission work rested on different assumptions: first, that federal policy affected their work only inasmuch as it would either help build schools and hospitals or else get in the way of administering justice to the region; and second, that because the Franciscans had lived in the Southwest for decades, they took a very long view of their work to bring Catholicism (in particular the spirit of St. Francis) to a region wracked with problems.

Thus in first few issues of *Franciscan Missions of the Southwest*, the Franciscan editors chose to dispel bigoted notions about Native Americans. "The Indians of the Southwest, in particular the Navajo, are not the lazy lot of humanity as which our American Indians in general are pictured to us," an

---

157. Introduction, *The Franciscan Missions of the Southwest: Official Organ of the Franciscan Branch (Cincinnati Province) of the Preservation Society* 1 (1913): 1.

editorial explained. "On the contrary, a glance at the advertising section shows flourishing business establishments, in the interior of Navajo country as well as on its borders, whose constituents are almost exclusively Navajo Indians, and who all were eager to avail themselves of the opportunity offered to them to advertise."[158] The Franciscans sought to promote the Najavo to their readers as spiritually fulfilled persons whose culture was so sophisticated that the friars spent years learning and translating their language. Reports filed from these missions stand as commentary on the constancy of the Franciscan presence among the Navajo people and witness to their lives as they moved from being wards of the federal government to being a nation within a nation.

Among the most significant early interlocutors for these missions was Father Anselm Weber, OFM, who served as the superior of the mission from 1900 to 1921. Weber was joined by Berard Haile, OFM, who wrote extensively on the Navajo language and religious customs, including a series on sacred Navajo ceremonies. Weber and Haile collaborated on the writing, editing, and publishing of *Franciscan Missions of the Southwest* to discuss their work among the Navajo and (to a lesser extent) the Pueblo. As religious historian Ross Enochs notes, "In this journal, they recounted their long journeys on horseback to visit the Navajos and stay in their hogans, their houses. Through their writing they showed that they were very close to the Navajo people and won their trust."[159]

Reports from the Franciscans often dispeled assumptions common to many Americans that Indians were indolent and their women servile. Enochs explains: "The missionaries described the women as having almost total control of the household and children, and the missionaries also noted that women owned property and livestock."[160] These reports also noted that the missionaries were having little success in evangelizing the Navajo adults, so the friars decided to focus their evangelization efforts on the children. Therefore school construction and administration became a consistent feature in accounts of the missions. In 1902 the Franciscans built St. Michael's boarding school in the Black Creek Valley of Arizona with financial help from Mother Katharine Drexel, who was canonized a saint by the Roman Catholic Church in 2000. However, because the Franciscans were perpetually underfunded, they relied more on government schools to educate Navajo children, an arrangement that the parents of those children apparently preferred. According to Haile, "the Navajos asked for a school in which the Catholic sisters would teach their children. He said that the Navajos were pleased when they found out that nuns were coming to teach their children in the schools

---

158. Ibid.
159. Enochs, "Mission to the Navajos," 50.
160. Ibid., 51.

because they believed that they cared about the children more than the government teachers."[161]

Weber wrote one long recollection on the origins of religious instruction within Indian government schools in the early 1900s. He recounted how originally federal laws restricted the Franciscans from giving religious instruction to Navajo children while in the school. Those rules changed in 1910 under a new administration in Indian Affairs. Teachers would be allowed to instruct pupils in denominational religion if the instructors received the permission of the parents or legal guardians of the children. So Weber recounted traveling "about a thousand miles" on horseback throughout Navajo country, where he received permission to teach 198 children the Catholic faith. He explained that he "divided them into two classes": "In the lower class I gave this instruction exclusively in their own tongue, whilst in the upper class I used both, the Navajo and the English language." Instruction in this manner took place two nights a week and on Sundays. Fort Defiance became, along with St. Michael's, the two primary posts from which the Franciscans built relations with the Navajo through schools, churches, and ultimately hospitals and community centers.[162]

The Navajos greatly resented the forced removal of their children from their homes and their enrollment in government schools. The Franciscans approached the same situation from a different perspective. As Weber's recollection suggested, the friars offered Navajos day schools and boarding schools—but both were optional and not forced on the tribes. The friars used their magazine to promote what they saw as somewhat difficult but necessary work among tribes. In other words the friars understood the delicate nature of their mission among a people who had been mistreated for many years. In a 1916 issue of *The Franciscan Missions of the Southwest*, Weber offered a statement from a Navajo father to confirm the bittersweet nature of their work:

> When we were young everything was much different from what it is now. Our children know nothing of how it used to be. . . . You priests teach them the white man's religion; they forget more and more the Navajo ways and by and by will become like Americans. We see all these changes, and we cannot stop them: they are bound to go on. We are not opposed to these changes so far as our children are concerned: they are for their good. We are satisfied that they go to school and learn something; we are satisfied that they pray the same as you do, but we old folks are too old to change.[163]

---

161. As quoted in Enochs, 53.

162. Father Anselm Weber and Father Egbert Fischer, "Our Mission Work at Fort Defiance, Arizona," *The Franciscan Missions of the Southwest*, 3 (1915), 10, 12.

163. Anselm Weber, OFM, "On Navajo Myths and Superstitions," *Franciscan Missions of the Southwest* 4 (1916): 45, quoted in Enochs, "Mission to the Navajos," 54.

In the third issue the Branch Society reported that its promotional efforts had increased membership in the society to 6,500 people and 110 financial sponsors. News items in the third issue dwelt on the number of so-called pagans (mostly children at the schools) brought into the Catholic Church. Interestingly almost all these children attended government schools, paid for by federal money allocated to manage Native tribes but used for both their education and the building of chapels in at least two of the schools. Almost all the teachers at these government schools were Franciscan brothers and sisters who also provided instruction in becoming Catholic. At the same time, Franciscans entreated the Mexican population in the region—another group sorely discriminated against—to return and renew their commitment to the Catholic Church. Added to these two groups were immigrants from cities in the East that had grown overcrowded with poor workers. The early issues of *The Franciscan Missions of the Southwest* reveal that the Franciscans undertook work among groups largely forgotten by the rest of America—Native tribes and Mexicans—and shed light on the deeply problematic treatment of Native tribes by the federal government. Such experiences provided a compelling narrative for those who encountered them in the pages of the friars' magazine.

In each issue of *The Franciscan Missions of the Southwest* in the early twentieth century, one can see the steady expansion of Franciscan work throughout the Southwest. St. Michael's Mission and School remained the center of Franciscan work for many years. But there were also missions in Tohatchi, New Mexico, and Chin Lee, Arizona; the Sacred Heart School of Gallup, New Mexico, in a desolate and poor region of the Southwest; the zealous Franciscans among the Pueblo Indians of Laguna, Cochiti, and Santo Domingo in New Mexico; and the Franciscan Sisters of Lafayette, Indiana, who traveled to Jemez, New Mexico, to set up their mission and new convent in Pena Blanca, christened in September 1900. By the Great Depression, the Franciscans had established a strong presence in the Southwest.

In 1938, the Franciscans of St. Michaels, Arizona, published a magazine called *Travelling the Padre's Trail*, taking over where the journal *Franciscan Missions of the Southwest* had left off in 1922. Like its predecessor, the newly renamed and relaunched magazine aimed to inform supporters of missions among the Navajo (primarily) about work done by the Franciscans. However, the magazine would over time turn from promoting mission work to profiling the role Franciscans played in the Southwest in general. That was a sensitive transition because it involved negotiating a relationship that was, in some ways, a zero-sum game—the Franciscans and Navajo had little genuine common ground in terms of religious practices, in the end only one side was asked to give up their religion. With some justification, religious historian Ross Enochs concludes: Just because the Franciscans "spent so many years collecting information on the Navajo religion does not mean that they had a high regard for it. Their familiarity with the Navajo religion only led them to see the Navajo religion as a primitive, superstitious religion."[164]

For example, one article described the eponymous Padre's visit to a hogan, the structure that Navajo families used as their main shelter. Made from logs and plastered with adobe, the hogan served as the place of all encounters from sleeping to eating to praying. "On his visits to the hogans the Padre frequently happens upon a 'sing,' or pagan ceremony," the author recounted. "And then the hogans that were so familiar and breathed such hearty welcome become strange and forbidding. Then the Padre realized that Christ has not yet become the head of the Navaho's home."[165] The rest of the article told of a practice by which the Navajo moved those close to death outside these homes, out of fear that someone dying inside them would change the hogans so much spiritually that the structures would need to be destroyed.

The discussion of Navajo customs continued in the next issue in an article "Strange Beliefs of the Navahos." The article seemed designed to underscore the exotic nature of Navajo life and the extent of help they needed to overcome what were apparently debilitating superstitions. "We do not hope or want to destroy the belief of our charges in spirits," observed this author, "but we do want to and must correct their concept, and thus bring about a transformation of their beliefs in the imaginary to a solid belief in the real, in God, the saints, the soul and things eternal."[166]

By the mid-1940s the magazine changed names again, becoming *The Padres' Trail*, and its format began to resemble other Franciscan magazines by including page numbers and dates of publication. The July 1946 issue honored the Navajo men who went off to fight in the American war effort. In the October 1946 issue the editors ran a story about the American Legion granting a charter to the Navajo veterans at Window Rock, Arizona. Members of Fort Defiance had been the first Navajo people to create an American Legion for their own nation, and it was their work that brought the American Legion to Arizona to honor those who had died in the war for the United States, the nation that had largely left them behind.[167]

For the forty-fifth anniversary of the 1898 founding of St. Michael's Mission, an issue of *Padre's Trail* emphasized the growth of the school founded by Mother (now St.) Katharine Drexel of the Congregation of the Sisters of the Blessed Sacrament for Indians and Colored People. Enrollment in the

---

164. Enochs, "Mission to the Navajos," 72.

165. "Home Sweet Home," *Traveling the Padre's Trail*, October 1938.

166. Father B. R. [pseud.], "Strange Beliefs of the Navajos," *Traveling the Padre's Trail*, February 1941, unnumbered.

167. "Editorial," *Padres' Trail* 1 (July 1946): 4–5; "The First American Legion," *Padres' Trail* 1 (October 1946): 10–11.

school increased steadily, becoming a significant alternative to the federally supported schools within which some Franciscans taught. St. Michael's also built a hospital that served thousands of Navajo at a time when such care was nearly nonexistent around other reservations. The tone of the *Padres' Trail* articles about the Franciscan mission described the efforts of friars and nuns in heroic terms. For example, "Despite severe handicaps in this humble beginning," wrote Thomas Shiya, "these friar-apostles to the Navahos expanded their work into the far-flung desolated areas of the huge reservation, using pack horse and springless wagon to reach the Indians in their isolated hogans in all kinds of weather." Shiya noted that from the original mission of "two priests and one brother, the missionary personnel . . . increased to 17 priests, 6 brothers and 36 Sisters from three separate communities." The number of churches and sanctuaries had also grown in number, as had the St. Michael's Indian School.[168]

St. Michael's Indian School appeared consistently as a topic of discussion in *Padre's Trail*. When the format of the journal changed in 1949 from six pages to sixteen, an article on the school had prominence because, as it stated, "the history of spiritual progress among the Navaho People has inevitably been linked with their Catholic education." By 1949 three hundred students were enrolled in the school, 291 of them as boarders, and not all were Navajo children; also present were eight Hopi, six Laguna, and children from "several other tribes." The article reported that in 1948 the first high school students graduated from St. Michael's. In addition to offering an overview of the school's history and some data on pupils and teachers, the article also addressed the influence of the school on the reservation. "These Navaho boys and girls," the authors assured readers, "are very eager to learn not only the religion but also the language and technical skills of the 'Belagana,' as they call the whites." The operating assumption was that the school would have a positive effect on the life of the children and their families. Thus it was not surprising to read, "The older Fathers on the reservation often remark that progress away from superstitions is quite evident in many cases due to Christian Education."[169]

However, at the same time that *Padres' Trail* published articles referring to the superstitions of the Navajo, the magazine also profiled the significant work of Father Berard Haile, OFM, for his extraordinary achievements as a Navajo scholar and linguist. Haile was among a small group of Franciscans who worked with the Navajo by learning and transcribing their language. And throughout the 1940s and early 1950s, the journal also ran articles on the paltry federal financial contributions to the reservation. For example, in 1953,

---

168. Thomas S. Shiya, "Brown Robes Carry on a 400 Year Work Hallowed by Tradition and Martyrdom," *Padres' Trail* 10 (December 1948): 1.

169. "Back to School," *Padres' Trail* 11 (1949): 4–9.

one editorial noted, "The President asked Congress for twenty million dollars for the fiscal year of 1953 in order to speed up the construction of essential roads, schools, and hospitals. Without these elements, other factors in the program cannot be realized. Instead Congress in an economy move, cut the appropriation to three million dollars and practically stopped the building program." The editorial further emphasized the lack of facilities, especially schools and hospitals, on the reservation. "To deny these people equal opportunity with the rest of American citizens," the journal reasoned, "is unjust and unfair. After all, the Indians are the first Americans, but too often the government treats them as cast-off misfits, and necessary nuisances."[170]

Many articles in the magazine spoke to the general plight of the Navajo as a forgotten people who lived in conditions a world apart from how most Americans imagined a modern person should live. Yet in the 1960s and 1970s the magazine began to make a perceptible attempt to close the distance between the Navajo Nation and white America by writing about the distinctiveness of the Navajo culture without qualifications. In the issue that celebrated the transition from the 1960s to the 1970s, editor Simon Conrad, OFM, wrote:

> One way of characterizing the Navajo world in the 60's is "Searching for Identity." In this context the trends of Navajoland paralleled those of the nation, but in a different way. On the national scene traditional institutions and patterns were shaken by civil rights violence, war opponents, campus riots, drugs and so forth. On the Navajo Reservation the forces of native religion, nationalism, partisan politics, militancy—emboldened by educators, anthropologists, lawyers, and other specialists—had a somewhat similar impact. There was a clash of these factors with the previously established pattern of federal paternalism.[171]

The editorial noted a sense of dislocation that Navajo experienced, contending with "Anglo-ization" from their involvement in schools like St. Michael's and a movement to preserve traditions that were in real danger of being dissolved by the acids of modern reservation life.[172]

Perhaps most significant in this Franciscan journal was the self-awareness that appeared among the friars themselves. For example, Conrad wrote: "As progress in basic education moved on, it was noticed that the Navajo Indians were not really achieving the results that were originally expected. Blame was put on a variety of factors: overlooking the fact that English was really a foreign language to the child—overlooking the Indian culture entirely and basing education on middle-class values which were also foreign to the children—not

---

170. Editorial, *Padres' Trail* 15 (1953): 3–4, 6.
171. Simon Conrad, "The Past Present in the Future," *Padres' Trail* 32 (February 1970): 2.
172. Ibid., 2.

giving the Indian child a sense of identity and self respect—and many similar reasons." Such a passage constituted a dramatic change in the fundamental way the Franciscans looked at and understood their role on the reservation. Doing so led to other observations about the mission itself: "Perhaps the greatest confusion of the people [in the mission] in finding their identity best explains the difficulty of mission work in the 60s," Conrad wrote. "There were no pat and easy answers to what approach to use in Christian witness. . . . The Navajo Tribe was being divided more and more among the educated and the uneducated, the young and the old. It was difficult to find an approach that could satisfy both." Looking into the future, he said, the magazine's editors hoped to ruminate in the pages about the meetings and discussions that would move along a reworking of their relationship to their historical neighbors.[173]

One way the editors proposed to do this was to emphasize the significance of St. Kateri Tekakwitha, a Mohawk Indian who lived in a region north of Albany, New York, in the late seventeenth century; she was beatified in Rome by Pope John Paul II in June 1980 and subsequently became a saint when Pope Benedict XVI canonized her in 2012. In a 1980 article about her, the editors offered: "In an age of distress and confusion, a young Indian girl points the way back to God." In 1980 on the occasion of her beatification, *Padres' Trail* used her story to introduce a slightly different narrative about the reasons Native Americans became Catholic. A highlighted section of the article asked readers to understand that "Kateri's beatification shows that God's presence was among the Indian people from the beginning."[174]

According to Catholic officials, Kateri was born to an Algonquin Christian; and though she was not raised Catholic, she was baptized at the age of twenty and ultimately escaped from her tribe through the help of Native Americans from the north who had converted to Christianity. Her baptismal name was Catherine, and she went by the Mohawk version of that name, Kateri. The mythology surrounding Kateri emphasized her willingness to dissent from her tribe, to commit herself to a vow of virginity, and to remain pious in her faith despite being tormented by non-Catholics, including those in her own family.[175]

The article fully endorsed the mythology that had grown up around this extraordinary story. First, according to *Padres' Trail*, "Kateri's beatification shows that God can be at work among Native American people even though their environment is without Christ." The writers argued that through the example of Kateri and by extension the history of Native Americans in the

---

173. Ibid., 7.

174. "In an Age of Distress and Confusion, a Young Indian Girl Points the Way Back to God," *Padres' Trail* 42 (October–December 1980): 7.

175. Ibid., 3–5.

United States, white Americans might come to see that it "takes heroic courage to embrace Christianity, and Christian values—for example virginity, when all one's relatives are opposed." The latter part of the article, which ran fifteen pages, addressed the beatification of Kateri in Rome, attended by representatives from Native tribes in the United States. Kateri symbolized for the magazine's editors, at least, a kind of bridge between the problems of the modern world and the clarity of faith that existed in a premodern world, shared by Native tribes in their traditional dress and by Catholics in their robes and customs. The article noted: "Kateri, the simple Mohawk Indian girl, was able to transcend the racial tension, unrest, injustice, and violence that existed all around her. She overcame by focusing on Jesus—on the cross. She went back to her roots in the forest and carved a cross on a tree—her altar."[176]

St. Kateri Tekakwitha's story served a number of purposes for *Padres' Trail* and the larger Catholic American culture into which it emerged. As an American Indian who chose the Catholic Church and sacrificed for her faith, she represented the best possible version of Catholic missionary history—a beacon for both Native Americans and Catholic missionaries alike. According to religious historian Kellie Jean Hogue, evidence suggests that many Native tribes directly supported the canonization of St. Kateri.[177] Robert Orsi argues that Kateri also served as a character in a civic narrative about American life that deliberately countered the prevailing Protestant view of US history. Here was a "figure," he writes, "who embodied and exemplified Catholic traditions most deeply at odds with the modern world and with the American story." As both Native American and Catholic, Kateri could not have been more foreign from the European and Protestant elite who dominated most of the American past.[178]

However, she also exemplified a persistent theme in Catholic culture: that of being something other than modern while living in the modern world. One can see especially throughout decades of Franciscan media an awareness that the modern world needs an alternative that maintains premodern traditions alongside an understanding that people will use such traditions within their modern context. Orsi points out: "To be modern is to be liberated from the past, which is understood to be at best irrelevant and at worst an obstacle to happiness, success, and fulfillment."[179]

---

176. Ibid., 6–7, 11–12.
177. Kellie Jean Hogue, "A Saint of Their Own: Native Petitions Supporting the Canonization of Kateri Tekakwitha, 1884–1885," *U.S. Catholic Historian* 32 (Summer 2014): 25–44.
178. Robert Orsi, "US Catholics Between Memory and Modernity: How Catholics Are American," in *Catholics and the American Century: Recasting Narratives of US History*, ed. R. Scott Appleby and Kathleen Sprows Cummings (Ithaca, NY: Cornell University Press, 2012), 25, 26.
179. Ibid., 14.

Interlude:
A Right to Be Merry

T he tension between modernity and a premodern church animated much of Franciscan media in the first half of the twentieth century. However, in 1956 a book appeared by a cloistered nun named Mary Francis that reveled in the stark, at times humorous, differences between the modern world and a community of decidedly independent if also premodern nuns.

Sister Mary Francis, PCC, was a cloistered nun at the Poor Clare Monastery in Roswell, New Mexico. When she was twenty-six, she and nine other young women dressed in their enclosure veils boarded a train at Dearborn Station in Chicago for a long journey to the American Southwest. It was November 1948 when the sisters left the chilly Midwest for the desert warmth of New Mexico. Waiting at their destination were two senior nuns: Abbess Mother Mary Immaculata and the novice mistress of the Order of St. Clare, who had been invited by Archbishop Edwin Vincent Byrne of Santa Fe to establish a monastery in Roswell. With the consent of Cardinal Samuel Stritch, the order established a monastery in an old white farmhouse that, as Mary Francis described it, was "just a very plain white frame building with a roguish red roof. An old-fashioned porch runs across the front and half of one side. The roof leaks when it rains, and nothing will prevail upon some of the windows to let themselves be opened."[1]

That roof played a major role in the story of Sister Mary Francis and the public's embrace of her particular Franciscan message. In 1956 the abbess mother asked Mary Francis to enter an essay contest that had as its prize $1,000. The monastery needed the money to fix the building's leaky roof. This Poor Clare began writing a story on the backs of labels peeled from cans of vegetables and fruits. As her account of cloistered life at the monastery grew, she began to send chapters to her aunt, who showed them to a dinner guest one evening. That guest was Frank Sheed, who with his wife Maisie Ward, had founded what became the preeminent Catholic publishing house Sheed and Ward in 1926. The publishers subsequently moved their operation from London to New York City in 1933, producing hundreds of titles in

---

1. Mother Mary Francis, PCC, *A Right to Be Merry* (New York: Sheed and Ward, 1956; San Francisco: Ignatius Press, 2001), 40. Citations refer to the Ignatius Press edition.

Catholic thought and theology, including many that promoted a more common approach to everyday Catholic living. Sheed read a chapter of Mary Francis's manuscript and asked for the rest. The resulting book, *A Right to Be Merry*, became a top-seller for Sheed and Ward and has been in print ever since. Needless to say, the roof was repaired.[2]

Mary Francis was born in 1921 in St. Louis (with the name Alberta Aschmann), where she attended the School of the Sisters of Notre Dame. She graduated and went on to St. Louis University but left before finishing her degree to enter the Poor Clare Monastery in Chicago in July 1942. In June 1943 she took her vows and her new name, Sister Mary Francis of Our Lady. She also began her career as a published author, completing her first book of poetry, *Whom I Have Loved*, while still a novice. She made her final profession in July 1947 and left for Roswell eighteen months later.[3]

A Right to Be Merry alternates between a first-person narrative and an exposition on the role of the Catholic Church in American life. The tone of the book is disarming, relating what it is like to live a cloistered life (something few readers would have experienced) with sincerity, humor, and warmth. It also exudes authority because it comes from a person who seems to have no stake in the doctrinal and institutional questions that necessarily occupy something as big as the Catholic Church. So Catholics who picked up Sister Mary Francis's book in the mid-1950s might have felt both closer to their faith and emboldened by the confidence that Mary Francis herself invested in that faith. This dual sensibility gave the book a profile not completely dissimilar to Thomas Merton's *The Seven Storey Mountain*, which appeared in 1948 and became a national best seller, chronicling his entry into a Trappist monastery. Both books reflected a broader trend in American culture in which people sought solace in faith from the anxiety induced by the Cold War. In short the book had broad appeal because it personalized a commitment to a faith in something larger and universal. In this way *A Right to Be Merry* anticipated the turn from devotional and doctrinal Catholic literature toward more personal and broadly spiritual literature.

In 1964, Mary Francis was chosen abbess of her monastery, thus becoming Mother Mary Francis, and in the preface to the 1973 edition of her book

---

2. Valerie Schmalz, "The Poor Clare Author Who Energized the Church," *Catholic Exchange*, June 24, 2006, accessed July 11, 2017, http://catholicexchange.com/the-poor-clare-author-who-energized-the-church; Archbishop Raymond Burke, "Be Not Afraid!: Death of a Holy Saint Louisan," Archdiocese of St. Louis, February 17, 2006, accessed July 11, 2017, http://archstl.org/files/archstl/images/stories/burke/columns2006/02-17-06-column.pdf; "Biography of Mother Mary Francis, P.C.C.," Poor Clare Monastery of Our Lady of Guadalupe, accessed July 11, 2017, http://poorclares-roswell.org/pages/mfm.html.

3. "Biography of Mother Mary Francis."

she seems to acknowledge that she offered advice as much as religious reflection. She wrote: "We are hearing and talking a great deal about options these days. So, here are two options for you, and an opportunity to exercise your keen sense of personal autonomy. Make up your own mind. Follow your conscience." That sentiment (or challenge), she said, could be read as an epilogue to the original 1956 printing. She offered readers a personal attachment to the book and, more broadly, to her Catholic faith.

In the first chapter of the book, Mary Francis related the fear and anxiety and excitement and joy of the sisters who traveled with her on a train to New Mexico. With the anticipation growing as they stood waiting to board the train, Mary Francis said, "Our hearts were turning toward unknown Roswell and unpredictable new beginnings. No one could shatter such a moment with a word. Then Sister Anne dropped her sewing box!"[4] This moment of levity also presented Mary Francis with an opportunity to describe just how important a sewing box is to a nun—"her greatest material treasures are in that box."[5] Her explanation demonstrated at once the profound simplicity of a cloistered nun's life as well as the nearly heroic self-sufficiency of these young women. In a world in which machines had changed not only labor but the household and even youth itself, these Poor Clares revealed that their originality made them almost the most modern women in Chicago. They seemed able to define who they were far better than those whose lives were circumscribed by an age of technology.

Much of the first half of the book deals with questions that many people presumably had about why a young woman in the modern era would choose a cloistered, celibate life of poverty and penance. Such a question offered an excellent way to structure the book—Mary Francis could play off people's assumptions and offer both a witty and an insightful narrative about things she knew best. For example, she dropped casual observations that revealed just how great the difference was between her sisters and other women. She recounted details from the train ride to New Mexico: "Sister Teresa complained bitterly about the way they plastered compartments with mirrors so that you could not look anywhere but out the window without seeing your own face. After fifteen years of not seeing her face" due to the vows she had taken, Mary Francis added, "she could not readjust to it now." Here were giggling young women who had adhered to a sense of modesty most likely antithetical to their contemporaries in America.[6]

Who were these women? First and foremost, they were Franciscans. In a chapter entitled "My Lady Poverty," Mary Francis declared: "Poverty was

4. Mary Francis, *Right to Be Merry*, 11, 21.
5. Ibid., 21, 23.
6. Ibid., 38.

truly 'most high' to St. Francis and St. Clare. Most high in the spiritual ideal of the Order, it must also take the highest place in the material side of the Franciscan life." Thus for women who chose a cloistered life, typical descriptions of their simple life hardly captured the essence of it—what they gave up in material possessions, they gained in "liberty of spirit and freedom of heart," Mary Francis wrote. "The monasteries of St. Clare are houses of a poverty not grim or drab, but bright and charming," she explained. When describing how to make mundane aspects of life beautiful, Mary Francis rejoiced in the Franciscan joy of what is common: "We do not paint things black where we could paint them white. We plant flowering tamarisk around our homemade incinerator because," she offered, "there is no reason why emptying the garbage should not be done with beauty and grace. . . . If poverty were thrust upon us, anything would perhaps be good enough. But we chose it, we espoused it. And we mean to clothe it in beauty."[7]

So if they constructed an identity out of imagined Franciscan ideals, they also lived as a small group of self-sufficient women—a rare exception in a country beset by a baby boom, with growing suburbs, and (especially within the Catholic Church) the elevation of the family to a sacred institution. Though her book stood as a comment about her times as much as about her community, Mary Francis wrote directly: "Life is so simple when we do not complicate it." Her stories affirmed special joy in finding one's calling. Their new home had very few conveniences, they even built their own cabinets and cupboards. Mary Francis had an uncanny ability to offer pithy and profound observations that connected with women outside the cloister. "If we had known theoretically before that the less material baggage one carries through life, the freer and gladder one is," she wrote, "We knew it experimentally that first year in Roswell. We have very little of anything but love and joy. And we needed little else."[8]

The second feature that defined these women was their decision to be cloistered. "What sort of girl elects to narrow the outer compass of her life to three or four walled-in acres? The neurotic? The lovelorn and disappointed? The selfish and shiftless? The social misfit? Such notions find easy quarter in many minds," Mary Francis acknowledged, "but it needs only a little common sense to reveal them all as preposterous." She explained forthrightly: "I was sixteen when I knew I had to be a Sister. I was twenty when I realized God wanted me in the cloister." But how and why? No vision guided her, Mary Francis asserted when recounting a pivotal conversation with a priest who helped her discern her calling. Her most crucial attribute was not piety or devotion to the Church but her sense of humor: "The ability to see *through*

---

7. Ibid., 70, 73.
8. Ibid., 43.

things and to know what is important and what is not, what is to be endured and why we endure it, what is to be tolerated out of compassion and what is to be extirpated out of duty, is dependent on one's sense of humor." Stating what followed this logic, Mary Francis noted, "A group of dour females with their jaws set grimly for 'perfection' and their nerves forever in a jangle would turn a cloister into a psycho-pathic ward."[9]

Still the severity of the cloister and the mystery of life within its walls demanded a more comprehensive explanation. Mary Francis acknowledged: "From outside the wall, perhaps the regulations concerning the enclosure do seem overdrawn. We speak at the parlor grille only to our relatives three times a year, or to priests; to others, only for some extraordinary reason, such as Maria Trapp [of the famous Von Trapp family] giving us recorder lessons, or Dr. Natalie White [a dramatist who wrote *A Billion Dollar Saint: A Farce in Three Acts*] coming to give me a private course in playwriting." Living behind a wall did not prevent playwriting, apparently. Yet all activities of cloistered nuns, while seemingly proscribed by rules that establish a physical environment, are a manifestation of their faith. That point, Mary Francis explained, grew as a result of a life of contemplation with the aim to create "the closest possible union with God." Such an aim, she wrote, "necessarily makes extraordinary demands on its pursuivants."[10]

The book addressed directly the question of why any modern young woman would leave "the twentieth-century world to enter a thirteenth-century Order." Mary Francis used a frankness that made her point well. She wrote not so much in defense of her world as in defense of her ability to accomplish what she set out to become. One gets the sense she could have become anything she desired—in her case that was a cloistered nun. "There is really only one lesson in monastic life," she explained, "the lesson of love. Each day, the postulant with a true vocation masters more of its content. If she is intelligent and basically humble, she will appreciate the corrections given her and accept them with love. If she is too stupid and incurably proud to realize that only good material is considered worthy of perfecting, she will not be kept in the cloister anyway." The sense of confidence that the monastery was not a prison for lost souls or the sad default for hopeless girls pervades the book. Mary Francis dismissed assumptions she believed others made about those who entered the cloistered life and those who ran it. But in doing so she took care to relate that all was not bliss; rather life in the monastery could be hard, uncomfortable, and even stressful. She and her sisters, though, grew together and could fail together and find joy in their struggles together.[11]

---

9. Ibid., 55, 55.
10. Ibid., 62.
11. Ibid., 88–89.

Mary Francis wrote carefully and frankly about celibacy as well. Elia Kazan's steamy movie *Baby Doll* came out in 1956, the same year that this book was published. The main character is a newly married, young woman of the Tennessee Williams-style South, called Baby Doll. She has allowed herself to be married to a misbegotten suitor but will not allow him to take her virginity until her twentieth birthday. The sexual tension of the film helps exaggerate the deviancy of a repressed Southern community. Mary Francis and the Poor Clares offered an alternative to that sensibility in almost every way. If the idea of sexuality for women had changed by the mid-1950s, even the Poor Clares had something to say to women of the time. "Virginity is not only a giving, but a receiving," Mary Francis offered. "If properly understood, it is a glorious enrichment. A woman who knows herself to be completely cherished is a woman of confidence and poise. This carries over into the spiritual life and gives a Poor Clare interior confidence and spiritual poise in whatever sorrows and trials may lie ahead. . . . She knows she is loved, cherished, chosen. That is really all a woman needs."[12]

A Right to Be Merry obviously offered observations and positions on gender, sexuality, and the status of women religious in a time of transition for women in America and, more specifically, for American nuns. Historian Rebecca Sullivan provides critical context for understanding the conversation to which Mary Francis's book contributed. It was one of many accounts that appeared in print and on film that purported to reveal the life of nuns. Sullivan writes that "while convent reforms had begun at the start of the decade [1950s], the organizational initiatives of sisters were not well publicized. . . . Thus, in the fifties, although there was a sense that sisters were making changes to their way of life, it had yet to be well articulated or assessed by the mass media."[13] Sullivan does not discuss *A Right to Be Merry* at length but does note that the book might be seen as a useful counterpoint to the more popular and more controversial best-selling book, *The Nun's Story*, by Kathryn Hulme, which came out the same year and was subsequently made into a popular and critically acclaimed Hollywood film in 1959. "At a point where they [women religious in the US] were hoping to receive some recognition for their efforts," relates Sullivan about *The Nun's Story*, "along came a novel that seemed to prove the public's greatest fears. It reinforced negative attitudes towards the convent as an imposing asylum where women were subjugated and demeaned in the name of religious obedience."[14]

---

12. Ibid., 118.
13. Rebecca Sullivan, *Visual Habits: Nuns, Feminism, and American Postwar Popular Culture* (Toronto: University of Toronto, 2005), 96–97.
14. Ibid., 98.

In fact both books, *A Right to Be Merry* and *The Nun's Story*, shared time atop the best-seller list published by the Jesuit magazine *America* from 1956 through the summer of 1957. Yet unlike Mary Francis's book, *The Nun's Story* came under fairly intense scrutiny for its depiction of the cloister. Hulme's book was a slightly fictionalized account of a former Belgian nun named Marie Louise Habets, who was called Sister Luke in the book and film. Hulme and Habets spent the latter part of their lives together as life partners when, following World War II, they worked for Catholic Relief Services helping throngs of displaced persons. Hulme recounted the real-life struggle of Habets who as young nun before the war had traveled from a cloister in Belgium to become a medical assistant in the Congo. The book's most controversial theme dwelled on Habets's conflicted spiritual life, detailing her struggles with religious vows by suggesting that such a commitment undermined the intellectual lives of women and, in the case of Habets, led to a profound moral crisis during the Second World War. Habets returned to Belgium just as the Nazi invasion of western Europe swept through her homeland, killing her father, a Belgian doctor. Told to remain neutral by her superiors, Habets found it impossible to keep her religious vows and received a dispensation from her order to join the resistance against the Nazis.[15]

The book review editor for *America*, Father Harold C. Gardiner, published a laudatory review of Hulme's book. Letters from readers of his review demonstrated that the story had courted some controversy. One writer exclaimed that in her book club a majority of the women "loved the book as a beautiful and moving story of spiritual struggle"; another wrote with justifiable wonder to ask why some Catholics "seem to delight in the gossipy trash [of a] *Peyton Place* . . . [but] assume such an offended attitude toward a really good book of the stature of *The Nun's Story*. . . . Why is it that [some of] my Catholic friends regard the book as a story of failure, whereas my non-Catholic friends come to me with tears in the eyes, describing it as a book of intense faith?" Other readers were less impressed: "To many of us it seems the story of a laywoman (not under final vows, always wavering) who was educated by a religious order, nursed back to health by the order—and all the while she sojourned in different convents which she now misrepresents. May I recommend that the too, too chivalrous critic-Reverend Father that he is—be given time out to visit a convent and meet Sisters as we know them?"[16]

In a symposium on the book and the film, also published by *America*, Hulme responded to her harshest critics. She admitted that writing such a

---

15. Ibid., 95–96.
16. "Reactions to *The Nun's Story*" (letters to the editor), *America*, January 26, 1957, 482–83.

defense grated against her "writer's principles," but she felt compelled to con tribute it as an "act of gratitude" toward *America's* decision to run opinions that demonstrated something beyond the "'sound and fury' of certain parochial criticism." She explained that what her critics seemed to miss was "that I was writing exclusively of *one nun* and of *her* response to her situation, and that I was describing a European order of twenty-five years ago consid- erably more rigorous in discipline then than now, and certainly different from many American congregations." Indeed it was Hulme who referred to Mary Francis's book, though somewhat indirectly. In defense of her characterization of the cloister as severe and rather anti-intellectual, Hulme retorted: "If my nun protagonist did not seem to some critics as 'merry' as nuns *they* knew, this was simply because my principal character saw nothing playful or merry about trying to please God."[17]

Indeed amid the criticism of *The Nun's Story*, Sullivan points out, could be found criticism from other nuns who "expressed concern over the damage the book could do to vocations. This was," Sullivan notes, "at a time when vocations were deemed at a crisis level and congregations were taking tentative first steps in recruitment drives and quasi-marketing efforts to improve the public image of the convent."[18] The fact that both books appeared before Vatican II illustrates the kind of changes already underway. Writing in 1988, Mary L. Schneider, OSF, explains that in 1954 the Sister Formation Confer- ence "established a broad base of support and dialogue for change [affording] the first opportunity for serious and extended cooperation among religious communities on both the regional and national level." Known as "operation bootstrap," the conference and the movement it fostered directly addressed the kind of issues exposed by the reception to books such as *A Right to Be Merry* and *The Nun's Story*. Schneider points out that "most of the spiritual writing about religious life was permeated by a deep-seated distrust of 'worldly education' and 'intellectual pride.' To combat this theology, the 1955–56 regional meetings had as their theme 'Spiritual and Intellectual Elements in the Formation of Sisters'—with a view to their integration."[19] Nuns like Mary Francis and Sister Luke represented more than their particular orders or even the realities of Catholic women religious, though. The fact that both became images in American culture reflected a broader debate over the role of women in American life and, further, how Americans in general had increasingly come to be defined by consumption and mass culture.

17. Kathryn Hulme, "Author's View: 'The Nun's Story'—A Symposium," *America*, June 27, 1959, 468.

18. Sullivan, *Visual Habits*, 104–5.

19. Mary L. Schneider, OSF, "American Sisters and the Roots of Change: The 1950s," *US Catholic Historian* 7 (Winter 1988): 63–65.

Thus the literature represented by *A Right to Be Merry*, *The Nun's Story*, and another minor best seller, *Bernie Becomes a Nun* (also published in 1956) addressed the complexity of young women's choosing to enter (or being chosen by) a religious order. "In a sense," Sullivan writes, "vocation books achieved a certain level of symbiosis between the allure of the individual in public life and the conventions of middle-class domesticity, fired up by new forms of liberal religiosity that became the organizing principle of postwar Catholicism."[20] If striking that balance between religious life and American consumerist culture seemed a difficult proposition, such a balance was precisely what this genre of Franciscan media sought to achieve. Where Franciscan little magazines and devotional works from *Immaculata* to Mary Francis's book existed uneasily (and deliberately) between modern and traditional Catholic worlds, Franciscan general interest magazines searched for a way to create a modern, Franciscan alternative to mass circulations magazines that dominated the American market.

---

20. Sullivan, *Visual Habits*, 126.

Chapter 3:
Franciscan General Interest Magazines

irculation remains a way to measure the success, influence, and even the nature of a periodical. Between 1945 and the late 1990s (just before the Internet exploded in popularity), certain Franciscan periodicals enjoyed wide readership and were designed for families—meaning they had sections to attract the attention of men as well as women, children as well as parents. Such magazines quite clearly attempted to appeal to that mythical Catholic reader about whom Brendan Mitchell and others ruminated at the Franciscan Educational Conference in 1959. In their search for broad appeal, these general interest magazines also developed innovations not cultivated by the Franciscan publications dominated by the personalities of their editors. Thus rather than follow a more deliberate profile that aligned with an editor or the history of an order, these magazines often served as catchalls for issues and stories that affected Catholic readers. Their connection to a specific Franciscan identity could be obscured by their desire to reach a more general audience. At the same time, such magazines demonstrated how a Franciscan message might appeal to audiences beyond an order or parish or institution.

FRANCISCAN MESSAGE

For example, in July 1947 a new journal called the *Franciscan Message* began publication as "the Magazine for the Common Man to Answer the Problems of His Heart." In a genre that included *St. Anthony Messenger*, *The Lamp*, and the *Franciscan Herald and Forum*, the *Franciscan Message* incorporated many elements that defined general-interest magazines, such as sections that offered advice for men, women, and teens, as well as fiction that sought to convey clear moral messages. Father Fulgence Masiak, OFM, served as the first editor of the magazine, and Julian Arent, OFM, was the associate editor. The *Message* was published by the Franciscan Fathers of Pulaski, Wisconsin, a province descended from Brother Augustine Zeytz, OFM, who had founded a Franciscan friary in 1889 to minister to the Polish population north and west of Green Bay, Wisconsin. In 1939 Rome approved the Assumption of the Blessed Virgin Mary Province, allowing it to develop a college seminary in Burlington, Wisconsin, and a major seminary in Cedar Lake, Indiana. The friars of this order reached Polish communities in various cities of the upper Midwest and Northeast, and they began mission work in the 1950s in Greenwood, Mississippi, among the African American population and as well as in the Philippines. From the late 1940s through the mid-1950s, the *Franciscan Message* usually published fewer than thirty pages per issue, with physical dimensions smaller than other general-interest periodicals.

The first issue began with an editorial declaring the standard Franciscan greeting: "May the Lord Give You His Peace!" Masiak and his staff intended this to be more than a mere salutation: "The word *peace* may have received in our generation a significance and meaning which prompts one to smile cynically at its mere mention. Small wonder, with diplomats at international conferences mouthing the word publicly with reckless abandon all the while in secret meetings their actions and agreements lead directly to everything but peace; leaders of political parties glibly promising peace and then traitor-like . . . surrendering trust tendered them by the people." The magazine seemed to give voice to the anger of the Polish community in the US that perceived concessions made at the Yalta conference as a betrayal of Eastern Europe following the Second World War. Such statements also gave credence to the *Message's* intention to advocate for the common man.[1]

"The *Franciscan Message*," the editors declared in the second issue, "is a magazine of the common man. It tries to suit his pocketbook, his thoughts and language, his interests and his heart. It aims to be nothing else than St. Francis speaking to the Twentieth Century." In the early post–World War II period, the American magazine market was flooded with periodicals. Aware of this situation, editors tried to distinguish their periodicals from the field by providing readers with a clear idea of what they held in their hands. The editors were not simply blunt about the mission of the *Message*; they also appeared willing to make clear the social significance of that mission. "We repeat, the *Franciscan Message* is interested primarily in the man on the street, in the Catholic whom you might label plebeian if you will. We want to get down to earth with such people, sympathize with their problems, laugh with them, cry with them, be little brothers to them as St. Francis would have been." They emphasized their effort to make common cause with the common man: "Let us get it straight from the very beginning that we are interested in the problems of the common man, no matter what his race, creed, or color may be. With St. Francis we believe that you can find good will among men, if you begin by showing it yourself."[2] In that issue appeared essays entitled "God Is Color Blind" and "The International Con-

---

1. "May the Lord Give You His Peace!," *Franciscan Message* 1 (July 1947): 1–3.
2. "Memo to Our Readers," *Franciscan Message* 1 (August 1947): 1.

science Today," plus sections that invited readers to ask questions and send comments.

Each issue often began with a brief, unsigned editorial on the inside of the front cover, with the rest of the pages filled with essays that ran perhaps two pages each. Although some of the topics might be considered fairly mainstream for a Catholic journal, such as a report on Stalin's successors, the magazine also kept readers informed on Franciscan activities not only from the province that produced the magazine but also from nationally syndicated media such as *The Hour of St. Francis*, a radio program produced in Los Angeles that had begun syndication in 1947. *The Hour* consistently asked editors of Franciscan magazines to publicize the stations that carried it. Compared to other Catholic magazines during the early Cold War, however, the *Franciscan Message* did not run many articles on communism and anticommunism. More common were brief essays about the Third Order; fiction stories; advice sections such as "They Ask Me This," in which readers could submit questions on a variety of topics; and a column called "Out of the Mouths of Babes," for which women submitted cute stories about children.

As a magazine begun in the early days of the Cold War, it also had a social angle, encouraging readers to be cognizant of their obligations to their parish and their families—duties that the editors assured readers would bring them a final kind of peace, personal peace of mind and spirit. "Thus we see that our times are characterized by a desperate need of peace," the first issue proclaimed: "peace among the community of nations and races, peace among the social classes, peace among families and within families, and peace for the individual heart."[3] The magazine assessed the approach other Franciscan periodicals took and decided to provide its Midwest readers with a measure of social justice coverage, through essays that explored Marian doctrine.

For example, in May 1950 the *Franciscan Message* ran a cover with an ink drawing of an ark labeled "State of Grace" sitting atop a mountain, while waves labeled "H-Bomb" and "Deluge" lapped around it. The caption read: "Worried? Return to the Ark." Inside the thin magazine was an opening story written in a question-and-answer format regarding the message of Fatima, entitled "Mary Needs Your Help." The Fatima reference might have been familiar to most readers, but the *Message* reminded them of the miraculous visions of the Blessed Mother in 1917 witnessed by three shepherd children and the messages that they delivered on her behalf. Emphasizing the significance of Mary in the lives of Catholics, the editors implored readers to understand that the message of Fatima—"penance, prayer, and reconciliation"—mattered to their time and to them personally. Like other magazines the

---

3. "May the Lord Give," 2–3.

Message also emphasized how significant it was to make praying the daily Rosary a fundamental part of one's life.[4]

Over time the editors of the *Franciscan Message* ran longer essays that attempted to underscore the complex life of common people. For example, an article in 1957 by Father Bruce Malina, OFM looked at Frank Flick, the founder of Flick-Reedy, a highly regarded and successful company located in Bensenville, Illinois, near present-day O'Hare International Airport, that became one of the largest manufacturers of machine tool–grade air and hydraulic cylinders—some of which were used in the United States space program. The point of the essay was to highlight Flick's self-avowed devotion to Catholic principles of business. He had an operation that for its time was quite modern and, he explained, "worker-centered." It had a swimming pool, ponds stocked with fish, large rooms for community meetings, and an ecumenical chapel dedicated to St. Joseph. Flick proudly pointed to the fact that in addition to grounds that contained a golf course and bowling alleys, his corporation also provided courses in basic economics, driver improvement and safety, "political action," and the "Flick-Reedy Public Affairs Program." As Malina concluded: "The success of Frank Flick's economic endeavor lies in his being a capitalist as well as a laborer. By combining both these facets, he can reason accurately in either direction."[5] Flick and his plant won awards for design and intention—for example the physical plant had glass walls to create more connections among employees, and seventy-five percent of the workers took part in a profit-sharing program. In the late 1950s, the *Message* held up Flick as a model of the Catholic businessman, though by the mid-1960s, Flick would be cited for obstructing a vote by his workers who attempted to unionize.[6]

In the December 1961 issue the editors ran a story called "Heroism Comes in Different Sizes" that discussed racial segregation of housing in San Francisco through the experiences of one family who had taken a principled stand against such treatment of blacks and by doing so lost their jobs as apartment managers. That piece signaled a shift in general editorial tone among many Franciscan publications, including *St. Anthony Messenger* and *The Way*. In the early 1960s the *Franciscan Message* was edited by Father Marius Zurat, OFM, then a young priest who was ordained in 1956 into the Franciscan Fathers of Pulaski but later left the institutional priesthood in 1973. Under his direction the *Message* provided nuanced positions on social issues with articles

---

4. Cover, *Franciscan Message* 3 (May 1950); "Mary Needs Your Help," *Franciscan Message* 3 (May 1950): inside front cover.

5. Father Bruce Malina, "Frank Flick: Economic Humanist," *Franciscan Message* 15 (November 1961): 213–18.

6. Kenan Heise, "Obituary: Frank Flick," *Chicago Tribune*, April 2, 1986.

and essays on papal encyclicals, asceticism, home schooling, Catholic education, ecumenism, poverty, race relations, and the shifting position of the laity.

The *Franciscan Message* enthusiastically greeted the Second Vatican Council in 1962 and ran a very good piece in January 1963 in which Father Camillus Hay, OFM, tried to reveal to readers the deep commitment to a spirit of ancient Christianity that imbued the Council proceedings. He intimated that the Council was not a secret gathering of Catholic officials conspiring to produce more dogmatic pronouncements. "It will be the function of the council," he explained, "to remove human imperfections and disfigurements from the Church so that men may more easily recognize in her the characteristics of Him whose bride she is: Christ's love, His compassion, His understanding of men and their problems."[7] He sought to shift the focus from the pageantry showcased in secular coverage (and many Catholic outlets) to the quiet moments of the Council: such as the reciting of the prayer *Adsumus Domine*, the opening of the New Testament on the altar between two lighted candles, and the apparent unity among factions of bishops, all singing together no matter what labels outside observers attached to them.

In an opening editorial in February 1963, Zurat characterized the service the magazine provided as one of preparing "informed, alert" Catholics: "Being an informed and alert Catholic means that you are aware of the many problems that exist—social, economic, and moral. Though they are difficult problems, and often defy simple answers, you have found at least an awareness and understanding of them." He made clear that the magazine had a evangelizing mission as well, encouraging readers to "try to share your knowledge and good fortune with others" by passing on their copies of the magazine and getting others to become regular subscribers.[8]

Though the *Franciscan Message* picked up themes followed by many Catholic leaders of the 1960s—such as contraception and the "plague of secularism"[9]—Franciscan media were more than an echo chamber. William Gulas, OFM, became the new editor of the *Franciscan Message* in October 1963, explaining that the magazine had an obligation to the "millions of Catholics who have not gone beyond high school in their formal education" and thus were not among the rising number of college-educated Catholics whom other magazines addressed.[10] Gulas and his staff began a

---

7. Father Camillus Hay, "Looking Back . . . to Better Understand," *Franciscan Message* 16 (January 1963): 320.

8. Father Marius Zurat, "Dear Reader," *Franciscan Message* 16 (February 1963): inside front cover.

9. See Father Raymond, OFM, "Secularism," *Franciscan Message* 16 (February 1963), 397.

10. William Gulas, OFM, "Getting Acquainted," *Franciscan Message* 17 (October 1963): inside front cover.

more concerted effort to take up issues raised by the increased profile of the laity in the Church. In fairly short order the magazine received letters praising them for "wiping the mold from the *Franciscan Message*"[11] and for publishing an "alert publication"[12] that had a "sensitive feeling for the need of the time and our people": "You're alive—with the rest of us," one reader wrote.[13]

In 1965 the *Franciscan Message* received the Catholic Press Award for general excellence in journalism. The announcement read: "*Franciscan Message* scores for both its purely devotional copy and its related general copy. A picture story of the new liturgy is not only technically well done but also performs a thoughtful service for the layman. A very knowledgeable article, 'Illiteracy in the USA,' is representative of the well-written and well-researched material contained in this magazine." Gulas counted the *Message* as part of general, across-the-board improvement made by Catholic periodicals in the 1960s, attempting "to report on the Church and the world as they really are rather than by pietistic reveries of the past." He admitted that the magazine's efforts hadn't always succeeded—sometimes just failing to hit the mark, at other times racing too far ahead of its readership. But overall he claimed that reader responses and subscriptions had demonstrated approval of the magazine's development.[14]

Into the 1960s the *Franciscan Message*, like other family publications, published a remarkable amount of material by and about women. In the 1940s and 1950s such articles had touched on themes that accorded with traditional gender roles, in essays on marriage, children, and family life generally. Historian Jeffrey Burns points out that Catholic lay women influenced debates about social and political issues in particular sectors of American Catholic culture. Clearly such influence did not extend to areas dominated by Church officials who were men and who rarely shared their authority, even with nuns who ran various Church operations. Nonetheless Burns documents how Catholic lay women "continued to articulate the Catholic theory of the differences of the sexes, while [their] activities suggested a growing disjuncture between ideology and practice." One outlet for such observations was journalism—"perhaps the greatest outlet for Catholic laywomen," Burns notes.

---

11. Cornelius Birchman, "Use Pages for Witnessing," *Franciscan Message* 18 (July 1964), 40.

12. Frank Magisterio, "The Message Has a Message," *Franciscan Message* 18 (July 1964), 40.

13. Jacob Rock, "Accurate Picture of Love," *Franciscan Message* 18 (July 1964): 40–1.

14. "Franciscan Message Receives 1965 Catholic Press Award," *Franciscan Message* 19 (July 1965): n.p.;William Gulas, editorial comment, *Franciscan Message* 19 (July 1965): n.p.

"One is struck by the ubiquitous presence of women writers in Catholic journals during the 1950s."[15]

Indeed Franciscan general interest magazines provide evidence of that observation. For example, in 1962 the *Franciscan Message* published an article by Nora Bishop, "My Retarded Child Is a Crown Not a Cross," that recounted stories from mothers with children who had Down syndrome.[16] The *Franciscan Message* also included social problem stories, like one by Lynn Alexander that began: "Patty's eyes were two big mournful blue buttons as she watched the old sedan turn into the driveway. She regarded her husband behind the steering wheel, with something like pity as she realized that the leash on her anger had grown short." Patty's husband had arrived home late again and spoiled the dinner she had made. Alexander used this moment to craft a cautionary tale about marriage, hoping that her young female readers might consider looking beyond or at least into the daily problems that plagued all couples. Writing about the unrealistically high expectations of her young married couple, she remarked: "It was work and misunderstandings and, often, bitterness. It was a pickle instead of the peach it was painted to be!" Her story ended in ambiguity: Patty began packing to "go home to mother," saying to her husband, "'I thought maybe you'd do better and' she gulped, 'I'd do better too.'" While other magazines published stories in a similar vein, Alexander's narrative had little overt religious counsel and was willing to wrestle openly with the messiness of modern American life.[17]

The magazine also included commentary about marriage and sex in a section called "They Ask Me This." Although the editors invited discussion about life, the idea of holiness, and the mysticism of Catholic saints, in this column they also printed questions and answers that dealt with the intimate lives of families. The section byline had a simple nofication: "This feature is conducted by an anonymous Friar Minor, (OFM), who will reply to questions in the order of their receipt. Private answers to personal questions. Write this column care of this magazine."[18] In March 1952 the magazine ran a long exchange (two pages) on the question of "what the Holy Father said about 'rhythm' when he addressed the Italian Catholic Union of midwives in Rome." The Friar Minor responsible for the column wrote: "True marriage demands the giving of a permanent, uninterrupted, not temporary or fluctuating right to the actions necessary for the begetting of children. When such rights are not

---

15. Jeffrey M. Burns, "Catholic Laywomen in the Culture of American Catholicism in the 1950s," *US Catholic Historian* 5, nos. 3/4 (Summer/Fall 1986): 389, 391.

16. Nora Bishop, "My Retarded Child Is a Crown Not a Cross," *Franciscan Message* 15 (June 1962): 546–52.

17. Lynn Alexander, "Going Home to Mother," *Franciscan Message* 3 (May 1950): 324.

18. "They Ask Me This," *Franciscan Message* 5 (March 1952), 275.

given, are consciously excluded from the marriage contract, there is no valid marriage contract." The friar went on to acknowledge exceptions to this understanding, including the medical condition of the woman, the economic condition of the family, the history of birth defects in previous children, and whether the parents are so dependent on others that having another child would be imprudent.[19] Nearly ten years later another woman wrote in to ask: "Does a wife have to obey her husband when he comes home intoxicated and begins to make demands of her?" The friar answered: "An intoxicated husband has very little right to exercise his authority as husband or father. He has lost the dignity that was his." But the priest added that if the husband's "demands" were reasonable, the wife had "an obligation to fulfill them."[20]

Perhaps more useful than marital advice from priests were essays from Catholic women on race, justice, and peace. In a 1962 piece "If You Want to Oppose Communism . . . Don't Be Radical," Alice Ogle, a frequent contributor to Franciscan magazines, eviscerated the uber-patriot position by vigorously arguing that nationalistic chauvinism born out of a will to oppose communism had led to catastrophically anti-Christian positions. In the mid-1950s the United States had changed its national motto to "In God We Trust" and added it to the currency, and had inserted "under God" into the Pledge of Allegiance—attempts to weaponize American religious freedom and religious identity against communism. Yet Ogle observed: "You can't help but wonder how anyone would have the presumption to decide all by himself that God is inevitably on our side." She asked, "What exactly are we doing to deserve that?" In her article she brought in Thomas Merton and quoted from a recent biography of Soviet premier Nikita Khrushchev; referred to her many "non-Western" friends in San Francisco; and incorporated the thoughts of a variety of theologians. For her time Ogle stood as one of the few Catholic women given a platform to write about topics other than the family or children.[21]

She took up another issue more forcefully in 1963 in "A Woman Looks at the Lay Apostolate." The term "lay apostolate" identified those laity who took the most active part in working with Church officials to help advance Catholic teaching in parishes and society. Ogle herself had lived this role in print, writing for the *Franciscan Message* as well as other Catholic and secular magazines. Described as a housewife from California, she began wryly: "It seems only yesterday that we were told to stay at home and mind the baby and be happy as a housewife. And it seems only yesterday that we were criticized for taking a job, whether we owed a monumental medical bill that was keeping us and our

---

19. They Ask Me This, *Franciscan Message* 5 (March 1952): 274–75.

20. They Ask Me This, *Franciscan Message* 15 (September 1961): 140.

21. Alice Ogle, "If You Want to Oppose Communism . . . Don't Be a Radical," *Franciscan Message* 15 (June 1962): 530–31.

husbands awake at night, or simply because the kids were all in school and we were bored with our lives. Now, suddenly, it is all right to spend time away from home but only if we're apostles!" The Church's recognition that the laity, even women, could participate more fully in the Church belied the fact that—as she quoted another female columnist for *The Sign*—"there is still an offish quality about the way clergy and laymen both consider us."[22]

It was 1963, and the Church had begun to encourage women to get more involved with parish life. But how? Experience dictated little, Ogle observed; women rarely insisted that they could take more serious roles in the Church. Ogle weaved together comments from President John F. Kennedy, Vice President Lyndon B. Johnson, a panel on the status of women in the United States, nuns who taught at the College of St. Frances in Jolliet, Illinois, and Pope John XXIII to make the case that the time had clearly come for women to act. "It's up to us, ladies," she declared. "You can become an active lay apostle if you begin by doing no more than shopping for a blind neighbor or passing out the scientific facts on alcoholism to the miserable wife of a drunkard." She went on: "You're an apostle when you . . . resist efforts of bigoted neighbors to ban Negroes from your neighborhood . . . and when you say a warm 'hello' to strangers you meet going in and out of church." The arc of her columns for magazines such as *Franciscan Message* made her an intellectual, but the fact she wrote such essays for a Franciscan journal gave her the additional identity of a lay woman evangelizing for social justice.[23]

Florence Wedge, who lived in Baltimore, Maryland, often wrote about marriage and other topics generally lumped together as women's issues. For example, Franciscan Publishers, who produced the *Franciscan Message*, also printed pamphlet-sized books by some of its common authors, including Wedge, who wrote *Hand in Hand to Holiness, God and Your Lonely Heart, Help Yourself to Good Habits*, and *Sixty Shining Halos*, the latter of which was advertised as a "wonderful aid to parents and teachers who wish to introduce their youngsters to the exciting world of the saints."[24] Wedge wrote dozens of short books and pamphlets for Franciscan Publishers in Pulaski.

By the early 1960s Wedge expanded her work. In one essay from June 1962 "Every Christian Must Walk the Tightrope of Justice," she offered a subtle take on how Catholics must manage competing claims—justice and charity, Church and society, faith and politics. "There is justice in thought, in word, in action," Wedge wrote. "There is injustice in culpable silence when

22. Alice Ogle, "A Woman Looks at the Lay Apostolate," *Franciscan Message* 16 (March 1963): 410, 412.

23. Ogle, "A Woman Looks at the Lay Apostolate," 414. See also Alice Ogle, "Racial Justice and Dr. James Carey," *Franciscan Message* 16 (July 1962): 30–35.

24. "Books about Marriage," *Franciscan Message* 15 (June 1962), 539.

the occasion demands that we defend another's good name or speak up in his defense when he is falsely accused. There is likewise injustice in lowering others in the esteem of their fellowmen by sins of slander, detraction, and malicious gossip. Clearly, too," she concluded, "the field of justice extends to include people of all races and creeds and social positions." Wedge's observations seemed to reflect—and perhaps were intended to interpret—the evolution of one kind of Catholic culture to another: away from the authoritarian Legion of Decency, no longer a subculture of American society, and interested in a politics that went beyond combating communism. She concluded: "Why is justice so important to our lives as Catholics? Here is one reason. Our sanctity as lay people is intimately bound up with our vocation to serve others. . . . On the way to Christian perfection we meet the double challenge of personal growth in virtue and the needs of our fellow creatures. These two must be integrated into a single way of life." [25]

Wedge seemed to understand that for lay people to grow active in the Church, they needed appeals that would inspire them to act not merely as churchgoers but as apostles. She wrote: "Many Catholics view their parish as a group of buildings to which they must betake themselves to hear Mass, receive the sacraments, or solicit advice or help in emergencies. A growing number of Catholics view the parish church as a convenient place to be baptized, married and buried." They lack, she argued, "personal relationships with priests and fellow parishioners . . . they lack pride in their parish . . . They have no roots." Wedge declared that in the effort to generate lay participation, the Church needed to remind the laity that they are part of the same Church created by the original Apostles and that the mission remains the same: "to help save not merely our own souls, but as many other souls as possible." Wedge appealed to the emotional attachment the laity needed to have with the parish as "the Mystical Body of Christ." "This body of Christ is as real as our parish is real," she declared. "It is throbbing with the very life of Jesus. It is an extension of Himself and His work in time and space, His plan for making millions one with Him." Wedge wrote this essay in the midst of the profound changes to the Mass wrought by the Second Vatican Council.[26] In an essay a year later on the need for priests to face the congregation, she emphasized the element of lay participation in the essential operation of the faith: "Wider participation in the liturgy is our right as sharers in the priesthood of Christ. In the pews are untapped reservoirs of liturgical love and involvement. An altar facing the people could do much to release those pent-

---

25. Florence Wedge, "Every Christian Must Walk the Tightrope of Justice," *Franciscan Message* 15 (June 1962): 536.

26. Florence Wedge, "The Proper Attitude Toward One's Parish," *Franciscan Message* 17 (June 1964): 558–60.

up potentialities for the good of the Church and of the world we are commissioned to consecrate to Christ."[27]

Anne Tansey brought an equally critical eye to the role of the Third Order in a 1966 essay for the *Franciscan Message* entitled "How Apostolic Is the Third Order?" Tansey was a writer and member of a Third Order fraternity based in Cincinnati. A friend's question about the work done by tertiaries in the area prompted Tansey to find out what those groups actually accomplished in relation to their stated devotion to Franciscanism. Her conclusions did not cheer her. She noted that the Third Order often received good press because it appeared to be an expression of lay Catholic action, such as the creation of the AIU tertiary apostolate. "However," Tansey reported, "a regional Father director in the Middle West told me he has striven in vain to interest tertiaries in his province in the A.I.U. It is quite possible that many tertiaries have never even heard of this program of action." "Of course," she added, "many prefects and spiritual directors know that 'Negro' is a controversial word in many fraternities. Any program with interracial overtones is rejected summarily."[28]

Tansey suggested the social activities of tertiaries had a systemic problem: "Relatively few tertiaries . . . of the 88,243 in the United States are willing to 'involve themselves' actively in the social programs of the Order. They are not willing . . . to teach religion to public school children in slum areas. They will not engage in the home visitation program for interracial understanding nor do convert work among the disadvantaged." The reason for this lack of activism, Tansey argued, was that the "great majority of tertiaries and fraternity directors are completely satisfied with . . . token approaches to charity." When she posed her explanation to a priest he pointed out: "Let's face it, they were taught to live in a ghetto, to be concerned with their own little souls to the exclusion of all else—to hate the world and not be of it—not to give a damn for anyone else's soul except the immediate family, etc. The closest you came to getting into contact with anyone else was the poor souls and you prayed for them." Tansey's biting critique of the failings of tertiaries led her to a simple conclusion: most tertiaries thought they lived out the precepts of Christianity, but "one wonders," she asked sardonically, "if one can live so apart from the struggle in the streets."[29]

Tansey was a writer who published in other magazines, secular as well as Catholic, just like Ogle and Wedge. She also wrote a book, *Mother Seton, Native Daughter*, and, not surprisingly, published a pamphlet based on her research on apostolates titled *Living Your Faith: Apostolic Spirit*. She also con-

---

27. Florence Wedge, "Mass Facing the People," *Franciscan Message* 18 (July 1965): 9.

28. Anne Tansey, "How Apostolic Is the Third Order?," *Franciscan Message* 16 (March 1966): 8.

29. Ibid., 8–10.

tributed to the discussion of the role of women in the Catholic Church. In a 1969 essay for *Franciscan Message* entitled "Can the Church Afford to Lose Its Women?" she highlighted the differences between the careers women had (and were expected to have) in secular society and the assumptions about women's role, work, and leadership in parishes specifically and in the Church more broadly. "They want their qualifications recognized," Tansey contended, "and want dignity and respect due their womanhood and lay status." Tansey did not remark generally about the problematic status of women in the Catholic Church but argued that the significance of the problem lay in the treatment of women in parishes, where a great deal of the work of the Church had always been done. She noted that religious education classes run through parishes were suffering from a decline in the number of women willing to teach in them. Low morale plagued the programs because, Tansey explained, the women teaching had "less freedom of action, little or no participation in decision making, and in some instances an overabundance of supervision." Tansey observed: "Priests should attend less to women's head coverings and more to their zeal."[30]

In this survey of women in parishes, Tansey also related one woman's frustration with parish leadership: "In my job I make important decisions every day, but in CCD [religious education classes] I am treated like a retarded child. I must even submit my lesson plans for a Sister's inspection." Another woman remarked: "The parents never seem to care about the religion of their children; why should I care?" Yet another former catechist told Tansey, "I learned during my two years of service that the Church belongs to priests and Sisters and we have no part in it. Why should I force myself where I am not wanted?" Tansey pointed out that the question regarding the proper role of women in the Church had exposed a rift among its officials, with some welcoming women into the liturgy and others citing a law (which evidently never existed) denying women any role. "There is resentment among women," she said, "for having been unjustifiably kept down in the Church in the past but this would pass if the situation were to be corrected, if fewer pastors would make a burning issue of forcing women and girls to wear hair covering in church, and would turn their zeal instead to feeding the poor." If this observation did not state plainly what was at stake for Church officials, Tansey concluded her essay with a strong warning: "The average Catholic woman . . . is to be found working every place but in the Church. What will this mean for Christendom? For the Church?"[31]

---

30. Anne Tansey, "Can the Church Afford to Lose Its Women?," *Franciscan Message* 19 (May 1969): 28–31.

31. Ibid., 32–33.

The *Franciscan Message* continued to publish into the early 1970s, having successfully provided a venue to discuss the effect Franciscan values might have on social issues and to demonstrate the pluralism of Franciscan values in action, in particular through the publication of works by women who wrote on a variety of topics. In this way it was similar to another Catholic magazine, *Integrity*, the mission of which, according to Burns, developed from advocacy for women serving as leaders of their families to "a policy of stressing the primacy of the human person against the requirements of the institution." Burns notes that another contributor to the magazine, Abigail McCarthy, "exhorted women to 'be present' in and to modern society" and that "citing papal directives, [she] argued that women had a right to be in public life and to participate in government. Women were called to be leaders of popular causes—civil rights, migrant labor, low income housing—realms previously considered as beyond woman's normal sphere."[32]

Even though the *Franciscan Message* became a barometer for social changes in the Church, particularly in regard to women, it suffered a fate similar to other periodicals, Franciscan and otherwise, in the 1970s. According to Brother Jude Lustyk, OFM, the archivist of the Franciscan Fathers of the Assumption Province in Pulsaki, Wisconsin, "The editors of the *Franciscan Message* and the full membership of Franciscan Publishers made a strong recommendation to the provincial leadership to discontinue publication. Sharply increased costs of paper and other publication materials (notably, the upward spiraling postal rates) combined with an ominous drop in readership, were cited as reasons for its termination. After a thorough review and discussion of the facts, the Provincial Council decided to cease publishing the monthly effective January 1, 1975."[33]

THE LAMP

The Franciscan Friars of Atonement in Graymoor, New York, began publishing a magazine in 1903 with the charge to offer "a Catholic magazine devoted to Christian unity." From the beginning *The Lamp* had a mission to reunite Christian Churches, and in particular to reunite the Anglican (or Episcopalian) Church with the Roman Catholic Church. The main force behind this plan was Father Paul James Francis, an Episcopalian priest who founded the order of Franciscans at Graymoor. Famously, on October 28, 1900, the Graymoor Franciscans "proclaimed publicly for the first time that the Anglican Communion . . . should reunite with Rome and accept the supreme authority of the Pope, whom Graymoor acknowledged as 'the divinely constituted

---

32. Burns, "Catholic Laywomen," 394–95.
33. Brother Jude Lustyk, email to author, December 14, 2015.

center of a reunited Christendom.'"[34] By 1902 most of Father Paul's previous congregants and religious colleagues had abandoned him and his direct appeal for reunification. "To pierce this wall of silence," Edmund Delaney wrote in 1973, "Fr. Paul decided to publish a monthly magazine, to be called *The Lamp*, that would keep alive the Graymoor message of Christian unity."[35]

Eventually the magazine grew into a general-interest Franciscan publication. Its mission, however, remained a physical part of the magazine through the phrase "*Ut Omnes Unum Sint*" ("That All May Be One") that was printed on every page of every issue, a practice that lasted the full thirty-seven years Fr. Paul edited *The Lamp*, according to Delaney. In a profile of the magazine, Delaney made clear that Fr. Paul sought not individual conversions from the Anglican Church to the Roman Catholic Church, but a corporate reunion. He accepted two conflicting ideas: that Christians owed their full allegiance to Roman Catholicism, and that the Anglican Church had a rationale to exist. In short, Fr. Paul preached unity, not alienation. Writing in 1973 Delaney pointed out that "time has shown that *The Lamp*'s position was very strong . . . [for] the notion of corporate union is the foundation of the ecumenical movement."[36] Although the circulation of *The Lamp* was quite small during its early years, those who read it sat in high places in both the Episcopal and Roman Catholic Churches. Fr. Paul, the Graymoors, and their magazine officially entered the Roman Catholic Church in 1909, though the magazine continued to advocate for reunion.

By the 1940s an era of ecumenism, if not Christian unity, had dawned in the United States, and *The Lamp* developed into a Franciscan family magazine. It was similar to *St. Anthony Messenger* in size and layout—with some color spreads and some advertising (though exclusively religious). In the 1950s it included sections called "Mostly for Men," "Mostly for Women," and "Teen Topics." It also ran a column called "One Faith—One Lord" that continued to pray for the unification of Christian Churches.

Like other Catholic general interest magazines, *The Lamp* took queries from the laity, welcoming questions regarding their faith. In *The Lamp* that section was called "By the Light of the Lamp." Through the mid-1950s *The Lamp* printed and answered three or four questions on a single page. The editors of *The Lamp* reprinted simpler questions such as "Does the Roman Catholic Church allow a woman to marry her dead husband's brother?" The answer given was no, "unless she gets a dispensation." Another question centered on the obligations of an "excommunicate"—they too were obligated

---

34. Editorial, *The Lamp* 1 (1903): 1.
35. Edmund Delaney, "Why *The Lamp* Was Founded Seventy Years Ago," *The Lamp* 70 (February 1973): 16.
36. Delaney, "*The Lamp* Was Founded," 17.

to attend Mass. One reader wondered if the incense burned in Church was the same as that sold in stores—generally not the same, came the answer. Occasionally *The Lamp* did print a question with some complications. One woman asked, "Having been married for a couple of months, [if] one discovers that her husband is the father of an illegitimate baby, would this be sufficient reason for an annulment in the eyes of the Church?" The answer addressed the term "annulment," a decision that could only be reached by ecclesiastical authority; and according to this analysis, a wedding ceremony would not be affected (and declared illegitimate) just because the groom had an illegitimate child.[37]

The Lamp changed the format of this column slightly in January 1959; now called "Question of the Month," the column comprised a longer response to a single question from a reader. In the new column Father Roger Matzerath, SA, answered questions about obtaining an annulment, eating meat on Fridays, and talking to children about pregnancy and childbirth. As with most magazines of this kind, family and child-rearing issues were central. A letter from "Mrs. CZ" conveyed a bit of desperation over having two children in less than two years. Mrs. CZ asked whether the Church recognized any legitimate way to practice birth control other than the rhythm method—considering, this young woman added, that "before marriage we were told that it was wrong to refuse one another marital rights." Matzerath responded by congratulating this mother on her children and her desire to give them all the attention they deserved. He also praised her for wanting to avoid "artificial birth control in all its forms." The heart of the matter, though, was the issue of "marital rights." Matzerath counseled that rights have two parts—in the abstract and in application—and he encouraged Mrs. CZ to move toward a more practical application of the marital rights: he advised her to say no more often to her husband.[38]

The Lamp ran essays on what the editors considered the bedrock of family life: marriage and women. Joseph Breig, a Catholic journalist who wrote for many Catholic outlets from the 1950s through the 1970s, wrote an oddly titled essay, "How Holy Is Marriage?," as a way to castigate Catholics for failing to take their faith seriously. Though not blaming his readers directly, Breig asserted: "Marriage is a sacrament and its ultimate reason-for-being is the making-holy of human beings: in this case the husband and wife, the children. And then the community, because the community is an extension of the home; the world's civilizations are, or ought to be, extensions of it. . . . Holy

---

37. Anonymous, letter, and response, By the Light of the Lamp, *The Lamp* 55 (January 1957): 23.

38. Mrs. CZ [pseud.], letter, and Father Roger Matzerath, SA, response, Question of the Month, *The Lamp* 56 (November 1958): 25.

marriage of men and women who see that the purpose of marriage is holiness will go far toward the consecration of the world and the restoration of all things in Christ."[39]

Breig's perspective was generally politically conservative, as reflected by his consistent support for the Legion of Decency and his later opposition to US Supreme Court busing desegregation decisions and the landmark 1973 decision in *Roe v. Wade*.[40] He reflected a debate over secularism that emerged during the 1960s by reminding Catholics that despite what they might have learned from other media, they were religious beings more than secular ones. "We talk about 'religious vocations' and the 'calling to the religious life,'" observed Breig. "But because of the ambiguity of the word 'religious,' there is an inevitable implication that the life of the laity is *not religious*, but *secular*." Breig argued that the activities of the Church are not relegated only to those offices with titles, but rather to all Christians, who are obliged to participate in the life of the Church—"a participation," he reminded his readers, "which has its own rights and place, its own privileges and duties, its own reason-for-being and uniqueness, as surely as does the participation of the Bishop, the Priest, the Brother or Sister, or the members of what is called (for want of a worse word?) a secular institute."[41]

Continuing the theme of tension with modern society in 1963, April Oursler Armstrong wrote an essay a few months later with another provocative question as a title: "Can Modern Woman Be Happy?" Although the title gestured toward a philosophical discussion, Armstrong's tone sounded decidedly judgemental, perhaps offering an indirect riposte to Betty Friedan's landmark book *The Feminine Mystique* published earlier that year. She reminded women that while Pope Pius XII proclaimed that "no field of human activity can remain closed to women . . . she may reach out into politics, the arts, sports," these activities, Armstrong qualified, "always come after her responsibilities to her husband and children." Her point was simple: happiness outside the house was a ruse. Armstrong understood that women might think they could find real joy, but she argued that they should be wary of worldly contentment and reject any notion that they could attain happiness in this world. In the end Armstrong advised readers: "Modern woman, as old-time woman, takes Mary as a model of perfection. But imitating Mary does not make anyone feel guilty for wanting to be more than a housewife. Mary's mind and heart soared

---

39. Joseph A. Breig, "How Holy Is Marriage?," *The Lamp* 59 (May 1963): 5–6.

40. See, for example, *Swann v. Charlotte-Mecklenburg Board of Education*, 402 US 1 (1971), accessed July 26, 2017, https://www.law.cornell.edu/supremecourt/text/402/1. See also *Roe v. Wade*, 410 US 113 (1973), accessed July 26, 2017, https://www.law.cornell.edu/supremecourt/text/410/113.

41. Breig, "How Holy Is Marriage?," 4.

far beyond recipes. She was the medium of God's expression of love, as we must be in our time. . . . She was all things to God. She became all things to all men. Both triumphs came through surrender of her entire being to God's use, and the belief that all things were possible."[42]

Into the mid-1960s *The Lamp* continued to promote Christianity as a bulwark against the trends that affected modern American life, from principles for virtuous living to advocacy of spanking kids, from federal funding for Catholic schoolchildren to "faith in the space age."[43] In the May 1961 issue *The Lamp* ran two essays from leading conservatives that framed a debate over education in terms of creeping secularization and the significant role played by private schools, especially religious ones. The first essay came from one of the fathers of modern conservatism and a Catholic convert, Russell Kirk, who denounced secularization and what he believed was the overemphasis on creating a unitary form of public education.[44] The other essay came from Leonard Manning, a constitutional law professor at Fordham University, who critiqued what he saw as a contrived distinction between religion and the state.[45]

In the first essay Kirk rejected "the hostile critics of private schools" for falsely claiming that private education failed to advance American democratic ideals. He noted that "by the end of 1961, about one child out of every six . . . will be attending a church-related or private school." He also noted that in the South, "private schools sprang up rapidly . . . [due to] looming integration of public institutions." Kirk praised the growth of private schools in order to counter, he contended, "the increasing secularization of public instruction . . . [and] the growing discontent with the quality of the public schools." Kirk set up a dichotomy that revealed the direction of modern American conservatism. To him education came down to choice: "One of our principal objects of our federal and state constitutions," he declared, "is to guarantee variety and freedom of choice—actually to protect that 'divisiveness' which the disciples of John Dewey denounce. A deadening uniformity, an enforced conformity to some secular abstraction of 'equality' and 'socialization,' is not the mark of American politics or American thought." To see education as a free enterprise was to protect Americans from the loss of "American freedoms" that, he assumed, resulted from the competition between nonpublic schools. But if a federal aid bill targeted money only for public schools, Kirk felt certain that

---

42. April Oursler Armstrong, "Can Modern Woman Be Happy?," *The Lamp* 59 (August 1963): 4, 7, 22.

43. Ernan McMullen, "Faith in the Space Age," *The Lamp* 57 (July 1961), 5-7, 26.

44. Russell Kirk, "The Great Education Debate: The 'Divisive' Charge," *The Lamp* 57 (May 1961): 5.

45. Leonard F. Manning, "The Great Education Debate: 'Is Aid Constitutional?'," *The Lamp* 57 (May 1961): 7.

the "increased tax-load . . . might succeed in forcing church-connected and private schools out of existence."[46]

Manning's piece—the second essay on education in the May 1961 issue—was less fiery and even a bit sarcastic in framing how opposing camps in the debate over federal funding for education viewed each other. He introduced caricatures of both sides to get at a larger and more significant point—the idea that the US Constitution strictly separates the activities of church from state. The context for Manning's remarks was President John F. Kennedy's attempt to navigate a multi-billion–dollar federal aid program to schools that stipulated funds could only go to public or non–church-related schools. Kennedy had declared that the Constitution made it clear that the federal government could not provide funds directly to church-related schools without violating the separation of church and state. To this Manning replied: "The Constitution speaks neither of schools nor, for that matter, of any wall of separation between church and state. The First Amendment simply states that 'Congress shall make no law respecting the establishment of religion, or prohibiting the free exercise thereof.' It is a courageous thing, to be sure, but ill-advised for the President to cull the meaning of that rather unclear clause from the obiter dicta of one judge written in one case decided by the Supreme Court of the United States."[47] The case Manning referenced was *Everson v. Board of Education of the Township of Ewing* (1947), in which the Court decided that federal funding for busing children to religious instruction did not violate the First Amendment—but also that a "wall of separation" existed between religion and the state. Manning pointed out that no existing tradition walled off the activities of the state from those of religious institutions; in fact the history of the country exhibited quite the opposite. However, like Kirk, Manning sought to call attention to the shifting narrative that had grown dominant by the early 1960s (at least)—that the United States seemed to have an established secularism that stood in opposition to a tradition of American Christianity that the editors of *The Lamp* clearly promoted.[48]

Among the many examples of a creeping secularism, perhaps the most paradoxical was the emergence of human exploration of space. In a 1961 essay entitled "Faith in the Space Age," Ernan McMullin, a young professor of the

---

46. Ibid., 4, 5, 6.

47. Manning, "Great Education Debate: 'Is Aid Constitutional?'," 7. For more from Manning on this issue, see Leonard F. Manning, "Aid to Education-State Style," *Fordham Law Review* 29 (1961): 525.

48. *Everson v. Board of Education of the Township of Ewing*, 330 US 1 (1947), accessed July 20, 2017, https://www.law.cornell.edu/supremecourt/text/330/1. For the best work on the history and specific debates that *Everson v. Board of Education* sparked, see David Sehat, *The Myth of American Religious Freedom* (New York: Oxford, 2016), especially 236–39.

philosophy of science at the University of Notre Dame, laid out for readers a line they probably already accepted:

> In a former time, the only ultimately satisfying pattern man could see in his world was given it by his religious faith. . . . Nowadays, a different ideal of explanation is preached, with spectacular practical success: things act thus because they are made up in such-and-such a way; a thing has the constitution it has because of a long series of modifications, following traceable laws, down through millions of years. This sort of explanation is far more immediate than the theological one, so that it can easily come to appear the *only* satisfactory way of making something intelligible.[49]

McMullin went on to become highly regarded for his ability to speak to the intersections, tensions, and compatibility of science with religion. In this essay, written early in his career, he suggested that science had opened up new avenues for theology and that religion—especially Christianity—had been consistently enriched by scientific revolutions of the past. Ultimately, McMullin declared, "It *is* true that the Christian will not be able to yield the unquestioning allegiance to temporal values that the unbeliever must profess. For the Christian, there *is* something more important than the search for earthly happiness, more important even than the promotion of earthly happiness of the greatest number."[50]

McMullin's observations about the relationship between the exploration of the heavens and the reality of heaven was part of a stream of literature that emerged at this time within Catholic thought. Historian Catherine R. Osborne relates that through the liturgical and educational movements of the 1950s into the 1960s, "Catholic Americans shared with their Protestant counterparts a set of concerns about the proper relationship of science and religion and about the theological implications of the seismic advances in technological capability being made in the twentieth century; they also shared the urge to respond to secular scientists who attempted [Osborne quotes historian James Gilbert] 'to control the discussion, to situate it inside a scientific framework exclusively.'"[51] The fact that *The Lamp* ran an essay from McMullin addressing how Christians might consider the reality of space exploration demonstrated the willingness of the editors both to engage their times and to do so with important thinkers such as McMullin.

Into the 1960s *The Lamp* offered its readers essays from high-profile thinkers, including H. A. Reinhold, who wrote an essay on ecumenism in the

---

49. Ernan McMullin, "Faith in the Space Age," *The Lamp* 57 (July 1961): 5.
50. Ibid., 7.
51. Catherine R. Osborne, "From Sputnik to Spaceship Earth: American Catholics and the Space Age," *Religion and American Culture: A Journal of Interpretation* 25 (Summer 2015): 219.

November 1963 issue in which he recounted an "Evening of Ecumenical Witness," an event held at the Municipal Auditorium in San Antonio, Texas. Reinhold was widely recognized as leader in the liturgical reform movement in post-1945 America and a successor to the most prominent American proponent of the relationship of liturgical prayer and social issues, Dom Virgil Michel, the Benedictine monk who died in 1938.[52] Reinhold told his readers to overcome the disunion between Catholics and Protestants through the common act of prayer. "We ourselves, can do no better than pray, this prayer should be of the kind and level of the Mass 'For reunion in faith' (*Ad tollendum schism*). Look it up in your missal," he preached. "From the Introit to the Communion antiphon this is a masterpiece."[53] The last decade of *The Lamp*—from the mid-1960s to the mid-1970s—saw a fuller expression of such ecumenical promotion as the magazine returned to its roots.

In 1967 Father Charles Angell, SA, became one of the final editors of *The Lamp*. The changes that had developed under his predecessors, in particular Father Ralph Thomas, SA, accelerated and solidified under Angell's leadership. For example Angell wrote an astonishing editorial to introduce the January 1971 issue on contemporary heroes, praising those who would not be canonized but whom people should follow nonetheless. He added: "Recently the Friars of the Atonement decided not to push for the canonization of their founder, but rather to use the resources and energy which would be required in the lengthy proceedings involved to help the poor."[54] By the early 1970s *The Lamp* came to resemble *The Way/Catholic Viewpoints*, publishing essays on Merton, Dorothy Day, Martin Buber, Hans Küng, César Chávez, and other leaders in social justice. Profiles of such figures were penned by a variety of religious writers—a few of whom were Catholic, but many of whom were not, including the religious historian Martin Marty and the theologian Robert McAfee Brown. In his editorial Angell explained that the list was not one of "saints for our times [but] of people struggling like us to make it somehow," echoing the way Franciscans related to the laity.[55] Though he understated the stature and work of people such as Küng and Martin Luther King, Jr., Angell's editorial leadership completed a shift away from an older manner of celebrating ancient values to one that was willing to draw from every corner of life to imagine what true fellowship might become.[56]

---

52. Joseph P. Chinnici, "Virgil Michel and the Tradition of Affective Prayer," *Worship* 62 (May 1988): 228.

53. H. A. Reinhold, "In These Ecumenic Times," *The Lamp* 59 (November 1963): 22.

54. Charles Angell, "The Fellowship of the Holy Spirit: People Who Count Today," *The Lamp* 69 (January 1971): 1.

55. Ibid.

56. Charles Angell, "'For God's Sake Break the Hellish Circle of Poverty,'" *The Lamp* 69 (February 1971): 1.

Angell also reported on a conference sponsored by the Graymoor friars titled "Women's Liberation: What Does It Mean?" Speaking at this extraordinary gathering were Day, Sister Mary Luke Tobin, superior general of the Sisters of Loretto and observer at Vatican II; Betty Friedan; Cynthia Wedel, president of the National Council of Churches; and more than 250 clergy, religious, and lay people. Angell noted that many of the women who spoke echoed Wedel's own observations and conviction: "I would rather see women and men joining together" Wedel declared, "to develop the creative new forms of ministry needed for a renewal and growing and a far more effective church of tomorrow."[57]

Angell also assessed how lay attendance at Catholic mass and Protestant services related to political or ideological shifts to the left among church leaders. He observed that in early 1970s the most conservative Churches were "booming" and the "more liberal easygoing churches have been declining." Angell made this observation in light of a study undertaken by Dean M. Kelley, an executive at the National Council of Churches. "I think the author has laid his finger on this fundamental explanation of this situation when he says," Angell related, "that the indispensable function of religion is explaining the meaning of life in ultimate terms. . . . I think it is probably true that while some of us have been fighting for racial justice, world peace and the needs of the poor as our Lord told us to do, we have not been emphasizing enough some other very fundamental tenets of Christianity." Along with other religious intellectuals of this era, such as Lutheran minister and editor of *Worldview* Richard John Neuhaus, Angell acknowledged that "when the church engages in social activism it must ask itself in a very hard-headed way: 'How will this activity help make clearer the ultimate meaning of life to our members?'" Indeed what came to be called the Religious Right arose, gained force, and gathered followers by merging social and political activism with messianic verve. "That is why," Angell concluded, "some of our churches are losing members to fundamentalist sects that claim to have a straightforward answer to the complex problems of life."[58]

The 1970s were hard on Franciscan magazines, because they, like many secular publications from *Life* to the *Saturday Evening Post*, lost circulation and found rising publication costs (especially the price of paper) to be debilitating. Even so, in the September 1972 issue, Angell announced that his magazine had won an award from the Associated Church Press for best series of

---

57. Charles Angell, "What Are Christians Doing?," *The Lamp* 69 (February 1971): 26.

58. Charles Angell, "Do Churches Prosper in Proportion to Their Strictness?," *The Lamp* 70 (August 1972): 1. For the rise of the religious right and the intellectuals who have debated it, see Steven P. Miller, *The Age of Evangelicalism: America's Born-Again Years* (New York: Oxford University Press, 2014), especially 9–31.

articles for the January 1971 issue on the fellowship of the Holy Spirit. Although he was proud to have published this collection on spiritual leaders, from Merton to King to Day, Angell added "one last word of warning." He explained that while he was "renewed in spirit and full of gratitude for the favorable judgments on *The Lamp*, honesty necessitates this reminder—we can only continue publication if our circulation remains large enough to warrant the heavy expense of the magazine."[59]

A survey sponsored by the magazine offered a snapshot of both the kinds of readers that patronized Catholic periodicals and the problems that beset such magazines. The readership consisted mostly of older, female, and long-term subscribers. A majority of the readers claimed no particular ideological or political persuasion—that is, they were neither conservative nor liberal—and many wanted the magazine to be a "meeting place where Christians of many traditions can exchange ideas." Those who responded to the survey confirmed that *The Lamp* had stayed true to its original mission of bringing a message of unity to Christians who practiced their faith in different Churches. But by the 1970s the role *The Lamp* played in mediating debates about the place of Christianity in turbulent times lost ground to the overt and explicitly sectarian mouthpieces of the Christian right and left alike. And so by the mid-1970s this magazine came to an end.[60]

FRANCISCAN HERALD AND FORUM

The *Franciscan Herald and Forum* was the most significant journal for the tertiaries, and through it we witness one way Franciscans contended with the development of new roles for the Third Order in the postconciliar era. At the center of this discussion was Father Mark Hegener, OFM, who had been an editor of the *Franciscan Herald and Forum* since 1947. Throughout his long career in publishing, he became a leader among Franciscan editors in creating as many avenues as possible to promote Franciscan thought and prayer. Hegener was ordained a priest in 1945 and earned a degree from Marquette University's school of journalism. He was assigned to Franciscan Herald Press working with Father James Meyer and Father Philip Marquard. At the press Hegener helped transform the *Franciscan Herald and Forum* into an illustrated periodical that looked similar to *St. Anthony Messenger* but sought to serve tertiaries in the United States. He became the chief editor of the magazine in 1955 upon Meyer's death.

---

59. Charles Angell, "Lamp Readers Have Their Day," *The Lamp* 70 (September 1972): 3.

60. Ibid., 1; Thaddeus Horgan, "Why the Atonement Friars Publish This Magazine," *The Lamp* 71 (February 1973): 33.

Hegener's legacy reflected the didactic style of his editorials. For example, when the issue of public funding for parochial schools emerged yet again in the early 1960s, Hegener provided a vigorous analysis of what he thought was at stake. He argued that three basic constituents had a say in the matter: parents, the Church, and the state. The situation in the United States, while not grave or comparable to undemocratic countries, nonetheless posed challenges to the basic understanding of educating children, Hegener believed. Parents and by extension the Church had by right and principle the ultimate authority over the education of their children; but Hegener argued, "The facts are that the non-public schools are not allowed to flourish . . . only to exist. The economic measures against them by non-tax (that is, non-state support) are such that the future of non-public education (that is, the future of freedom of choice in education) remains dim if justice is not done." Hegener advanced an idea popular among conservative Catholics in the early 1960s: that the US Constitution did not forbid direct financial support for Catholic school students. "Legislation," he contended, "has established in the public schools a new kind of secular-humanist religion, oriented and organizing all knowledge with man alone at its center." He urged tertiaries to get involved and speak out on the subject, presumably in favor of federal funds for Catholic schools.[61]

No contemporary issue consumed him as much as the implications of the Second Vatican Council. In response to the official announcement convening the Council, he ran an especially significant editorial titled "A Petition for Action." He discussed a petition sent by the commissaries general of the four Franciscan obediences that emphasized the role the tertiaries could and should play in efforts to rejuvenate the Church. Seizing upon discussions regarding the role of the laity in the Catholic Church, Hegener pointed out "how badly the Third Order is needed 'for all Christians' to inculcate 'the spirit of poverty, of charity, of penance and joyfulness'; how beneficial it is 'for the diocesan clergy'; what it can do for the promotion of 'the solution of the Social Question'; and what an 'inspiration to Catholic associations' it can be." Such work—now called Catholic Action—had to be done, Hegener asserted, "within the framework of the Church, and specifically under the direction of the ordinaries—the bishops." Speaking against what he viewed as "moral individualism," Hegener wanted Catholic Action to be collective action, to work within the Church and not merely in the name of the Church.[62]

Hegener's editorials throughout the mid-1960s charted a consistent course for tertiaries as the most natural leaders of the movement to involve

61. Mark Hegener, OFM, "Issue of Our Time," *Franciscan Herald and Forum* 62 (February 1963): 67.

62. Mark Hegener, "A Petition for Action," *Franciscan Herald and Forum* 62 (December 1963): 323.

the laity in the reformation of the Church. In a 1965 editorial entitled "The Church in the Modern World" (evocatively using the title of the Council's final document, *Gaudium et spes*), Hegener's argument practically lept off the page in response to the Council's call for Catholics to get involved in enacting the Gospels in their daily lives. Rather than peripheral to social action, he declared, Franciscans had been "deeply involved in the matters of the world . . . from the beginning." He contended that "the Third Order is not a watered-down or diminished form of the Franciscan spirit, but it is a whole and integral part of the Franciscan family, the one lived by laymen engaged in the life of the world." More crucially for him and the mission of the *Franciscan Herald and Forum*, Hegener believed that answering the call of the Council implied reforming the Third Order as well.[63]

For most of 1966 the *Franciscan Herald and Forum* concerned itself with discussions of the fate of the Third Order in light of changes, and rumors of changes, related to Vatican II. Citing the "parallelism between the seminary crisis and the Third Order crisis," Hegener argued that "the crisis, it seems to us, is caused by the fear of taking the plunge. And the 'plunge' means the total involvement which charity demands. This is the heart of the matter." Hegener believed that the concurrent dramatic drop in vocations to the priesthood and decline in Third Order commitments reflected a church in trouble. In February 1966 Hegener took up what he called "one of the most depth-shaking, if not breath-taking letters to be addressed to tertiaries all over the world." In that letter the general directors of the Third Order of each obedience challenged the tertiaries to "completely overhaul" the Third Order. At issue was how the Third Order should change according to the conclusions reached at the Second Vatican Council. To advance this directive the *Herald and Forum* asked its readers to complete surveys, explaining that answers would guide the Third Order as it began to reconsider its Rule and ritual.[64]

The *Franciscan Herald and Forum* published two separate questionnaires: one for Third Order members, and a second for directors, moderators, and leaders. The questions reflected the nature of the crisis—namely, that Vatican II had inaugurated a vigorous discussion about commitment to the faith and to the leaders of it. Members answered questions about their commitment to the Third Order, and leaders rated which parts of the Franciscan Rule they

---

63. Mark Hegener, "The Church in the Modern World," *Franciscan Herald and Forum* 64 (February 1965): 1–2. See also Second Vatican Council, *Gaudium et spes* (Pastoral Constitution on the Church in the modern world), promulgated by Pope Paul VI on December 7, 1965, accessed July 26, 2017, http://www.vatican.va/archive/hist_councils/ii_vatican_council/documents/vat-ii_const_19651207_gaudium-et-spes_en.html.

64. See Mark Hegener, "A Sign of Growth," *Franciscan Herald and Forum* 65 (February 1966): 33.

advanced. For example tertiaries were asked to select an answer that best described their "view of the Third Order": either "a new way of life" or "an intensification of my Christian life." Among the most revealing questions posed to Franciscan lay leaders was "Do you think the rule should contain challenges, or regulations? Should it give general directives, or precise points to be observed?" In sum opinions solicited by the questionnaires reflected the drift toward prioritizing personal commitments to Franciscanism instead declaring oneself a secular Franciscan simply because one pledged to follow the rules that governed the Third Order.[65]

In editorials that seemed designed to address the question of discipline, Hegener began consistently to return to questions about how friars and tertiaries should make their way in a world beset by ambiguity, revolts, and issues that seemed to grate against Church doctrine. In an editorial denouncing what he called "ecclesiastical gibberish," Hegener argued against "the inverted, ingrown, solipsistic churchman so engrossed in himself and in his supposed rights and prerogatives that the real apostolate goes begging by comparison." He referred to a new wave of "churchmen" as "navel-gazers" who "defied, decried, and ridiculed" the Church in the "name of freedom in the Church." Obviously frustrated by what he saw as hollow declarations for change, Hegener dismissed what he saw as the bandwagon effect of the 1960s: "Those who are constantly harping about the nation are not the people making America strong. . . . In a parallel manner we have the same thing going on in the church: a generation of solipsistic, negativistic, withdrawn people who stand along the sidelines as the troops march by and 'critique' the parade and its strength because they have no heart for the marching and no good words to express themselves."[66]

What Hegener related through such editorials is what historian Daniel Rodgers calls an "age of fracture." Rodgers writes about the period that gave Hegener such fits: "Across multiple fronts of ideational battle, from the speeches of presidents to books of social and cultural theory . . . conceptions of human nature that in the post–World War II era had been thick with context, social circumstance, institutions, and history gave way to conceptions of human nature that stressed choice, agency, performance, and desire."[67] Hegener lamented these changes in 1967: "The existence of so much is being challenged, that it is not surprising that the very existence of anything like a

65. Mark Hegener, "Overhauling the Third Order," *Franciscan Herald and Forum* 65 (August 1966): 241–50.

66. Mark Hegener, "Ecclesiastical Gibberish," *Franciscan Herald and Forum* 66 (July 1967): 193–94, 203.

67. Daniel T. Rodgers, *The Age of Fracture* (Boston: Belknap Press of Harvard University Press, 2011), 3.

Third Order should be rolled in with relics and rosaries, statues and saints, and dropped on the ecclesiastical dump heap in the name of renewal." The assumption that lay Franciscans had a clear role to play in the life of the Catholic Church drifted into ambiguous territory as the terms that had helped organize the Church itself were reimagined. Hegener noted with some scorn that the role of priests and seminaries, never mind that of lay Catholics, no longer seemed clear in an era that, he concluded, was "fast falling into humanistic secularism which worships the individual on the one hand but tends toward a mood of anti-life."[68]

Hegener's editorials highlighted an interesting conundrum for Franciscan media. If a new era of spiritual independence proclaimed "no need for any other organization, institution, society or movement in the Church to convey the formulation of the people of God," then Hegener wondered about the necessity, much less the relevance, of the Third Order or even of media to advance any kind of formal understanding of Catholicism. "The new May pole concept of the Church in which all God's children happily dance about, intertwining themselves into one happy and brilliant braid . . . is," he declared, "a fantasy!" For many years Catholics had shown genuine interest in the teachings of their Church and in participating in, understanding, and carrying forward the traditions of the Church. "Witness the many books on the sources of Franciscan spirituality and life published in the last twenty years!" Hegener noted. And he would know, because he and Franciscan Herald Press had done a great deal to promote Franciscanism in the immediate postwar era and would continue to do so through the 1990s.[69]

But what if no one listened anymore? Writing to those fellow Franciscans whom he believed interpreted the example of St. Francis through the lens of contemporary conceptions of individual freedom, he reminded his readers: "Against all the idealism of Francis, his orders could not go on as in the halcyon days of its founding brethren, when thousands applied for membership. It had to be 'structured'; rules had to be made. The spirit had to be bound!" Was Francis the antidote for an age in which "anything goes" and people were exhorted to "do [their] own thing"? Hegener reasoned that "the man whose life is governed by the interior inspiration of the Holy Spirit will be pre-eminently docile, that is, willing to learn the truth from those empowered to teach it." He concluded that the simplest rule was the commitment to the Gospels, and that this commitment both freed friars from being obsessed with contemporary problems and allowed them the freedom to follow their con-

68. Mark Hegener, "Laying It on the Line," *Franciscan Herald and Forum* 66 (1967): 161.

69. Mark Hegener, "Franciscan Renewal Today," *Franciscan Herald and Forum* 66 (1967): 129, 136.

sciences, for that meant following the Gospels.[70] The shifting ground of modern culture left Hegener, like so many others, perplexed—and more resolutely committed to an older way.

Yet Hegener continued to be informed by the "crisis in the Church." Pope (now Blessed) Paul VI's 1968 promulgation of his encyclical *Humanae Vitae* ("on human life") provided another moment to comment on what seemed to be a developing rift between Church officials and the laity.[71] Although Pope Paul VI had proposed to resolve the birth control issue for Catholics with his encyclical, quite the opposite occurred. Historian Mark Massa explains: "In issuing *Humanae Vitae*, Paul VI had overridden the majority opinion of a blue-ribbon international committee which his much loved predecessor, Pope John XXIII, had appointed. The majority on that committee had favored a change in Church teaching that would allow some forms of contraception."[72]

In his editorial reacting to *Humanae Vitae*, Hegener argued that many observers wanted to see a conflict between hierarchy and laity, pitting the "autocratic" mentality of Vatican I with the more humane and open mentality of Vatican II. However, as in his earlier editorials, Hegener viewed that dichotomy as false. He argued that the Church had not changed substantially; rather it upheld a paradoxical pessimism about human nature. In this paradox "the Church preaches poverty of spirit and [yet] promotes human progress on every level," Hegener reminded his readers. "It teaches us to be patient in suffering, but provides hospitals and asylums for the sick. It teaches a laborer and servant to be obedient, but champions the rights of the laborer as worthy of his hire." But the society in which this paradox existed had changed so remarkably, according to Hegener, that actions once associated with the radical evil of Nazism were being performed in the name of progress: "The disdain for human life is crass and manifests itself in the escalating abortion rate, the attempts to legitimize mutilation to control population, the menace of euthanasia programs. We have offset Hitler's gas chambers for destroying the aged and feeble with health programs and Medicare, Unesco against the millions of displaced persons."[73] Hegener's stunning indictment was a clear harbinger of the culture wars sparked by changes and debates in the 1960s.

---

70. Mark Hegener, "Freedom, Authority, Holy Spirit," *Franciscan Herald and Forum* 67 (June 1968): 162–63.

71. Pope Paul VI, *Humanae Vitae* (Encyclical on the regulation of birth), July 25, 1968, accessed July 26, 2017, http://w2.vatican.va/content/paul-vi/en/encyclicals/documents/hf_p-vi_enc_25071968_humanae-vitae.html.

72. Massa, *American Catholic Revolution*, 32.

73. Mark Hegener, "Where Do We Stand?," *Franciscan Herald and Forum* 67 (1968): 353–55.

Not surprisingly Hegener continued to find much to oppose in American Catholicism following Vatican II. He continued as editor of the *Franciscan Herald and Forum* into the 1980s and, just as important, led a publishing surge at the Franciscan Herald Press. According to Open Library,[74] Franciscan Herald Press published nearly 575 works through the early 2000s, with the bulk coming out in the 1970s and 1980s under Hegener's directorship. Many of its titles related to the life of St. Francis and Franciscan spirituality; and many also, especially in the 1970s and 1980s, were written by conservative Catholics. Of course the *Franciscan Herald and Forum* and its publishing company were not alone in the struggle to make sense of the role Franciscans played in the in age of fracture.

ST. ANTHONY MESSENGER

The relationship between editorial position and readership framed the history of Franciscan magazines that sought to be popular. No other magazine reflected that relationship in all its complexity better than *St. Anthony Messenger*. The most popular of the Franciscan monthlies, *St. Anthony Messenger* integrated a consistent layout, including sections devoted to readers' opinions and questions, with editorial positions that demonstrated changes within Catholic culture in America. Like most Franciscan counterparts, *St. Anthony Messenger* maintained anticommunism as its standard editorial position. For example, in the mid-1930s, Hyacinth Blocker wrote many essays warning his readers that communism was an even more insidious and expansive menace than they might assume. Blocker wrote an essay on the Spanish Civil War as that conflict began to harden into a fight between far-right antidemocratic forces, led by General Francisco Franco, and supporters of the Spanish Republic. That latter group became fatally associated with far-left factions, including communists supported directly by the Soviet Union. While Blocker acknowledged that the communists did not successfully orchestrate a political coup, he argued the standard Catholic line of the day by declaring that the coalition that did hold political power—the Popular Front—was little more than a ruse for "an embryonic Soviet regime."[75]

Blocker's characterization of the forces opposed to the Popular Front was more generous. He called the Franco-led counterrevolution the "so-called Right factions," and rather than finding fault in them for launching a civil war, Blocker remarked, "If nothing else, the war now raging in Spain has awakened Europe to the imminent menace of Communism everywhere." Interestingly

---

74. See https://openlibrary.org.

75. Hyacinth Blocker, "Seeing Red: A Little History and a Solemn Warning," *St. Anthony Messenger* 44 (November 1936): 372.

Blocker took exception not merely to the antireligious animosity of communism but also to its "universal revolution against our present economic system." *St. Anthony Messenger*, like other Catholic magazines, had a somewhat conflicted relationship with capitalism. But in the face of the challenge presented by communism, the editors easily folded support for capitalism into a general defense of the civilization Catholics seemed required to protect.[76]

Blocker wrote the essay to disabuse the "busy man and woman of today" of the notion that communism was some distant threat. It could happen here, he bluntly declared. And it could happen gradually, through the education of children, the indoctrination of workers, and the insinuation of the government into every aspect of an American's life. "A new national soul . . . everyone as exactly alike as the buttons on your shirt," Blocker wrote, "all poured into the same mold; mechanical robots with no initiative, no mind of their own. That is the consoling existence offered man by Red visionaries."[77]

"The serpent," Blocker warned quite chillingly, "is crawling through our own country, waiting for the opportune moment to strike." After reading a book from Jesuit priest Michael Kenny entitled *No God Next Door*,[78] Blocker declared that "Communists are in our army, our navy, our universities, our factories, our unions and all our professions." Indeed, more than fifteen years before the emergence of Senator Joseph McCarthy, Blocker implicated Harold Ickes, secretary of the interior under Franklin D. Roosevelt, as a supporter of communist economic theories and warned that some American labor unions were only one step removed from Moscow. All these revelations led Blocker to conclude: "Unless Uncle Sam cleans house soon, he may find himself so enmeshed in the intricate webs of Communism spun about him that escape will be impossible." But it also led him to place the Catholic Church alongside some strange bedfellows. He wrote that "so far a few leaders and groups have raised their voices to sound the note of danger in America: Father [Charles] Coughlin, the American Legion, the Catholic Church, and several small and isolated parties"—many of which parties few Catholics would have recognized as kindred souls. Nonetheless Blocker's analysis illustrated the ideological transition that would establish the image of Catholics as archetypical Cold Warriors.[79]

Also like most other Franciscan periodicals (and almost all other American magazines) during the 1940s and 1950s, *St. Anthony Messenger* addressed essays to those many families with men serving in the armed forces, expressing sympathy especially with their mothers. Historian Daniel Hurley contends

---

76. Ibid.
77. Ibid., 373.
78. Michael Kenny, *No God Next Door: Red Rule in Mexico and Our Responsibility*, (New York: William J. Hirten, Co., 1935).
79. Blocker, "Seeing Red," 377.

that the *Messenger* earned the reputation for being among the best "all-around family" magazines in the United States, a distinction made evident by how often the magazine addressed the toll that military service took on families as well as the stress of the Cold War.[80] For example, during World War II the *Messenger* ran a section called the "Honor Roll" listing the names of sub-scribers' sons, brothers, and husbands who had been killed in the line of duty. In April 1945 Father Severin Lamping's column "The Tertiary Den" devoted space to expressions of grief over casualties of war, printing letters mostly from mothers about those they had lost. Such letters consistently appeared in the *Messenger* as they did in many other periodicals of the era.

However, Lamping was not beyond highlighting letters that spoke about the horrors of war. In an April 1945 letter titled "War Against War," the writer declared, "I for one say that there is so much we can do to stop wars, if we want to. People don't like wars, but if they don't, why do they take such a tolerant attitude toward war?" Lamping replied: "We should . . . beware, lest a false patriotism blur our vision and make us heed more the words of war mongers than of the Pope."[81] Indeed Pope Pius XII's Christmas message of 1944 had reiterated the Catholic Church's position against wars of aggression and pointedly remarked on the deplorable state of world affairs. When another letter in April 1945 expressed deep concern over the deplorable state of human affairs, Lamping replied: "Can we say in truth that the world is civi-lized?" "And education?" he continued: "It ennobles only when to it is joined the religious and moral training of the individual."[82] Thus although the *Messenger* did not offer a new philosophical or theological position on war, it did provide lay Catholics with a place to register their complicated views on war.

In 1946 Father Victor Drees, the new editor of *St. Anthony Messenger*, took over from Hyacinth Blocker and made certain that the *Messenger* con-tinued to stand as a bulwark against communism. Though the magazine ran profiles of people and events abroad, almost all of them fit into a narrative of anticommunism for domestic consumption. Hurley noted in his historical ret-rospective of the magazine that this drift had implications for the way the magazine treated someone such as Dorothy Day, co-founder of the Catholic Worker Movement and a famous pacifist. According to Hurley, coverage during the Cold War of Day in the *Messenger* "changed from being a cham-pion of the poor into a 'fellow traveler.'"[83] More generally though, the mag-

---

80. Hurley, "St. Anthony Messenger," 15.
81. T.W., "War Against War" (letter), and Severin Lamping, response, The Tertiary Den, *St. Anthony Messenger* 53 (April 1945): 32, 34.
82. Anonymous, letter, and Severin Lamping, response, The Tertiary Den, *St. Anthony Messenger* 53 (April 1945): 35.
83. Hurley, "St. Anthony Messenger," 16.

azine ran stories such as the January 1951 article by Leonard Foley, OFM, titled "Korean Sacrifice," which introduced the life and death of a Franciscan priest, chaplain Herman G. Felhoelter, OFM, during the Korean War by detailing the atrocities of the soulless communist enemy. The layout of this story also included a poem, boxed off and inset on the page, entitled "Marx and Mohammed." It read, in part: "From the East the Menace comes again . . . And Marx's minions fain would ride, As Mohammed's hosts, through a bloody tide. . . . To whom shall we look, O soldier saint, If not unto you when men's Faith is faint? For your Seraph-Seal is mightier far Than the Crescent or Sickle's scimitar."[84] An issue later in 1951 ran a long story by John Rossi, titled "Poland's Big Sister," that used a scene of children pretending to be different countries as an allegory for the tragic fate of those people living under communism.[85]

Like the *Franciscan Message*, *St. Anthony Messenger* maintained its identity as a family magazine by keeping its content safely consistent with official church positions on the Cold War, communism, funding for Catholic schools, and the pope. The magazine's position began to fracture, though, in response to emerging social imperatives posed by the Civil Rights Movement and more widespread concern about poverty, the underclass, and the developing world. Leaders in Franciscan media understood that they needed to address changes to the American cultural landscape.

A painting of St. Anthony and the Blessed Virgin from 1780 introduced the June 1960 issue of *St. Anthony Messenger* as "the National Catholic Family Magazine." The issue included articles on how to rate Catholic schools, the increasing use of vitamins, and moonlighters. The next month, the magazine looked different. A new layout and new mindset greeted readers of the most popular Franciscan magazine. The cover image did not include one of the Franciscan saints but rather a contemporary photograph of Father Bertrus Grassmann, OFM, in the distinctive brown robes with the Franciscan cord, surrounded by a group of people from the Zuni tribe. The issue announced articles on political conventions, space travel, and alcoholism. One month apparently separated the past from the contemporary. By 1961 the covers grew increasingly edgy, as did the content. For example a drawing of Christ in anguish with the crown of thorns dominated the March 1961 issue. Inside readers found articles on divorce, poisoned air, and Catholicism in India. The essay on divorce was written by "a Catholic woman who experienced the tragedy of a broken marriage and came closer to God through her suffering."

---

84. Liam Brophy, "Marx and Mohammed," *St. Anthony Messenger* 58 (January 1951): 24.

85. Leonard Foley, "Korean Sacrifice," *St. Anthony Messenger* 58 (January 1951): 23–25; John L. Rossi, "Poland's Big Sister," *St. Anthony Messenger* 58 (December 1951): 16–18.

Though not a moralistic tale of sin, the essay did not describe divorce as an individual right either. Rather the author tried to depict a sense of the suffering that comes with any divorce and provided stories from her own life to humanize the different ways divorce happens and can be handled. Ultimately the moral of the story was that her own divorce led her to believe that it was God's will for her to suffer through such a fate to find spiritual enlightenment and a closer relationship to God through the Catholic Church. She also met another man to marry.[86]

Hurley explains that personnel changes in the mid-1960s produced lasting differences in the magazine. "In late 1963, Provincial Sylvan Becker, OFM, asked Father Leonard Foley . . . to become editor," Hurley notes. "Kieran Quinn, OFM, was appointed art director. Almost immediately Father Leonard recruited one of his most promising former students, Jeremy Harrington, OFM, to be the associate editor, while Father Kieran hired Larry Zink . . . to develop a new graphic look for the magazine."[87] The most visible sign of these big changes was the cover for the November 1964 issue, on which St. Anthony was shrouded in black and purple, in shadow and light. That issue also introduced book and movie reviews that differed markedly from those produced by watchdog groups such as the Legion of Decency and the National Office for Decent Literature. In one of his first editorials Foley declared that the *Messenger* would discuss "the major movements and events in the Church—the leadership of Pope Paul and the Council—as well as the problems of everyday bill-paying family life; the problems of prayer as well as family budgets, of racism as well as the 'new' Mass. We will take many looks at Pope John's famous four pillars: truth and love, justice and freedom, particularly as regards marriage and education, authority and race."[88] The editorial shift reflected an interest in seeing the magazine as a work of social criticism as well as religious communication.[89]

Under Foley and Harrington this family magazine became a significant source for tracing how Catholics might, as one editorial declared, enter into a dialogue: "Today we need the honest exchange of ideas and opinions to heal the serious conflicts that divide us and to solve the problems that confront the Church, our communities, our nation, and our world. To take sides like children and do nothing but shout taunts at those who disagree with us is

---

86. Anonymous, "Divorce and the Will of God," *St. Anthony Messenger* 68 (March 1961): 23–26.

87. Hurley, "St. Anthony Messenger," 16

88. Hurley, "St. Anthony Messenger," 16.

89. On a similar change in the San Francisco–based magazine, *The Way of St. Francis*, later called *The Way/Catholic Viewpoints*, see Jeffrey Burns, "John O'Connor and the 'New Age' of Catholic Journalism, 1960–1967," *U.S. Catholic Historian* 25 (Summer 2007): 109–26.

too dangerous and unChristlike in 1965." Like the editors of other Franciscan magazines, Foley and Harrington struck a tone that tended toward moderation and reflected what their readers evidently felt as well.[90]

Harrington explained that the magazine made a decision under Foley to change from a devotional magazine that supported vocations to a journalistic magazine that engaged with issues significant to readers.[91] In addition to running sections that they hoped would appeal to the entire family, from articles on the pope and reflections on saints to religious fiction and advice columns, the magazine continued its broad approach. It also ran an extensive section of letters to the editor in which, over time, one can see responses to the magazine's evolution in layout (generally greeted positively) and to its editorial drift. Of course letters arrived that charged the magazine with having "joined the ever-growing group of 'liberal' Catholic magazines"—thereby jeopardizing some of its subscriber base. However, such a charge reflected a basic conundrum for all Catholic media: simply reporting on the events in the Catholic Church and American society seemingly led to conclusions about ideological slants.

For example, *St. Anthony Messenger* ran a positive editorial about ecumenism. Rife with quotes from Church officials and examples from recent Church history, the editorial certainly advanced a particular view of the ecumenical movement and in the process legitimized the somewhat radical notion of considering "what . . . Catholics can learn by a Christian attitude toward other Christians." "For a start," the editors offered, "we can learn about, and respect, their holiness." Pointing to the "selfless dedication of the Salvation Army and the raw courage of the ministers who marched in Mississippi," the editors asked readers to recalibrate their religious sensibilities away from competition toward mindsets of charity and community. The *Messenger* suggested that Protestants' knowledge of the Bible and missionary work demonstrated the power of the sacraments all Christians held in common.[92]

Because *St. Anthony Messenger* enjoyed a profile as a popular magazine, letters sent to it were often significant as social history. For example, in the spring of 1965, an article on "The Psychology of Childhood Confessions" by a pediatrician provided at least one letter writer with material to imagine that teaching children about Catholicism might entail more than rote memorization of the catechism. "It has helped me feel more definite and less 'guilty,'" Mrs. Robert Walsleben admitted, "perhaps about the type of religious training

---

90. "Dialogue: Getting to Know You," *St. Anthony Messenger* 72 (January 1965): 36–37.

91. Fr. Jeremy Harrington, OFM, interview with author, February 8, 2016.

92. "What Can We Learn From Protestants?," *St. Anthony Messenger* 72 (January 1965): 36–37.

I'd want for my children who are young but already learning." Following this letter, the editors added some encouragement: "You not only 'could' impart interest and love of God in your children by whatever talents you have, you by all means SHOULD. You are the most important teacher God wants your children to have."[93]

In the same July 1965 issue, the editors chose to print letters responding to an essay run in the May 1965 issue written by Madelyn Bonsignore, a leading figure in the Christian Family Movement (CFM) describing how she had nearly sacrificed her life to march in Selma, Alabama. One letter praised the essay and the heroic actions of its writers; the other letters, published with names withheld, struck a different tone. The editors included a note of apology about the tenor of the hostile letters and issued a challenge: "We apologize to our Negro brothers and sisters for printing these letters. . . . We want our readers to know what kind of letters we DID get. What kind of letter didn't YOU write?"[94] Most of the letters denounced Bonsignore's decision to march for civil rights as selfish at best and race baiting at worst. One said, "Is this why you publish *St. Anthony Messenger*, to praise a woman who should have been home with her family? The good Fathers beg us for money to educate boys to become priests who parade in the streets with niggers against their benefactors."[95] Other letters followed suit, most castigating a woman for "leaving" her family to take up a struggle with people who, a few letters pointed out, were not part of her community. "I resent and refuse to allow rabble-rousing and distorted literature into our home. As a former resident of an integrated community, I will peacefully fight to repulse the influence of the 'African Culture Integrationists,'" wrote another writer, whose sentiments echoed others by imploring the editors to "keep out of politics and economics and remain steadfastly in religion."[96] Yet this era made the personal political— from the family and prayer to race and gender.

In 1967 the associate editor Harrington moved up to become editor and inaugurated a section called "I'd Like to Say," in which the magazine paid ten dollars for every contribution by laity with this caveat: "There will be no comment added by the editors, whether we agree with the opinions or not."[97] The attention to lay opinion had defined *St. Anthony Messenger* over its history and continued in new ways under Harrington. It also became a forum of sorts to rally Catholics to consider the politics of the Church. Harrington wrote in

93. Mrs. Robert Walsleben, letter to the editor, and editors' response, *St. Anthony Messenger* 72 (July 1965): 4.

94. Editors' Note, letters to the editor, *St. Anthony Messenger* 72 (July 1965): 5.

95. Name withheld, letters to the editor, *St. Anthony Messenger* 72 (July 1965): 5.

96. Name withheld, letters to the editor, *St. Anthony Messenger* 72 (July 1965): 5.

97. "I'd Like to Say," *St. Anthony Messenger* 75 (July 1967): 31.

one editorial that unlike periodicals of the past, magazines were increasingly not solely an expression of their editors. What he wanted was a place for debate and encounter—"If the Church has a dirty face," he explained, "she must know about it before she can wash away the smudges." That kind of approach suggested a flexibility that took advantage of an age of fracture rather than finding reasons to retrench within it.[98]

What some Catholics were thinking was captured in December 1968 when Tom Schick of *St. Anthony Messenger* published the results of a reader poll. The poll found that readers of the *Messenger* were, on average, younger and more Catholic than those of *The Lamp*, and most were interested in how Vatican II had affected and might continue to affect their lives as Catholics. "A majority of Catholics," Schick reported, "approve of the new Church. They think Vatican II struck a pretty happy medium in updating." Respondents reported that they generally found themselves talking "more about religion," and most tried "to keep informed about the Church and the changes taking place." One reader said: "I don't know enough about the changes that were made [through Vatican II] but I would like to." Schick also reported that among those who were interested in changes happening within the Church, most found out about those changes from publications like the *Messenger*.[99] Thus the editors smartly calibrated the magazine to address the general need among the laity for more information not merely about the Church and their faith, but about how their role as laity had changed.

In the conclusion to his article Schick made a few observations that demonstrated the evolution of Franciscan media in post–Vatican II America. "You, our readers, have shown that you *want* to be heard," Schick noted. And though readers had written to *St. Anthony Messenger* for most of its history, Schick suggested that perhaps dialogue rather than doctrine was the purpose for Franciscan media. One reader, Schick reported, "thanked us for 'the *first* opportunity' to express an opinion. 'My feelings and judgments,' he said, 'have never been solicited until this time.'" Aware of the debate over implementing Vatican II, Schick wrote: "Often innovations have been decided upon and they have been 'enforced' with little regard to adequate instruction and preparation, and without sufficient care for showing why the changes are being made. Often the voices of legitimate and significant minority groups have been ignored in an attempt to have total 'one-wayness' in the Church."[100]

---

98. Jeremy Harrington, "The People and Views You'll Discover," *St. Anthony Messenger* 75 (February 1968): 1.

99. Tom Schick, "The Results of Our Survey," *St. Anthony Messenger* 76 (December 1968): 18.

100. Ibid. 21

Where the magazine stood on social trends could be seen in its ability to integrate women into discussions about the future of the Church, such as running dozens of short essays mostly by women in the "I'd Like to Say" section. Although men could contribute to this section, the vast majority of contributions came from women. And somewhat like the letters to "The Tertiary Den," this section provided yet another glimpse of Catholic women thinking through changes in the Mass, Catholic schools and religious education, problems with parish life, and priests and celibacy. Women writers also continued to contribute to the magazine, including the prolific Alice Ogle, who wrote a long-form essay that argued against the death penalty.[101]

In one of the first issues that ran "I'd Like to Say," one woman wrote to express her "sadness at seeing the changes in the Church" and having "suffered through a guitar mass recently . . . stumbled up to the communion rail hardly sure I was at Mass—trying not to cry but truly grieving for all the Church has taken from us. Must the changes be so radical?" she asked.[102] But another writer told of her overwhelmingly positive experience of attending a "Teenage Mass" at which "young people literally filled the church to overflowing, and their music (complete with guitars, drums, and a young, female vocalist) was the most inspiring I ever heard." This format of offering contrasting if not directly conflicting opinions about the Church and, in some cases, the changes wrought by Vatican II became a mainstay for the *Messenger*.[103]

These evident conflicts among the laity gave Harrington a chance to address the potential role Catholic media might play mitigating the identity crisis the church experienced from the late 1960s into the 1970s. Harrington contended that an "information gap" existed between Catholic officialdom—who initiated changes in everything from the liturgy to Catholic sisters—and the laity, who "protest the introduction of unexplained and nonunderstood departures from past practice or belief." For a Catholic press, such a problem offered a chance to affirm its purpose in Catholic culture. Harrington wrote that the editors of *St. Anthony Messenger* believed that there was justification for the protests heard from the laity and that the parishes could barely keep up with the job of teaching their parishioners how to implement the changes. But in a moment when the relevance of the Catholic press should spike, Harrington and his colleagues were "utterly dismayed by the current plight of the Catholic press." Rather than a boom in publications, "the real situation is that

---

101. See special issue, "The Parish in Time of Crisis," *St. Anthony Messenger* 77 (1969).

102. Elizabeth McAndrew, "I'd Like to Say—Think of Us," *St. Anthony Messenger* 77 (1969), 16.

103. Joan M. Schowen, "I'd Like to Say—The Other Side," *St. Anthony Messenger* 77 (1969), 16.

in the last 10 years 100 Catholic magazines have ceased publishing because there is not demand for them or their finances made it next to impossible to continue publication. More distressing is the fact that even in the last eventful year, 10 Catholic magazines were put out of business by ever-mounting production and mailing costs coupled with plunging circulations."[104]

In the past, magazines such as *St. Anthony Messenger* provided significant insight into the everyday life of Catholics. But changes in the Church forced that profile to evolve. For Harrington large social problems demanded attention from a sophisticated mediator like the Catholic press. What he found, though, was that "when a Catholic magazine publishes news or reports opinions these people do not like, they sit down and write caustic cancellations of their subscriptions. In effect they are building for themselves a make-believe world where everything is just as they would have it. They live in a dream world far removed from reality. Then when reality catches up with them, they are angry again because nobody told them what was what."[105] Harrington envisioned a future in which the press would engage controversy because it could not avoid it, but hoped that its readers would be sophisticated enough to accept this new reality because they wanted to participate in creating a new Catholic Church.

Harrington and the editors who preceded him at *St. Anthony Messenger* also understood that they operated under certain cultural constraints. First and foremost they produced a general interest magazine with a readership made up largely of women. The province in which the magazine was published had a mission anchored in the values of St. Francis. And while the *Messenger* did not actively seek out particular political positions, readers could and did read Franciscanism as being political. So the magazine ran articles on working with the poor in the United States and abroad. Essays and stories explored movements for peace, racial justice, and the environment, but almost always these pieces anchored coverage in the Gospels. In a later interview Harrington said that those who worked at the magazine "tried hard to be 'popular,' easily understood, and appealing to 'ordinary Catholics' [such as] a Sunday Mass congregation." The editors and many writers were Franciscan friars who heard confessions and said Masses on Sundays in parishes. "We had," Harrington noted, "pastoral experience and knew the concerns of the people."[106]

At the center of many discussions mediated by the magazine was the place and definition of the family in the Catholic Church. One key influence on Christian views of the family was the Christian Family Movement, which began a decade before Vatican II and helped redefine the Catholic Mass, the

---

104. Jeremy Harrington, "We Need Each Other," *St. Anthony Messenger* 77 (1969): 2.
105. Ibid.
106. Fr. Jeremy Harrington, OFM, interview with author, February 8, 2016.

role of the laity, and the limits of change among Catholics as a social group. In his history of CFM Burns explains that young couples in the 1950s joined to "transcend and transform not just their own family life but their culture." As an organization CFM never grew very large—having perhaps fifty thousand members at its height—but it possessed a sensibility that bridged the period from Catholic Action in the 1930s and 1940s to the Vatican II Catholicism of the late 1960s and 1970s. Burns writes that CFM "refused to allow couples to be content with their lives as they were and insisted that families take responsibility for their Church and world." The CFM combined the organizing principle of the family and the energy and inspiration of Catholic Action to create a potent social and political agenda that sought to make the world an "easier place for families to be good, human, and healthy."[107]

During its heyday from the mid-1940s through the mid-1970s, CFM served as one way for Catholics to grapple with interlocking issues of family life; social issues such as race relations, changing roles for women, and contraception; and the implications of Vatican II for the future of the Catholic Church. The fate of the CFM illustrates the complexity of appealing to family issues in a time of flux for many American Catholics. The idea of the family had a fundamentally conservative connotation—it envisioned specific roles for men and women and assumed that Catholics held certain convictions on issues such as contraception. CFM declined, as Burns points out, primarily because of "the malaise that affected Catholics, particularly liberal Catholics, in the early 1970s." For *St. Anthony Messenger* the crisis of Catholic identity similarly marked a new epoch in the magazine's history.

In an editorial in July 1972, Harrington wondered where Catholics got their values, suggesting one possible source was media such as *St. Anthony Messenger*. Harrington reported on a talk in Collegeville, Minnesota—the site for annual retreats for US Catholic bishops—by the well-regarded Yale theologian George Lindbeck, who argued that "Churches have not been very successful in getting their members to make their own the values preached by the Church." Indeed Harrington introduced his brief editorial by citing a poll that demonstrated that Catholics do not necessarily follow their Church on "birth control, abortion, divorce and remarriage." In addition to disagreement over those issues, Lindbeck pointed out that "study after study show that churchgoers in all the major Christian denominations are, on the average, more prejudiced than non-churchgoers."[108] In response Harrington wondered how Catholics would determine what they believe and how to see their

---

107. Jeffrey M. Burns, *Disturbing the Peace: History of the Christian Family Movement, 1949–1974* (Notre Dame: University of Notre Dame Press, 1999), 4, 7, 10.

108. George Lindbeck as quoted in Jeremy Harrington, "Where Do We Get Our Values?," *St. Anthony Messenger* 79 (July 1972): 11.

Church from their worldview. Harrington asked three questions. First, "how effectively does the Catholic Church in the US influence the values of its members?" Second, do Catholics want their Church to play a prophetic role in their lives, challenging them to consider how to create values? And finally, how would lay groups and educators, in addition to the clergy and the Mass, communicate values "as an essential function of a parish"?[109] In an editorial directly below this one, Harrington offered the Vietnam War as one of those test cases for the formation of Catholic values.[110] And while that particular war did produce conflict among Catholics as well as other Americans, other issues proved to have broader and longer resonance.

Among the issues most controversial was the changing role of women in both society and the parish, long a concern of Franciscan media. For example, in 1971 and 1972 the magazine ran issues devoted exclusively to women—historically the most significant group of its readers. The articles included "Women's Lib in a Christian Perspective," "Changing Sex Roles in Our Society," "Woman in the Bible," "Good-Bye to a Male Church," "The Womanly Woman—A Man's View," and "Nine Prominent Women Speak Out." To begin the March 1971 issue Harrington offered an editorial entitled "Confessions of a Male Editor." Harrington admitted that he had not taken seriously most issues that concerned a vast number of women, but he said he changed after an especially "spirited" discussion among his editorial advisory board. "At stake," he explained, "is what we as men and women expect of ourselves, what we teach our children about the meaning of being a male or female in our society." The issue included nearly fifty pages of essays and reflections by and about women in the Church and American society. As Harrington suggested, the decision to run the issue grew out of the need for the magazine's readers to hear about and engage with these matters. Throughout the 1960s and 1970s, the magazine also made an effort to hire more women editors, have women serve on the editorial board, and encourage women to write articles for the magazine. For most of its history *St. Anthony Messenger* made engaging its readers a priority and a signature characteristic of the magazine's relationship to Catholic culture. But never before had the magazine treated the group that made up the majority of its readers as a subject of intellectual analysis.[111]

---

109. Jeremy Harrington, "Where Do We Get Our Values?," *St. Anthony Messenger* 79 (July 1972): 11.

110. Jeremy Harrington, "A Case in Point: Forming Our Attitudes on Vietnam," 79 (July 1972): 11.

111. Jeremy Harrington, "Confessions of a Male Editor," *St. Anthony Messenger* 78 (March 1971): 1; see also Karen Wullenweber Hurley, "Wanted: A Chance to Serve, a Look at Women and the Church), *St. Anthony Messenger* 78 (March 1971): 19–24; Harrington, interview with author, February 8, 2016.

Karen Wullenweber Hurley, a long-time assistant editor at the *Messenger*, wrote one of the lead essays in the March 1971 issue, entitled "Wanted: A Chance to Serve, a Look at Women and the Church." Just as older and newer understandings of the Catholic Church were clashing, perceptions of women in the Church contained an internal and nearly eternal conflict between the practical role women had played in the Church—namely subordinate in every way to men—and the contributions women might make to the mission of the Church. Hurley noted that as much as Vatican II had created new opportunities for the laity in the Church and new conversations about the future of the Church, it also further exposed a major problem. "Regardless of Pope John's intentions," she observed, "the renewal which followed Vatican II only contributed to feminine discontent. The Aggiornamento may have opened many Church doors to lay men—opportunities to serve as lectors, commentators, deacons, parish administrators—but women's positions remained unchanged." Hurley pointed out that before changes to the Church in the 1960s, lay men as well as women "shared the same plight of 'second-class citizenship.'" In a sense Catholic women thus encountered a double dose of inequality in the late 1960s and early 1970s. They were largely left behind in Church reforms for the laity and also felt even more acutely the distance between their role in the Church and the changing role of women in American society as political feminism began to have some effect.[112]

A year later the magazine ran an issue with a cover story about women and work, written by Sidney Callahan, who at the time was the author of two books: *The Working Mother* (1971) and *The Illusion of Eve: Modern Woman's Search for Identity* (1965). In the decades since that article appeared, Callahan earned a doctorate in psychology and became a distinguished scholar in ethics, religion, and women's studies. In her essay "Every Mother Needs to Work," Callahan engaged with a debate raging over the role of women in society and directly tackled one of the questions with which Catholics had wrestled throughout the twentieth century—whether there was an ideal composition and function of the family. By addressing women and their relationship to the Church, *St. Anthony Messenger* quite squarely contended with its own identity as a family magazine.[113]

During the 1970s into the 1980s the magazine published essays on contraception, abortion, the role of women in the Church, the rising rate of divorce, the declining attendance at Mass, and the general sexual revolution. The *Messenger* ran long interviews with luminaries such as John Tracy Ellis as well as debates among readers over contraception, Catholic schools, and so-called protest priests such as Father James Groppi of Milwaukee, Wisconsin.

---

112. Hurley, "Wanted," 19–21.
113. Sidney Callahan, "Every Mother Needs to Work," *St. Anthony Messenger* 80 (June 1972): 32–37.

Letters from readers continued to be revealing. For example, a young man wrote into the "Wise Man's Corner" column in the summer of 1972 to ask if homosexuals could become priests. He asked: "Should I forget about the idea of priesthood because of this deviation or should I follow my desire and continue striving to serve the Lord?" The Wise Man consulted a fellow priest before printing a response that strongly recommended the young man choose another way to serve the Church outside of the priesthood.[114]

St. Anthony Messenger also captured reactions to the controversial Papal encyclical *Humanae Vitae*.[115] Disagreement over how the Catholic Church addressed contraception erupted publically after the 1968 encyclical, but it had simmered privately among some Catholic theologians and the Catholic laity long before that, as one could see in the pages of the *Messenger*. Over its history the magazine had moderated conversations between women and priests that expressed the complicated understanding of Catholic doctrine on contraception. Underlying such exchanges was a particular kind of acceptance of truth in the Church. Massa observes: "Given the presence of faith on the part of the person receiving such teaching, the Catholic moral argument went, the believer could and should be able to understand the reasons adduced to justify the Church's teaching on moral matters."[116] Yet as one can see from the arcs of arguments in Franciscan magazines over the way Catholics both lived and received their religion, the translation of doctrine into practice was not so easy. Thus while Catholic theologians critiqued *Humanae Vitae* through a heightened historical consciousness in which truth was contested, Catholics writing to the *Messenger* debated the encyclical's implications in a world influenced by decades of liberal thought and their own lived experience.

In December 1973 *St. Anthony Messenger* ran long letters in response to an essay from Karen Hurley titled "Let's End the Silence on Birth Control" in which she defended *Humanae Vitae* as a "radical challenge" to contemporary sexual mores and individualism. The encyclical, she argued, "challenges our desire to shape our own future rather than cooperate with God so the unknown mystery of *his* plan can unfold."[117] Hurley acknowledged that many of her readers might dispute the Church's teaching on sex, and Harrington noted in a brief editorial that "the letters have been serious. Many of them moving. The majority agreed with the article, but some argued an opposing

---

114. "Can a Homosexual Be a Priest?" (letter), and response, The Wise Man's Corner, *St. Anthony Messenger* 80 (July 1972): 47.

115. "Letters to the Editor," *St. Anthony Messenger* 81 (December 1973), 3-5.

116. Massa, *American Catholic Revolution*, 33.

117. Karen Hurley, "Let's End the Silence on Birth Control," *St. Anthony Messenger* 81 (October 1973), 11.

view with vigor."[118] Consistent with the magazine's history and mission, the editors ran three pages of letters as a way to illustrate the diversity and sincerity of opinion about birth control.[119]

While the editors showed equanimity in running the letters, the writers were nonetheless pointed in their opinions. A letter from Mary R. Joyce of St. Cloud, Minnesota argued that "sex-related drug dependency is not liberation"; contraception, she declared, was a scheme of the "money-hungry, male chauvinist establishment" designed to confirm the view of St. Thomas Aquinas and Aristotle that women are "defects of nature."[120] Leonard Bowman of Davenport, Iowa, echoed other readers by questioning Karen Hurley's contention that contraception interferes with "God's creation." Bowman mused, "After I think about it, then, the 'confidence in God' suggested in the article starts to look a bit like an unreasoning attempt to abandon responsibility. . . . Maybe, then, Ms. Hurley is not all that fair when she associates contraception with selfishness or amorality. Maybe that choice could be just as rightly associated with responsibility and highly sensitive moral judgment."[121]

Other letters addressed how Catholics understood (or should understand) the Church's teaching and God's will. Some of the writers contended that a decision about birth control concerned not whether to use it, but whether to violate one's faith. "To the intelligent, informed Catholic," one wrote, "*Humanae Vitae* is not an imposition of morality but an expression of morality." This letter writer concluded that the Church was "only trying to do us all a favor. She is continuing to protect her people from unhappiness and regret by teaching, not imposing, a higher level of values which can truly bring an inner peace." After a "very-much unplanned-for fourth baby," the letter writer wanted readers to know that she "touched the angel's hand who brought her to me."[122] Another letter said: "Common sense should tell us that the generative faculty and instinct has to be disciplined or sublimated because, like fire, sex also is combustible and potentially dangerous."[123] "I am saddened," another letter said, "that so many Catholics miss this opportunity to witness for Christ in one of the most vital areas of the 70s—sex." She suggested that couples, such as one with six young children mentioned in Karen Hurley's article, could also consider "abstinence over

---

118. Jeremy Harrington, OFM, "In Harmony with the Universe," *St. Anthony Messenger* 81 (December 1973): 1.

119. "About Birth Control, I'd Like to Say. . ." (letters to the editor), *St. Anthony Messenger* 81 (December 1973): 35–38.

120. Mary R. Joyce, letter, in "About Birth Control, I'd Like to Say. . . ," 38.

121. Leonard Bowman, letter, in "About Birth Control, I'd Like to Say. . . ," 36.

122. Maureen Franca, letter, in "About Birth Control, I'd Like to Say. . . ," 37.

123. Christy Ann Maguire, letter, in "About Birth Control, I'd Like to Say. . . ," 35.

a period of months and even years." "With grace all things are possible," she added.[124]

In an almost full-page dissent, Sue Kane, who also wrote commissioned work for other Catholic outlets, attempted to complicate the assumption that Catholics ought to know God's will. She acknowledged that "an immediate turnabout in the official Church's attitude toward birth control cannot be expected," but she was encouraged by "a gradual awakening to the possibility that contraception may not be at all times contrary to the will of God is possible." She pointed to an apparent contradiction in what many Catholics took as the Church's teaching. "Contraception does not always, and of necessity, diminish the holiness of our bodies or their excellence as symbols. If it did," she reasoned, "abstinence should be considered immoral; rhythm should be considered immoral; and only intercourse that results in conception should be considered the right use of our bodies in marriage." Turning some of Karen Hurley's logic in on itself, Kane posed a challenge: assuming God is present when there are no barriers to conception, what does it mean "if the wife is barren, if the husband has a low sperm count"—"is God, then, absent also?" Indeed Kane wondered if the problem was less about God's will and more about the implications sex had for Church officials. "There is no official Church stand against false teeth, blood transfusions, organ transplants, polio vaccine or aspirin. The only medical interventions that the Church is known to disapprove of as 'unnatural' are contraceptives. There is something left unsaid in the clerical reasoning," she asserted, "and it is this: sex is one of the weaknesses of men, one of man's animal attributes and it needs justification." By running Karen Hurley's original essay and then the letters in response, the *Messenger* continued its tradition of dealing with ordinary Catholics and the ways in which they live their lives by illustrating the complicated fidelity both to the Church and to God.

In a later interview for this book, Harrington related that for him and his colleagues, "Vatican II told us to read the sign of the times." Among those signs was the evident rift among Catholics over a variety of social issues. The magazine, according to Harrington, attempted to keep a "Catholic centrist position," running articles such as "Equal Rights Amendment—Why Catholics Are Divided," and "Smeal vs. Schlafly: A Square Off on Women's Issues" (the latter referring to a 1986 debate between Phyllis Schlafly, who opposed feminism, and Eleanor Smeal, then president of the National Organization for Women). Harrington explained that he and the staff "recognized division among Catholics and between the laity (and some clergy) and the hierarchy. Our deliberate goal was to be a bridge between

---

124. Mrs. Robert Louderback, letter, in "About Birth Control, I'd Like to Say. . . ," 35.

liberals and conservatives in the Church, between generations, between pastors and the laity."[125]

Looking for ways to reach across such divisions, the friars at *St. Anthony Messenger* decided to introduce more variety in their publications. Unlike many other Franciscan magazines, *St. Anthony Messenger* did not suffer a precipitous financial collapse. Two reasons stand out to explain the magazine's ability to weather a storm that other publishers could not. First, like the other survivor from this period, the *Franciscan Herald and Forum*, *St. Anthony Messenger* had a media organization attached to it, St. Anthony Messenger Press. The press published dozens of books on a variety of topics from Catholic identity to prayer; and the press introduced new voices in the Church who grew into popular writers, such as Father Richard Rohr.

Second, the press also produced publications designed to address changes in parish life following Vatican II. Harrington pointed out that as costs for publishing the magazine went up, he looked for ways to reduce the size of the magazine and increase revenues by introducing new products. For example, in 1970 the press introduced *Homily Helps*, pamphlets tailored specifically for priests who, like their parishioners, needed to adapt to the new conditions of the Mass. Then in 1973 the press began offering a newsletter called *Catholic Update* as a way to address specific topics of interest to Catholics. This wildly successful initiative generated interest and income for the rest of the press's endeavors.

According to Harrington, it was Father Norman Perry's idea to create a way for the press to reach many more people than the 350,000 or so subscribers to the *Messenger*. Perry had served for many years in a variety of capacities, including associate editor and, perhaps most famously as the Wise Man for "The Wise Man's Corner," where he answered thousands of questions over the years. By 1992 the press had sold over 4.7 million copies of 220 paperback titles; had a subscription base of 350,000; and had developed 234 titles in and distributed over 110 million copies of the *Catholic Update* series. In the *Update* series, priests, brothers, and lay Franciscans who worked at the press turned out essays on topics such as "Why Stay Catholic?" by Perry; "Isn't Anything for Sure Anymore?" by Jack Wintz; "Do People Still Pray?" by Susan Onaitis; and "Is Sunday Mass a Must?" by Karen Hurley, to name but a few. In his interview Harrington added that even though an "*imprimatur* from the bishop was not required . . . we wanted it for the *Catholic Update*. We wanted to be accurate and faithful to Catholic teaching. Also, the *imprimatur* was our defense against clergy or laity who disagreed with what we published." The archbishop who provided official Church sanction of *Catholic Update* was

---

125. Harrington, interview with author, February 8, 2016.

Joseph Bernardin, who served in Cincinnati, Ohio, for ten years before Pope John Paul II made him archbishop of Chicago in 1982.[126]

For the hundredth anniversary issue of the magazine, Harrington and his editors included a long essay on the history of *St. Anthony Messenger* and articles that brought together reflections on Franciscan missionary work covered by the magazine over the years as well as profiles of celebrities who had been interviewed.[127] However, the issue also made clear that it was the family in Catholic life that animated much of the magazine's history. In retrospect, choosing the family made sense, and as John Bookser Feister noted, soon after the magazine's fiftieth anniversary the editors declared the *Messenger* "the National Catholic Family Magazine." From its inception the *Messenger* had focused on the family as a reflection of Church teaching in *Rerum Novarum*. But of course by the 1990s profound changes to the composition and function of the family in American life forced the *Messenger* to consider how best to treat or define roles for men, women, and children.[128]

Feister pointed out: "By 1942, *St. Anthony Messenger* had been transformed from a small, print-heavy booklet to a feature magazine chock-full of articles, recipes, 'modest' sewing patterns, columns and stories. In every issue one sees a steady emphasis on promoting solid, Catholic family values and strengthening Catholic families to practice their faith in the homes." Throughout the postwar era, the *Messenger* remained a significant presence in Catholic media, in part because it adapted to winds that changed both American and Catholic culture. In the 1960s "the magazine's editors," Feister noted, "became more willing to venture into controversy, cautiously to support some aspects of the women's movement, to continue the magazine's tradition of supporting liberal social politics but to remain firmly, some would say conservatively, pro-life and pro-family."[129] The broad appeal of *St. Anthony Messenger* helped to shape its mission—it spoke about the family because it sought to speak to family. The magazine continues to enjoy a healthy subscription base in 2017 and anchors Franciscan Media, a company that absorbed some electronic forms of American Franciscanism. Among the most significant expressions of Franciscanism came through the radio, television, and most recently, the Internet.

---

126. Harrington, interview with author, February 8, 2016; *Issue Directory for Catholic Update, March 1973–1992*, Offices of Franciscan Media, St. John the Baptist Province, Cincinnati, OH.

127. "100 Years of Good News," *St. Anthony Messenger* 100 (June 1992).

128. John Bookser Feister, "Family Says It All," *St. Anthony Messenger* 100 (June 1992): 24–27.

129. Ibid., 25, 26.

Chapter 4:
Electronic Evangelization

Father Hugh Noonan, OFM, and Father Romanus Dunne, SA, cataloged the great diversity of Franciscan electronic media in their reports to the Franciscan Educational Conference in 1959. The Franciscan radio presence dated back to at least the 1920s, with many friars speaking the languages of their communities. For example *Christ the King Hour* in Chicago was in Polish; Luke Ciampi, OFM, addressed listeners in Italian; other programs were translated into French and German. Although there were many examples of Franciscan outreach on radio and television (fewer of the latter), the three that established a substantial Franciscan presence were *The Rosary Hour* (a radio show), *The Ave Maria Hour* (a radio show), and *The Hour of St. Francis* (first a radio show and then a television program). Combined they reached millions of Americans, demonstrating a significant level of activity that before the 1960s placed Franciscans in a league with other religious programming. And with *The Padre's Hour*, Franciscan media could claim a radio show with a life span longer than any other produced by a religious denomination in American history, and one that further distinguished itself because it broadcast from an Indian reservation in both English and Navajo.[1]

However, even with such impressive credentials, Franciscan success on the radio never approached the reach and audience of the reactionary Father Charles Coughlin, who reportedly reached tens of millions of listeners during the 1930s with a combination of anti-elite, anti-Roosevelt, and anti-Semitic broadcasts; or the reach and audience of Bishop Fulton Sheen, who dominated the airwaves in the 1930s on the popular *Catholic Hour*. Sheen began his career on radio, developing his popularity, according to Irvin D. S. Winsboro and Michael Epple, through a combination of philosophical preaching and anticommunist lectures, expanding from the 17 stations of a single syndicate in the 1930s to 118 NBC affiliates by the early 1950s.[2] Sheen then

---

1. Father Hugh Noonan, OFM, "Achievements of the Friars in Radio and Television," *Communications and the Franciscan Message*, 100–105; see also Father Romanus Dunne, SA, "Radio and the Franciscan Message," *Communications and the Franciscan Message*, 113.
2. Irvin D. S. Winsboro and Michael Epple, "Religion, Culture, and the Cold War: Bishop Fulton J. Sheen and America's Anti-Communist Crusade of the 1950s," *The Historian* 71, no. 2 (Summer 2009): 213.

used his popularity from his radio program and his best-selling books to launch a popular, prime-time television program called *Life Is Worth Living*, running from 1952 until 1957 and attracting "a diverse audience of 30 million . . . on 123 television stations."[3] The most obvious reasons why Coughlin and Sheen enjoyed such success was their overt and at times aggressive engagement with contemporary politics. In short they played upon acute American fears. And while both ostensibly also evangelized through their programs, when Sheen decided to devote more time to his role as the director of the Society for the Propagation of the Faith, he retired from television.[4]

So while Franciscans did not have a superstar media personality in the heyday of radio, they did adhere more closely to the evangelizing mission that characterized all Franciscan media for most of its history. In his description of Franciscan media in the 1930s and 1940s, Noonan noted that on the radio, many Franciscan priests and brothers gave talks related directly to aspects of the Church calendar and specific Masses; others used airtime to lead people in meditations about St. Francis and St. Anthony or in prayers and hymns; and still others focused on catechetical talks or answered questions posed by listeners. Very few used these media appearances to discuss the news or contemporary events, other than addressing those issues that typically occupied Catholics, such as the family or the priesthood or the lives of saints.

Some Franciscans had fairly substantial stints on radio. Adrien Malo, OFM, broadcast out of Canada and focused on Church doctrine and Christian history. Ferdinand Coiteux, OFM, produced a fifteen-minute program in Montreal called *St. Anthony and the Sick*, which included prayers, hymns, intentions, and short sermons on the meaning of statements from St. Francis and St. Anthony. Giles Webster, OFM, did a brief program for almost fifteen years on Sunday mornings called *Catholicism in the News*, while Noel William, OFM, broadcast a Sunday High Mass with a sermon and commentary four times a year for twenty years from Emporia, Kansas. For fifteen years the Capuchins of the Province of St. Augustine ran a weekly broadcast from Butler, Pennsylvania on Church teachings; they included talks from faculty at the St. Fidelis Seminary. And Boniface Weckman, OFM Cap, aired a weekly spiritual instruction class for more than twelve years that occasionally invited guests for discussions and a question-and-answer segment from Charleston, West Virginia.[5]

In this chapter, I cover a representative sample of Fraciscan radio and television programs. Each program in the chapter had a distinctive feature that reflected other Franciscan programs, but not all were equal—some were produced by a small group for very low cost and had a relatively small audience

3. Ibid., 217–18.
4. Ibid., 230.
5. Noonan, "Achievements of the Friars," 102–5.

while others were products of Franciscan-secular joint efforts with budgets that rose to meet popular demand and technical expertise. Therefore, the bulk of this chapter is devoted to reviewing the production history of *The Hour of St. Francis*, a program that brought together many of the talents and hopes of Franciscan media while pioneering innovative ways to reach Americans through television.

THE ROSARY HOUR

Father Justin Figas created *The Rosary Hour*, the first and one of the most successful Franciscan radio shows. Figas was born into a Polish family in the mining town of McClure, Pennsylvania in 1886. While the coal region of Pennsylvania attracted thousands of Polish immigrants in the latter half of the nineteenth century, the largest population of Polish immigrants settled in cities in the US Northeast and Midwest. Estimates based on census data indicate that by 1930 a population of more than three million first- and second-generation Polish Americans lived in the United States. Staninslaw Hajkowski, author of a dissertation that includes a good deal of research on Figas, observes that in the 1920s and 1930s this massive Polish American population underwent a significant transition in identity. In Franciscan magazines such as *St. Anthony Messenger*, Catholics negotiated issues from Americanism to divorce. Figas's radio show became another site for such negotiation.[6] "This change from Polish to Polish-American or to an American-Polish perspective on religion," Hajkowski explains, "was noticed and addressed in an extraordinary way by two Franciscan orders working in the United States, the Capuchin Fathers from the Polish Province of the Assumption of the Blessed Virgin Mary and the Conventual Franciscans from the Polish Province of St. Anthony of Padua."[7]

Figas graduated in 1903 from the Gymnasium of St. Francis in Trenton, New Jersey, run by German Conventual Franciscans; he entered the novitiate of the order, taking the name Justin, and in 1906 moved to the province of St. Anthony that had been established for Polish-speaking Franciscans. This province assumed the care of the Polish communities in the United States from 1906 through the early 1940s, at which point it expanded beyond its base of Polish Americans because their identity became less attached to their national origins in Europe. The three primary geographic regions of the province were Baltimore, Maryland; Boston; and Buffalo, New York, which became home for Figas. Ordained a priest in 1910, he earned a doctorate in theology and served for brief time at the Basilica of St. Joseph in Milwaukee,

6. Stanislaw Hajkowski, "The Cultural Transition and the Attitudes of Polish Immigrant Families Towards Divorce and Parental Authority in the United States, 1931–1940" (PhD dissertation, The Catholic University of America, 2010), 66–67.
7. Ibid., 71.

Wisconsin, until he was appointed secretary of the Polish Franciscan province in Buffalo. From that position he was elected minister provincial in 1923 and was reelected six consecutive times. The Polish community of this city in western New York numbered more than two hundred thousand, almost half the city's total population, making its Polish population second only to that of Chicago in size. Among the many projects Figas coordinated was the building of the studio that broadcast *The Rosary Hour* in Polish.[8]

Figas's career in the relatively new medium of radio began with an invitation from the sponsors of a Polish variety show broadcast on WKEN in Buffalo on Sunday evenings in the 1920s. What started as an address to a Polish audience primarily in the Buffalo region lasting a few minutes each Sunday grew into a half-hour show called *Question Box* on WEBR by 1928. As a priest who ministered to a parish, Figas was acutely aware of the changes many in his community were experiencing, especially in regard to family life. Many of his early talks focused on issues such as divorce, raising children in America, and the economic woes brought on by the Depression. That economic catastrophe temporarily shut down Figas's radio career for two years until 1930, when he returned to his half-hour format at a production cost of $25 per program. Within a year Figas's show developed into *The Rosary Hour*, an hour-long format under a new radio network called the Great Lakes Chain. Formed in December 1931 to broadcast to the millions of Polish Americans who lived around the Great Lakes, this network based its operations in Buffalo and was transmitted by telephone lines to Chicago, Detroit, Pittsburgh and Scranton in Pennsylvania, and Cleveland, Ohio.[9]

Figas titled *The Rosary Hour*'s first episode "Our Parents." "This program, the first of its kind, will be entirely dedicated to our Polish fathers and mothers," Figas told listeners, "those quiet and humble pioneers who have adorned the Catholic Church by their deep and modest faith; who have enriched America by their hard and constant labors; who have by their practical approach to life earned the praise of foreigners; and who have left us godly Polish virtues as their legacy. I repeat, it is to them exclusively that I, with a heart overflowing with love, respect and gratefulness, dedicate this program."[10]

The new format and broadcast schedule—airing from 6 to 7 P.M. once a week—allowed Figas to deliver long sermons and to include a considerable amount of music—primarily the singing of hymns. The show also continued the "Question Box" feature, which like similar features in Catholic magazines

8. Ibid., 73
9. Ibid., 77.
10. Father Justin Figas, "Our Parents," *The Rosary Hour* (radio show), Microsoft Word transcript, December 6, 1931, accessed July 13, 2017, http://rosaryhour.com/December%206,%201931.docx.

could sound contrived but offered discussions relevant to immigrant Catholics in the Midwest. The animating spirit of many of Figas's program sermons, at least during the first few years, was the apparent clash of cultures (and generations) that emerged as immigrants raised their families in a time of cultural change. Hajkowski contends that Figas viewed his role as a translator of sorts who helped Polish Americans address their conflicted feelings about leaving behind traditions they had carried to the United States. He took a cultural pluralist view of his role, assuring his listeners that they should continue to express their ethnicity while they acclimated to the norms of American culture. Figas gave his reasons in his second broadcast:

> Right at the beginning I would like to make note that I am not trying to incite controversy among listeners. We are Americans both legally and politically. But at the same time we are Americans or American citizens of Polish descent. I am trying to prove—and I will prove—that Polishness and Polish descent never have been an obstacle for us to completely and perfectly fulfill our civic duties towards our adopted Homeland, contrariwise to the claims of some people who, I know not by what right, have turned themselves into the guardian angels of the freedom, loyalty and welfare of America.[11]

While Figas defended his community's patriotism, he was not above slighting another ethnic group, rejecting the notion that Poles might be comparable to Chinese Americans.[12]

Figas broached topics that ranged from the local circumstances of his listeners—their families, parents, children, neighborhoods—to issues that defined one of the most radical periods of American politics—working conditions, communism, and the politics of labor. Like some of his counterparts in print, Figas took a strong and decidedly reactionary stance against organized labor. In a two-part episode reflecting the fear of communism, titled "Wolf in Sheep's Clothing" and "The Victims of Wolves in Sheep's Clothing," he related: "Since last Sunday, I have received a few hundred letters asking me to speak at least once more about the agitators who sow ferment in the minds of workers, who under the guise of teaching and helping the masses of good and noble workmen, lead them astray by imbuing revolutionary rules in their hearts and minds; they expose people who are calm and innocent as lambs to the dangers of prison and deportation; to the loss of work and bread; often also to handicaps, and sometimes even to—death!" Such dire warnings were buttressed by letters

---

11. Father Justin Figas, "The Pole as an American Citizen," *The Rosary Hour* (radio show), Microsoft Word transcript, December 13, 1931, accessed July 13, 2017, http://rosaryhour.com/December%2013,%201931.docx.
12. Ibid.

he read over the air from Polish Americans who conveyed accounts of being terribly misled by labor organizers, whom Figas seemed to label generally as outside agitators most likely from the Soviet Union.[13]

Throughout the first few seasons of *The Rosary Hour*, Figas used his sermons as a bulwark against threats—real or imagined—that challenged Church assumptions regarding the primary role of the family and social issues. Figas navigated between the problems that plagued his listeners and his fidelity to tradition, seeking to steer people away from sources that promised more comprehensive solutions, such as the government, or more radical change, such as communism. In this way Figas's show illustrated an important dynamic in Depression-era America—the struggle between competing ideologies and systems to define what it meant to be an American and how that understanding was being shaped by millions of people who often believed themselves to exist outside of their country's national identity. Hajkowski contends: "There were two major external factors confronting every member of the Polish-American communities in the 1930s: the challenge from American culture and the Great Depression, both of which distressed the lives of American families until World War II. *The Rosary Hour*, which was aimed at working class Poles, devoted considerable radio time to address these issues related to everyday life." At the same time, Hajkowski notes, Figas addressed what the priest viewed as dangerous tendencies within the Polish community and family to let competing loyalties and vanity distract them from their piety. "Father Justyn addressed his program," Hajkowski observes, "to the working-class Polish-Americans who on one hand found themselves in a critical and exploitative socioeconomic situation in the 1930s and on the other hand were torn apart by the internal quarrels among differing Polish ethnic organizations."[14]

The outbreak of World War II and the Nazi invasion of Poland changed the topics of Figas's sermons. His first sermon following the blitzkrieg into his homeland began with a poem from the Polish poet Kornel Makuszynski: "bury your sad poetry under a boulder, so that no one hears complaints, as they will take you with the negroes to the shameful markets of the world, and then be great and silent, like a coffin, and in that silence, be Oh Poland, proud."[15] Figas cast Poland and much of Polish history as a reflection of Chris-

---

13. Father Justin Figas, "The Victims of Wolves in Sheep's Clothing," *The Rosary Hour* (radio show), Microsoft Word transcript, April 30, 1933, accessed July 13, 2017, http://rosaryhour.com/April%2030,%201933.docx. See also Father Justin Figas, "Wolf in Sheep's Clothing," *The Rosary Hour* (radio show), Microsoft Word transcript, April 23, 1933, accessed July 13, 2017, http://rosaryhour.com/April%2023,%201933.docx.

14. Hajkowski, "Polish Immigrant Families," 92–93.

15. Kornel Makuszynski, quoted in Father Justin Figas, "Poland Has Not Ceased to Exist," *The Rosary Hour* (radio show), Microsoft Word transcript, November 5, 1939, accessed July 13, 2017, http://rosaryhour.com/November%205,%201939.docx.

tian sacrifice and redemption. Poland during the war would become a national Lazarus, dead but in time resurrected because of faith. "Poland, that Poland which was always the bulwark of Christianity and Civilization," Figas declared to his listeners, "God picked as a victim for the redemption of the sins of all Europe which was drowning in the teachings of materialism and neo-Paganism. And the uprising, lifted up with the all powerful righteousness of the Creator!"[16]

A shift in emphasis took place within Figas's sermons as the war raged in the 1940s. Like many other American religious leaders, he found the American flag as well as the cross to be symbols on which to focus attention. What Figas reflected was a sense that, as one military historian also argues, "World War II taught Americans to get along."[17] In a sermon entitled "Our American Flag," Figas carefully but vigorously argued that his country's flag was red, white, and blue—not merely red and white (the colors of his parents' homeland, Poland):

> Today, as we speak of this patriotism I have in mind the United States, which is the real motherland for me, because I was born and raised here. I live here and work here. I am a citizen and partake of the citizen privileges. And it is here, God willing, that my remains will remain here. But to avoid a misunderstanding, I profess publically and honestly that I am not ashamed of my Polish heritage. I have never . . . [been] ashamed to admit that I had a Pole for a father . . . [and] a Pole for my mother, but boasted of that fact, and today I take pride in it. I love the homeland of my parents and I always will.[18]

For Figas the transition toward Americanization and away from ethnic pluralism came as a result of the war.

Figas built a sizable operation within his first few years. Helping him manage many of the details of the show was Maria Jung, the secretary of *The Rosary Hour* from the beginning of the program to Figas's death in 1959. Her primary duties in the early years were to maintain an ever-expanding mailing list of those who wrote into Figas and who would receive printed versions of the priest's radio talks. The amount of mail grew during holiday seasons, when requests for novenas were most common. And while Figas took care of his private correspondence, according to Hajkowski, his secretary and a fleet of volunteers handled the thousands of letters that praised the program. Those

16. Figas, "Poland Has Not Ceased."
17. Thomas Buscino, *A Nation Forged in War: How World War II Taught Americans to Get Along* (Knoxville: University of Tennessee Press, 2010), 9–11.
18. Father Justin Figas, "Our American Flag," *The Rosary Hour* (radio show), Microsoft Word transcript, March 14, 1943, accessed July 13, 2017, http://rosaryhour.com/March%2014,%201943.docx.

with questions to be addressed by Figas were sorted and given to a Franciscan friar who served as Figas's secretary for such matters. The program followed a fairly consistent order of hymns, sermon, and Figas's addressing questions submitted to the "Question Box." At its peak the show drew an estimated five million listeners, though on average it consistently drew a couple million listeners a week over twenty years on the air.[19]

Hajkowski sees Figas as a figure in a larger debate over the fate of the Catholic family in mid–twentieth-century America. Many episodes related to preserving an ideal of the Catholic family in the face of threats as varied as alcoholism and communism. At the time many made comparisons between him and Coughlin. Although both broadcast from the Midwest and claimed many Catholic immigrant families among their listeners, Coughlin was far more vitriolic in professing his ideological opposition against a variety of enemies. Figas was far less popular in terms of numbers but also had a longer career. He fit among those Franciscans who used media to address an audience that was of mixed ethnicity, was patriotic, and had fidelity to a Church that hoped to balance both.

THE PADRE'S HOUR

The longest-running Franciscan radio program was also the order's most unique. On May 8, 1958, at a small radio station in Gallup, Arizona, Father Cormac Antram, OFM, began broadcasting a half-hour Gospel show called *The Padre's Hour* in both English and Navajo, the language of a great swath of his audience. Antram was the only host until illness forced him off the air in 2012. Indeed for more than fifty years—excepting an eighteen-month period when another priest stepped in for Antram—the Navajo reservation listened to the same Franciscan priest. Reporter Leo W. Banks writes: "With its fascinating mix of Catholic and Navajo traditions, the show has been an integral part of Sunday mornings on the reservation."[20] Moving among small, makeshift studios around Arizona, Antram created a dedicated, multigenerational following among the Navajo by speaking in the language and translating Catholic prayers into Navajo. "The language is so difficult, it took 10 years to be able to carry on a basic conversation," he explained. "It's a tonal language, like Chinese, so the slightest change in tone can change your meaning."[21]

---

19. Hajkowski, "Polish Immigrant Families," 88–90.

20. Leo W. Banks, "The Holy Wind Talker," *Los Angeles Times*, March 23, 2003, http://articles.latimes.com/2003/mar/23/magazine/tm-navajo12, accessed October 2, 2017.

21. Cormac Antram, quoted in Banks, "The Holy Wind Talker," *Los Angeles Times*, March 23, 2003, http://articles.latimes.com/2003/mar/23/magazine/tm-navajo12, accessed October 2, 2017.

Antram was part of the legacy of Franciscans who worked and lived and learned among the Navajo. Unlike the friars who first served St. Michael's in Arizona and edited magazines and wrote books about their missions in the Southwest, Antram was born in the Southwest. He was born James Antram on May 16, 1926 in Roswell, New Mexico. He went to public schools before entering St. Francis Seminary in 1943 and graduated from Duns Scotus College in 1950, a year after he professed solemn vows in 1949. He studied theology at Holy Family Friary in Oldenburg, Indiana, from 1950 to 1954 and was ordained a priest in June 1954 by Archbishop Paul Clarence Schulte of Indianapolis.[22] Antram served many Navajo missions in New Mexico and Arizona, including St. Michael's and St. Francis in Arizona and St. Mary Mission in Tohatchi, New Mexico. In his biography of Antram, Father Ronald Walters notes that Antram was the "last of the Franciscans sent to the Navajo to become a fluent speaker of their language." He published two books, *Laborers in the Vineyard* and *Halos and Heroes*, and perhaps most significantly, he received permission from the Vatican to translate the Mass into Navajo. Befitting the program's small operation, Antram financed the radio program through small donations; in 2003 the program entailed a mere $125 per episode to produce. The Navajo translation for radio is "wind that talks," and when Antram's show traveled across the radio, it spoke a language familiar to its listeners.[23]

THE AVE MARIA HOUR

The second longest-running Franciscan radio program was *The Ave Maria Hour*, which began in 1935. By 1959 it had recorded 1,250 episodes and was carried on more than 750 stations domestically and internationally. *The Ave Maria Hour* was sponsored by the Graymoor Friars of Atonement in New York who, as Noonan observed in his 1959 lecture, created the "most truly Catholic dramatic program on the air."[24] The program remained on the air for another decade, to 1969, and dramatized stories from the Bible for more than thirty-five years, with professional actors playing the roles of religious characters. Founded by Father Anselm de Pasca, SA, the program dramatized the lives of Catholic saints in half-hour shows. According to Dunne, who was the director of the program by 1959, *The Ave Maria Hour* was successful from the first broadcast in April 1935, generating "more than 1,000 letters" a week.[25]

---

22. Ronald Walters, OFM, "Cormac Antram, OFM: 1926–2013," *Padre's Trail* 27 (October 2013): 7.
23. Ibid.; Banks, "Holy Wind Talker."
24. Noonan, "Achievements of the Friars," 99.
25. Dunne, "Radio and the Franciscan Message," 117.

The program's popularity paid for a large part of the operating expense of St. Christopher's Inn, a shelter for homeless and destitute men at Graymoor, and promoted the missionary work of the friars around the nation and world. The friars viewed the radio program as an evangelizing tool, helping to "break down some of the prejudice and misunderstanding many people have about our Faith."[26] As evidence of their success, Dunne quoted a letter from a young woman who wrote to the friars in July 1958: "I'm seventeen years old. But if it wasn't for your 'Ave Maria Hour,' I wouldn't be a Catholic—nor would my Mother and Sister," she confessed. The power of the dramatic recreations on the show had made her and her family avid listeners and later converts. She wrote, "I entered the Sisters of the Visitation, a cloistered group of nuns. I remember before my conversion I used to say lengthy prayers and would end by saying 'And if possible, God, God bless you.' Now instead I say, 'God bless the Graymoor Friars.'"[27]

The Graymoor friars' close proximity to New York City and its abundance of dramatic talent was crucial to the success of the *The Ave Maria Hour*. Dunne explained that he and his predecessors traveled to New York City each week to produce an episode of the show with actors who were members of the American Federation of Television and Radio Artists, a union that began in the wake of the 1935 National Labor Relations Act. Indeed the friars worked with all professional talent, from the actors to directors to the technical staff and musicians. In 1959 the show was recorded in a studio in Manhattan and then was sent to Connecticut for the final cut, after which 175 copies of the program would be sent to Graymoor for distribution to radio stations. Like *The Hour of St. Francis* and its productive relationship with Hollywood talent, *The Ave Maria Hour* benefited from the generosity of Broadway and television talent in New York City, including Bret Morrison, who was famous as the voice of *The Shadow*. But such talent was only as good as the material they had to work with. Writing the programs, Dunne admitted, was among the most difficult aspects of pulling off a good show. "The problem is to find qualified writers," he asserted, "who can present that material in an up-to-date way, in an interesting, instructive and entertaining manner, while at the same time adhering closely to the Catholic theology and philosophy contained in our message."[28] Indeed during the period in which Dunne worked, American Catholics had grown far less tolerant of weak cultural expressions meant to educate and uplift rather than entertain.[29]

---

26. Dunne, "Radio and the Franciscan Message," 117.

27. Quoted in Dunne, "Radio and the Franciscan Message," 117–18.

28. Ibid., 120. See also "'Ave Maria Hour' Marks Milestone," *Airtime: Publication of the Catholic Broadcasters Association* 8 (Spring 1965): 13–14.

29. For more on the conflict over aesthetics and taste among critics who were Catholic, see Haberski, *Freedom to Offend*, 61–89.

Remarkably this program cost only $90,000 a year. Yet the cost, relative to the expense of commercial media, was nonetheless substantial for the friars, who bore it almost alone. Other Catholic programs, most notably Sheen's *Life Is Worth Living*, had sponsors who carried the cost of production. The lack of funding for programs clearly posed a significant problem, as did another equally influential factor—taste. Dunne recounted that at the eleventh annual convention of Catholic broadcasters, Arthur H. Hayes, president of CBS Radio at the time, told the audience that "many religious and educational radio and TV programs today are 'three-D—dull, drab and dreary' and that the situation is due 'partly to an unwillingness of persons like yourselves to invest in progress which will compete honestly with commercial programs.'"[30]

Though Dunne had identified many problems that plagued Franciscan electronic media, by 1960 a new wrinkle seriously affected the way religious programs filled airtime. From 1934 through 1960 stations operated under a congressionally mandated obligation to broadcast "in the public interest." From the start of this policy, stations fulfilled that obligation by hosting religious programs. In the 1930s most radio networks decided—as historian William Fore explains—"to give time to the largest representative bodies which would speak on behalf of all religions. These groups were the National Council of Catholic Bishops, the Federal Council of Churches, and a coalition of three national Jewish organizations." Throughout the early post–World War II period, this was how many Franciscan programs found free airtime. The policy extended to television in the 1950s as it became a common appliance in homes. "The FCC gave 'public interest credit' to the networks and their stations for providing free time," Fore writes. "In fact, the networks themselves actually paid for the program production." But then in 1960 the Federal Communications Commission (FCC) ruled that local stations could begin to sell airtime and still receive public interest credit. The new policy favored those religious groups with the ability to raise funds to buy airtime, effectively dismantling the arrangement that had allowed a balance among the so-called big three faiths (Catholicism, Protestantism, and Judaism) since the 1930s. Fore notes that before the FCC ruling, "53% of all religious broadcasting was paid-time. But by 1977, paid-time religious broadcasting has risen to 92%." That shift had implications for most of Franciscan electronic media. In 1969 the increasing costs to produce the shows and, more significantly, to buy airtime forced *The Ave Maria Hour* to cease operations. However, today the Friars of Atonement run a website that allows listeners to access rebroadcasts of many programs produced by *The Ave Maria Hour*.[31]

---

30. Dunne, "Radio and the Franciscan Message," 124, quoting Arthur H. Hayes.
31. William F. Fore, "The Unknown History of Televangelism," *Media Development* (January 2007), https://www.religion-online.org/article/the-unknown-history-of-

THE HOUR OF ST. FRANCIS

For anyone paying attention to the power of media, radio had demonstrated the capacity to bring religion to millions of people. Religious historian Philip Goff reminds us that Charles and Grace Fuller's radio broadcast, the *Old Fashioned Revival Hour*, reached an estimated twenty million listeners in the United States and abroad. Goff notes, "At its height during World War II, [the Fullers' show] surpassed in popularity virtually every show on American radio."[32] Protestants in the United States had a variety of radio shows to choose from such as the Chicago Sunday Evening Club, as well as shows by evangelical Protestants such as the Fullers and Aimee Semple McPherson.[33] Thus it should not be surprising that Father Felix Pudlowski, OFM, a missionary to tribes in the Southwest, Third Order director of St. Joseph's Fraternity in Los Angeles, and a priest from the Santa Barbara Province, came to create another radio program to spread the Franciscan message: *The Hour of St. Francis.*

The Hour of St. Francis began as a mere fifteen-minute radio program on December 15, 1946.[34] The *Franciscan Herald and Forum* reported: "The program has been excellently prepared by our Los Angeles fraternity. Our local directors have arranged radio time and are setting up the machinery to take care of the correspondence that will naturally result from a program of this kind. But the success of the entire attempt," Hegener and his fellow editors reminded readers, "rests largely with you, the individual Tertiaries."[35] Many in the friar community had come to terms with the need to address, if not employ, the machinery of the electronic age—if only in service to a message with ancient but timeless resonance. Twenty years later another article from the *Herald and Forum* noted: "If ever a man needed a microphone and a TV screen, that man was St. Francis of Assisi. He burned with ambition to shout the good news of the Gospel from every street corner and crossroads

---

televangelism/reprinted at http://www.religion-online.org/showarticle.asp?title=3369 (March 2014); see "Ave Maria Hour: Enjoyed by Millions Since 1935," Franciscan Friars of the Atonement, accessed July 13, 2017, https://www.atonementfriars.org/communications_and_online_media/the_ave_maria_hour.html. Accessed, October 7, 2017.

32. Philip Goff, "'We Have Heard the Joyful Sound': Charles E. Fuller's Radio Broadcast and the Rise of Modern Evangelicalism," *Religion and American Culture: A Journal of Interpretation* 9 (Winter 1999): 67.

33. Michael Stamm, "Broadcasting Mainline Protestantism: The Chicago Sunday Evening Club and the Evolution of Audience Expectations from Radio to Television," *Religion and American Culture: A Journal of Interpretation* 22, no. 2 (Summer 2002), 233–64; Matthew Avery Sutton, *Aimee Semple McPherson and the Resurrection of Christian America* (Cambridge: Harvard University Press, 2009).

34. Karl Holtsnider, "History of the Hour of St. Francis and Franciscan Communications" (unpublished manuscript, 2012), 2.

35. "The Hour of St. Francis," *Franciscan Herald and Forum* 26 (January 1947): 29.

in the universe. But on foot and by voice alone, he could only cover a corner of his world."[36]

The Hour of St. Francis had a rather humble, though geographically significant, beginning. In 1946 Pudlowski had tried leading discussions about St. Francis in a hotel in downtown Los Angeles. But as Karl Holtsnider explains, "Working against him was the downtown location." Holtsnider had been a teacher at St. Elizabeth High School in Oakland and St. Anthony's in Santa Barbara and had also served as secretary of the Santa Barbara Province. He became one of the most significant members of a team of Franciscans who built the radio and television programs. Pudlowski, according to Holtsnider, figured that most people did not want to hang around Los Angeles when they could be driving the many miles home. So if Pudlowski couldn't keep the people near him, he would meet them in their homes. He contacted KGER, a radio station based in Long Beach, California, and with the financial help of lay Franciscans he began buying time for the short radio program that became *The Hour of St. Francis*.[37]

The original *Hour of St. Francis* played at decidedly unpopular times on Sunday mornings in a fifteen-minute time slot. Pudlowski typically conducted discussions about Franciscanism with a guest or other broadcast entertainment—music or a play. Within the first year he entered semiretirement due to poor health, leaving the door open for Father Hugh Noonan to transfer from Santa Barbara to Los Angeles. Noonan came to *The Hour of St. Francis* as a friar who had some experience with a radio program at an army camp in Trinidad. Noonan was a poet and former professor of English at St. Anthony's Seminary. His training led him to consider a different format for a radio program, one that emphasized his own background and used the extraordinary talent around him. Holtsnider explains that despite some initial trouble with "amateur" talent (i.e., other friars), Noonan worked on professionalizing his productions, entreating Fred Niblo Jr., the son of a famous Hollywood producer and director and an accomplished screenwriter in his own right, to help. Noonan also hired Pedro de Cordoba, a well-regarded Hollywood actor, to play St. Francis. From a studio in St. Joseph Catholic High School in Los Angeles, *The Hour of St. Francis* began to grow and get noticed.[38]

Noonan and his staff took care to line up support for *The Hour of St. Francis*. First, they campaigned for support from Church officials as well as fellow friars to publicize the program. Next, in October 1946 Archbishop John T. Cantwell of Los Angeles gave Noonan his official "approval and blessing" for *The Hour of St. Francis*, wishing it "wide influence of good through-

---

36. "The Hour of St. Francis," *Franciscan Herald and Forum* 44 (February 1965): 3.
37. Holtsnider, 1.
38. Ibid., 2.

out the country."³⁹ In the secular press, such as the *Los Angeles Times*, Noonan publicized the program as first a series of "dramatic sketches . . . written and produced by radio experts . . . with all professional casts." The initial press release promoted the involvement of Niblo and de Corboda and announced the first run of fifty-nine consecutive weeks broadcast over fifty-three stations. Announcing the Third Order of St. Francis as the show's sponsors, Noonan made clear that the program was "non-commercial . . . and unique in that it is designed to bring the impact of the Franciscan way of life to the modern world."⁴⁰ In the *Tertiary*, a newsletter for Third Order friars published by the Sacred Heart Province in Quincy, Illinois, *The Hour of St. Francis* received special coverage: "When news of this entirely new type of Catholic radio broadcast came to the notice of the Director, the Officers of your Fraternity were immediately informed and they, in your name, agreed enthusiastically to promote this program through proper planning and financing." The announcement noted that the episodes would be both "Franciscan . . . in general and Third Order of St. Francis in particular" as well as professionally produced. Echoing the line Noonan wanted to project in the early stages of the project, the *Tertiary* also emphasized that *The Hour of St. Francis* intended to attract Catholics and non-Catholics alike and that a duty of the tertiaries was to promote the program to build support for its syndication.⁴¹

The crucial next step was exposure. In literature sent to tertiaries to justify the expense of the program, the staff of *The Hour of St. Francis* explained that the program was to appear on forty-seven stations, though fewer actually launched the program on the target date of December 15, 1946. *The Hour of St. Francis* did catch a couple breaks. Figas agreed to give *The Hour of St. Francis* part of the time allotted to his own radio program, *The Rosary Hour*, which played on twenty-nine of the stations with which Noonan had negotiated. Other stations also signed on early, including WEAI in west central Illinois, which became the first official station outside Los Angeles to run the program—something it continued to do for the "entire fifteen years of its radio life."⁴² Noonan and his staff also made an effort to illustrate the immediate support the program had generated by reproducing excerpts from letters

39. Archbishop John T. Cantwell to Rev. Hugh Noonan, OFM, October 23, 1946, in clippings file, box 1, *The Hour of St. Francis*, in the Franciscan Communications Collection, Santa Barbara Province Archives, Santa Barbara, CA (hereafter Franciscan Communications).
40. Memo to radio editor, *Los Angeles Times*, December 9, 1946, in clippings file, box 1, *The Hour of St. Francis*, Franciscan Communications.
41. Father Ralph Scherrer, OFM, "The Hour of St. Francis," *The Tertiary* no. 18 (December 15, 1946), in clippings file, box 1, *The Hour of St. Francis*, Franciscan Communications.
42. Holtsnider, "History of the Hour," 3.

of approval received from Church officials, including the archbishops of Los Angeles, New Orleans, and Fort Wayne, and from members of the Third Order.[43]

Noonan made clear to his fellow Franciscans how crucial it was for as many of them as possible to make direct, personal contact with radio stations to promote the booking of *The Hour of St. Francis*. In a memo sent during the first few months of production, Noonan advised: "You have to go directly to the station, with plenty of ammunition of enthusiasm and conviction. Then you have to show them by actual test—by audition, that is, that 'The Hour of St. Francis' has as great an appeal as any religious program on the air." Noonan acknowledged that such forthright salesmanship might be a new endeavor for his audience, so he offered a few pointers. Demonstrating his educational background, Noonan had the recipients of his memo consider how to pitch the show through intrinsic and extrinsic motivations. Among the former Noonan emphasized the positive, wholesome nature of the episodes, intended to appeal to "all types of listeners"—not just Catholics, and not just for the benefit of "the three Franciscan Orders." As extrinsic motivations, Noonan suggested that his fellow Franciscans emphasize the need for stations to provide this public service by broadcasting programs from all faiths, stating that "'The Hour of St. Francis,' like St. Francis himself, appeals to non-Catholics as well as to Catholics" and so might appeal to stations that already aired another Catholic program. Moreover, any station that aired the program would get publicity for doing so in parish newspapers and announcements. Finally Noonan told his fellow friars to emphasize that *The Hour of St. Francis* could help the reputation of radio stations by contrasting the destructiveness of popular culture with the moral betterment these programs were supposed to deliver—"show the strong, frightening tendencies of our day," he wrote, and remind the station managers of the way that radio programs often received blame for "aiding and abetting these tendencies rather than combating them."[44]

However, like criticisms leveled at the priests who edited *St. Anthony Messenger*, *The Hour of St. Francis* also had critics who wondered why it didn't "confine itself to stories about St. Francis and other saints." In other words some found it inappropriate for the program to expand into social issues that had few direct references to Church doctrine. In a press release sent to Franciscan magazines, Noonan addressed this question: "For an answer, we go back to the original purpose of the program—to help solve modern problems

---

43. "St. Francis on the Airways," in file "Press Clippings and Releases," box 1, *The Hour of St. Francis*, Franciscan Communications.

44. Hugh Noonan, memo on *The Hour of St. Francis*, n.d., in file "Press Clippings and Releases," box 1, *The Hour of St. Francis*, Franciscan Communications.

in the spirit of St. Francis. The people with problems are not only Catholics, but non-Catholics. . . . We realize that those outside the fold also need the solid truth and high ideals of St. Francis." If any approach could unify Franciscans' use of various media, it was this "middle of the road" approach, as Noonan called it, to address modern life. "St. Francis did not confine his care entirely to the three Orders he founded," Noonan explained. "He spoke to [people] first in the universal language of sympathy, understanding and love; he helped them discover the basic truth that they were the children of God and meant for heaven; and then he led them gently to see that the Church held all the treasure of peace and certainty for which they were searching." Holding to this line did not make *The Hour of St. Francis* or other Franciscan media especially highbrow or partisan; rather than view people by religious denomination or by political and ideological shades, Franciscan media appealed to their basic, common humanity. It was an attempt to make Franciscan media popular as well as Catholic.[45]

With some success in signing up stations, Noonan needed shows to send to the stations. As a movie screenwriter Niblo could write drama, but he did not naturally write in the Franciscan voice. However, because Niblo could not type, Noonan hired Juanita Vaughn, a Third Order volunteer and a lay Franciscan, to be the script assistant. After Noonan asked her to try writing a script, she rapidly became one of the key writers for the series.[46] Along with Vaughn, Father Terrence Cronin, OFM, a friar who helped run the Franciscan Serra Retreat house in Malibu, California, also contributed to developing stories. Noonan wrote for *The Hour of St. Francis*, as did Pat Kelly, manager of the Los Angeles radio station WKFI and also the first moderator of the program.

Most remarkable, though, was Vaughn's contribution. She later told Harrington that she wrote nearly four hundred radio scripts during her time with *The Hour of St. Francis*. In the first half of 1948 *The Hour of St. Francis* produced forty-six scripts, of which Vaughn personally wrote thirty-one.[47] That output would have been extraordinary over almost any period, but Vaughn and the other writers had to produce two new stories every week to fill both sides of the sixteen-inch discs used to record the programs. In the days before audiotapes, the discs were sent to radio stations around the country (and the world) to fill fifteen minutes of airtime two times a week. Holtsnider recalls that the pressure to produce stories took a toll on the staff, and presumably most acutely on Juanita Vaughn. Sometimes, though, *The Hour of St. Francis*

45. Hugh Noonan, "Middle of the Road," n.d., in file "Press Clippings and Releases," box 1, *The Hour of St. Francis*, Franciscan Communications.

46. Holtsnider, "History of the Hour," 4.

47. Jeremy Harrington, "Television: The Men of the Hour," *St. Anthony Messenger* 73 (September 1965): 25; Library of Congress, *Catalog of Copyright Entries*, third series, vol. 2, part 2, no. 1 (Washington, DC: Government Printing Office, January–June 1948), 52.

received scripts unsolicited in the mail. For example, "in an envelope bearing a Philippine stamp, [Noonan] found a script sent in by a Jesuit missionary, Father J.B. Reuter. . . . It was one of the most popular stories ever recorded."[48]

As the staff accumulated an extensive list of scripts and the program built a following, Noonan also realized that listeners did not mind and even often requested repeated broadcasts of their favorite stories. Based on letters and feedback from radio stations, the staff began running episodes that seemed to be audience favorites, including one written by Noonan himself from his time as an army chaplain called "Goodbye, Soldier"; according to Holtsnider it had more than three thousand requests for copies of the script.[49]

"Goodbye Soldier" was recorded as the eighteenth program in series five, with each series containing around forty original scripts. The program hired actor Robert Ryan to play a veteran soldier who upon his return home must face the impending commission of his younger brother. Like all of these episodes, this one would have been introduced with dramatic organ music and a voice-over from Pat Kelly:

> With the timeliness of tomorrow's headline and the impact of a familiar name on a casualty list, "The Hour of St. Francis" brings its listeners Robert Ryan in the role of a returned soldier [announcer then included the station's name]. While his younger brother gets ready to leave for the armed forces, Steve O'Donnell travels in memory down the hard road which began for him the day he stood with one foot on the step of a train, and his watching family could think of nothing to say. The fear of what may happen to his brother grows in Steve's mind until his concern reaches a climax which will touch the heart of everyone who had ever said "Goodbye" to a young soldier.[50]

Produced in the wake of the Second World War, the episode reflects the conflicted memories of the Second World War, dealing with the demons from fighting the war and struggling with the difficult integration back into society. This particular episode echoed themes in *The Best Years of Our Lives*, one of the most popular films of the early postwar years because it somewhat romantically, though quite honestly, addressed issues faced by soldiers returning home. The fact that "Goodbye, Soldier" resembles a Hollywood film about the war is not surprising. The episode that had launched *The Hour of St. Francis* was "The Vagrant," written by Niblo. Like "Goodbye, Soldier," "The

---

48. Holtsnider, "History of the Hour," 3. Father Kenneth Henriques introduced the first taping system to *The Hour of St. Francis* in 1950.

49. "Goodbye Soldier," *The Hour of St. Francis* (radio program), series 5, episode 18, in *The Hour of St. Francis* Collection, Franciscan Communications; see also Holtsnider, 3.

50. "Goodbye Soldier"; "All Manner of Men," *Franciscan Herald and Forum* 44 (April 1965): 68.

Vagrant" story too resembles *The Best Years of Our Lives*, as it portrays a veteran who experiences trouble returning to life after the war, mainly because his wife has left him. He becomes a vagrant and a drunk but encounters a friar who introduces him to the spirit of St. Francis of Assisi. Because *The Hour of St. Francis* began airing in the early postwar period, many episodes dealt with World War II and the difficulty soldiers had adjusting to life at home. And just like *The Best Years of Our Lives*, many scripts for the show also came from accounts published in magazines and newspapers.[51]

Of course well-known aspects of the life of St. Francis served as the basis for episodes as well. For example, in the first series of scripts, episode twenty-six, titled "St. Francis Finds the Way," recounts parables from the life of St. Francis as recorded by his followers—"The Little Flowers of St. Francis." Similarly, "Poor Man's Gold" portrays "the effect of St. Francis's generosity on the life of Father Sylvester, preoccupied with building a church." But much more common than stories from the life of St. Francis were stories, as the series announcer often intoned, that brought "the ideals of St. Francis into contact with basic human problems, for which his ideals have a strikingly simple solution."[52]

It is hard not to be impressed by what the *The Hour of St. Francis* packed into fifteen-minute episodes. In episode five of the first series, titled "Marriage Can Work," the narrator asks: "Modern marriage—can it really be made to work?" The episode suggests a timeless answer to the problems of any couple—in this case "Harry and Virginia"—who treat marriage as something far less serious than a sacrament. Virginia realizes that her marriage is part of a long tradition that has roots and meaning beyond contemporary influences such as materialism and transient passion.[53] Other episodes deal with juvenile delinquency ("the fast-moving script relates how the life of a leader of a boy gang was vitally changed when he came into contact with the spirit of St. Francis of Assisi") and materialism ("the descent [of a banker] on the economic scale leaves him richest when he has nothing [which] makes the narrative paradoxically dramatic.") The show even dealt with euthanasia—in "The Ways of God," a doctor described by the narrator as an advocate of "doing away with the incurables, insane, and cripples" finds his ideals tested when he "delivers a crippled infant, the tenth child of a poverty-stricken tenement family.[54] With great reluctance, he starts the baby breathing, ushering him into life which has apparently no purpose but suffering. [Later] the boy reap-

---

51. "The Way Home," *Time* 44 (August 7, 1944): 15–16.
52. *The Hour of St. Francis* (radio program) episodes, in file "Press Clippings and Releases," box 1, *The Hour of St. Francis*, Franciscan Communications. Specific episodes of *The Hour of St. Francis* cited hereafter come from this archive.
53. "Marriage Can Work" *The Hour of St. Francis* (radio program), series 1, episode 5.
54. "The Ways of God," *The Hour of St. Francis* (radio program), series 3, episode 20.

pears in Doctor Martin's life, under circumstances which cause the doctor to wonder for the first time if the ways of God are not wiser than the judgments of men." In a similar vein, but with a different message, "Dream for My Daughter" depicts a father who has to come to terms with the fact that his daughter must "struggle to lead a normal life. Then his daughter tells him of her dream, a cherished ambition which brings the father to the point of thanking God for making his daughter different."[55]

Some scripts seemed to stay in step with the ideological temper of the times. An episode titled "Trouble with the Union" cast a communist union member as the skeptical witness to a "non-union 'miracle.'"[56] That script might have been more timely in the middle of the Great Depression, because by the late 1940s most unions had purged whatever residual influence the American Communist Party had had. In an episode on the fear of the atomic bomb, called "Brother Atom," St. Francis helps two atomic scientists make sense of their ethical obligations to humanity.[57] "Dark Journey," a story based on an article from *PM Magazine*, addresses the problem of segregation head-on by depicting the prejudice African Americans experience throughout their lives. The story follows a little boy who first encounters racism on a segregated bus and grows up to encounter prejudice and segregation in housing, work, and even religion. The episode ends with the now grown man observing his own young boy encountering the same expressions of racism that have thwarted him—"the same cloud darken[s] the life of his young son."[58] In "Promise Me Tomorrow," a "modern woman," Mrs. Cora Blake, stands in for all listeners who let "trivial activities" replace "worthwhile accomplishments" while fate lurks, in this story, literally around the corner. The story reaches its climax when Cora is struck and killed by a car whose driver has been, like her, busily going about business in a state of dire obliviousness.[59] *The Hour of St. Francis* criticized lapsed Catholics in "Out of the Depths,"[60] warned of the implications of the Supreme Court case *Everson v. Board of Education* (1947) in "They Never Told Me,"[61] and dismissed secularism in "Only the Fool."[62]

---

55. "Dream for My Daughter," *The Hour of St. Francis* (radio program), series 4, episode 12.

56. "Trouble with the Union," *The Hour of St. Francis* (radio program), series 1, episode 9

57. "Brother Atom," *The Hour of St. Francis* (radio program), series 1, episode 11.

58. "Dark Journey," *The Hour of St. Francis* (radio program), series 2, episode 16.

59. "Promise Me Tomorrow," *The Hour of St. Francis* (radio program), series 2, episode 20.

60. "Out of the Depths," *The Hour of St. Francis* (radio program), series 2, episode 21.

61. "They Never Told Me," *The Hour of St. Francis* (radio program), series 2, episode 22; see also *Everson v. Board of Education of the Township of Ewing*, 330 US 1 (1947).

62. "Only the Fool," *The Hour of St. Francis* (radio program), series 2, episode 25.

A good number of these scripts came from material already published. Danny Thomas starred in one called "Our Lady's Juggler," based on a French tale about a juggler who "gives thanks for a favorable answer to prayer by performing his tricks before a statue of the Blessed Virgin, with astonishing results."[63] The script for "The Last Sermon"—about the life of a beloved priest in an English port village—was taken from the opening chapter of *The Dry Wood* by Caryll Houslander.[64] Henry Wadsworth Longfellow's poem "Robert of Sicily" was transformed into a fifteen-minute script titled "King Robert of Sicily."[65] "I Met a Miracle" retells the story of John Traynor, a disabled veteran from the First World War who became a testament to the miraculous waters of Lourdes.[66] Other stories recounted the real-life experiences of Franciscan missionaries in China and southeast Asia ("Mission of Blood") or stories from popular magazines such as *Reader's Digest* and *Collier's*.[67] Overall many scripts challenged listeners to consider the assumptions they made about their own lives and their daily struggles and at least suggested that they might find a way to witness their own humanity and that of others in those struggles.

An especially poignant example of this mission radiates from the episode "Welcome Home, Soldier." [68] Jack Webb—who starred in the famous television show *Dragnet*—narrates a story about a disabled war veteran who comes back to his country following deployment during the Korean War. The program notes for the episode invite radio stations to tell listeners that they should ask all soldiers for forgiveness. "We, even more than the enemy, are responsible for what has happened to you," Webb intones. The episode unfolds as a remarkable critique of the social nature of war. It begins with Webb reading an open letter to Private Thomas T. Williams, a soldier who has lost parts of both arms and legs from frostbite because he had to crawl across a frozen lake after being wounded in battle. The script casts Williams as "an idea . . . a symbol. You're our conscience and our pride." Webb states that while Americans love to revere the Unknown Soldier, we need to face the known soldier—the one who will never again walk, drive a car, jump a fence, or "hold his girl in his arms." The episode asked Americans to realize that the Korean War was part of a collection of mistakes made by the nation, from "conference rooms and business offices to houses in restricted residential districts to the

---

63. "Our Lady's Juggler," *The Hour of St. Francis* (radio program), series 2, episode 14.

64. "The Last Sermon," *The Hour of St. Francis* (radio program), series 2, episode 18.

65. "King Robert of Sicily," *The Hour of St. Francis* (radio program), series 2, episode 19.

66. "I Met a Miracle," *The Hour of St. Francis* (radio program), series 2, episode 23.

67. "Mission of Blood," *The Hour of St. Francis* (radio program), series 3, episode 9.

68. "Welcome Home, Soldier," *The Hour of St. Francis* (radio program), series 5, episode 28.

slums." Williams is the product, so says the script, of a society too callous to care about the poor and too racist to see a contradiction in denying a black man the right to eat with white people but finding him American enough to die for the nation in Korea. The episode concludes with a meditation on sacrifice that forces listeners to consider their personal responsibility for veterans such as Williams. Williams reflects the kind of unselfish sacrifice that also made the death of Jesus transcend place, time, and the individual, the script intimated. Just as those who bore witness to Jesus's death shared a collective guilt, so too do Americans bear responsibility for the horrors of war. Among the last voices in the episode is a mother who says: "Am I going to let this happen to my boy?" The episode ends with a plea for peace.

The episode raised a question about the role religion played in understanding the meaning of sacrifice in the Cold War. Americans had a long tradition of finding national meaning through war; they believed killing and dying happened for noble ends, whether that be freedom from Great Britain, the end of slavery, or the defeat of fascism. The Korean War posed a different problem: the story of Thomas Williams suggested that while most Americans at the time believed in the struggle against an international communist enemy they also came to rue the Korean War—as polls showed that a majority of Americans did by 1953. As American fortunes in the war rose and fell in the fighting, the danger of escalation into a larger, global conflict scared many people around the world. Moreover, the failure to find a path to victory influenced President Harry S. Truman's decision not to run for president in 1952, just as it pushed President Dwight Eisenhower to make his own run, promising to "go to Korea" to bring an end to the war. In an era when religious leaders helped Americans interpret the Cold War and its hotter moments, many wondered what the Korean War meant.[69]

On the face of it the Korean War pushed Americans closer to God in new ways, so one might interpret "Welcome Home, Soldier" by looking inward to face one's own sinful nature. Jason Stevens argues in his book *God-Fearing and Free* that "America's image at mid-twentieth century was becoming a chastened adult's, his visage weathered by the sight of Europe, no longer so far-off, its blight forcing the once callow youth to look inward for his own sin." Unlike the episode about Thomas Williams, though, Stevens observes that the collective guilt created by the evils of war transformed America's role as a biblical agent. "His innocence," Stevens writes, referring to a chastened, matured America, "would no longer identify the nation with the revelation of Christ, as the second Adam, Adam reborn from History, but with the outgrown illusions of a purity never possessed. Adam was now a tragic hero bear-

---

69. Haberski, *God and War*, 37–39.

ing History as his cross."[70] Indeed other scholars also find the period around the Korean War as one that hardened or coarsened American theology, using religion's "spiritual weapons" in the Cold War and fostering an acceptance of technocratic expertise to grapple with, and largely make peace with, materialism and the darkness of human nature.[71]

Yet, in no uncertain terms, *The Hour of St. Francis* connected the guilt Americans ought to share for the sacrifices made by soldiers to the sacrifice in the Crucifixion of Christ—the Korean War neither redeemed American faith in its struggle against communism nor stripped the nation of its innocence, but rather revealed an unsettling truth about making appeals to a God who sacrificed his only son. When the mother in the episode asks whether she would let her son go to war, the script does not question her patriotism, nor does it implicate her as a communist sympathizer. Rather it relates her honest reflection to a wholesale questioning of the kind of society that treats its sons as sacrifices. A sacrifice for what? the program appears to ask. For the materialism that creates gross disparities of wealth? Or for a racism that divides people who are equal in war but unequal in peace? Unlike the war-hardened theologies and uses of religion that characterized America's spiritual Cold War, *The Hour of St. Francis* reminded listeners that religious witness might also pose a profound challenge to war.[72]

Judging by excerpts of letters reprinted in the *Franciscan Herald and Forum, The Hour of St. Francis* seemed to strike the right balance between sentimentality and religiosity. It appealed to people on different levels by dealing with issues that had contemporary relevance and historical significance in ways that made the religious message more accessible to the audience. And according to the magazine, at least one-third of that audience was made up of non-Catholics.[73] The program received hundreds of letters, most asking for scripts, and many praising various aspects of episodes. When Noonan and later Father Kenneth Henriques, OFM, sent letters to provinces asking for financial support, they often included excerpts from such letters. One letter from New York read: "My daughter, my son, and I listen to your program every Sunday morning. We find it very inspiring and you give us much food

---

70. Stevens, *God-Fearing and Free*, 8.

71. See T. Jeremy Gunn, *Spiritual Weapons: The Cold War and the Forging of an American National Religion* (Westport, CT: Praeger, 2009), 8; Eugene McCarraher, *Christian Critics: Religion and the Impasse in Modern American Social Thought* (Ithaca, NY: Cornell University Press, 2000), 89–119.

72. The best, most comprehensive book on debates over images and meanings of those images of soldiers as sacrifices is Jonathan H. Ebel, *G.I. Messiahs: Soldiering, War, and American Civil Religion* (New Haven, CT: Yale University Press, 2015), especially 1–24.

73. "All Manner of Men," 68.

for contemplation and discussion, and bring us nearer to God. This morning's program was most helpful to me spiritually." Another from Texas said: "This program, 'Because I Was Ambitious,' was most stirring and appealing, and I want to tell it to my Junior Department of girls and boys at Sunday School." And as an illustration of the ecumenical appeal of *The Hour*, an administrator of a Methodist congregation in Iowa wrote to say: "Thank you for the copy of 'Our Lady of the Americas,' which I enjoyed so very much as I heard it. Is it possible to become a member of a permanent mailing list? I am sincerely interested in anything about St. Francis and the good that continues through the centuries because of him." An officer from West Point thought the program did good "for God and country," and a woman who ran a Methodist Sunday school program in Mississippi wrote that it helped her teach about Christian democracy.[74]

With stations providing free airtime—that is, all stations who were required to allot public service time—great pressure was on Noonan to raise money to produce episodes for his growing list of stations. But the demand for episodes depended on other Franciscans voting to support their production. Amazingly, according to Holtsnider, the early fate of *The Hour of St. Francis* came down to a single vote at the lay Franciscan national congress in 1947, at which the conservative president of the organization made clear that radio programs had little to do with the mission of St. Francis and that he therefore did not approve of sending money from his organization to the production of radio plays. For Noonan the popular opinion of the group held his only hope for revenue. He proposed to have each professed member pay fifty cents to fund the production of the episodes. Amid procedural wrangling and political machinations, the members took a vote and by a small margin approved Noonan's plan. As Holtsnider describes, the need for funding was acute—the initial budget depended on the charity of very few Third Order donations and a special loan of one thousand dollars from the Franciscan Fathers of California. After this consequential vote, the central offices of the Third Order provinces supported an increase in funding for *The Hour*. Quite rapidly the program moved from being hosted by a handful of stations to airing on five hundred stations across the continental United States and a few stations overseas, including in India. By 1961 *The Hour* could claim more than four hundred scripts and was heard on more than five hundred radio stations.[75]

In addition to the initial fifty-cent fee on members of the Third Order to finance *The Hour of St. Francis*, friars of the First Order also contributed. So

---

74. Letters included in Rev. Kenneth Henriques, OFM, letter to Friends of *The Hour of St. Francis*, January 26, 1951, in file 2, "Correspondence," box 1, *The Hour of St. Francis*, Franciscan Communications.

75. Holtsnider, 4–5.

for example, the receipts for the fifth series of the program in 1950 and 1951 generated $7,785 from First Order provinces, including Immaculate Conception in New York, St. John the Baptist in Cincinnati, and Sacred Heart in St. Louis. From the Third Order the show received $21,896, with the bulk of that revenue coming from five key provinces: the three mentioned above as well as St. Joseph Province in Detroit, and St. Barbara Province in California. Each of these provinces contributed over $1,500, with Sacred Heart collecting $7,960 and St. Joseph and St. Barbara both bringing in around $3,500 each. Thus the combined income for the fiscal year was a bit shy of $30,000 to produce *The Hour*.[76]

Over that same period *The Hour of St. Francis* spent $27,000 to produce, record, and distribute the program. The total cost to produce the program, including pay for the talent involved in the show, was $7,000; $8,000 was spent on producing the records for the show. As an indication of how lean this operation was, the total amount spent on salaries for the staff was $1,500.03; compare that figure to the fact that postage and office expenses ran to nearly $4,500. A note at the bottom of the expense records for the fifth series declared: "This surplus [of $2,753] has already been used in producing the new series, the sixth. In fact *The Hour of St. Francis* needs a greater 'cushion fund' to take care of the carry over from one series to the next. In this period it really sweats it out trying to pay bills." The accountant for *The Hour*, who was also the author of the report and that comment, was Helen Payne, who according to Holtsnider and Vaughn worked minor miracles balancing the books for *The Hour*. Payne worked a day job as the secretary-treasurer for an insurance company in Los Angeles and volunteered time to *The Hour* to supervise mailings in addition to working on the program's finances. The inability to depend on a constant income plagued the radio program from the beginning. For example the difference in contributions from the Third Order from the 1956 series to the 1957 series was nearly $6,500. While the First Order made up for that loss (and then some), those who ran *The Hour* during this time—Noonan, Henriques, and Holtsnider—spent considerable energy and time figuring out ways to raise money. That problem intensified as the show's production shifted from radio to television.[77]

Part of the magic involved in creating *The Hour of St. Francis* entailed getting talent for the show, from writers such as Niblo to musicians such as Roger

---

76. Receipts for the *Hour of St. Francis*, series 5, 1950–51, in file 3, "Financial Statements," box 1, *The Hour of St. Francis*, Franciscan Communications.

77. Expenses for *The Hour of St. Francis*, series 5, 1950–51, in file 3, "Financial Statements," box 1, *The Hour of St. Francis*, Franciscan Communications; *The Hour of St. Francis* income/expense comparisons for 1956–57 and 1957–58, in file 3, "Financial Statements," box 1, *The Hour of St. Francis*, Franciscan Communications.

Wagner and Bob Mitchell. However, the names that captured the attention of listeners were the actors. That group included many of Hollywood's and Broadway's most recognizable voices, including Ann Blyth, Rosalind Russell, Charles Laughton, Ruth Hussey, Virginia Gregg, Gene Lockhart, Peggy Webber, Ruth Perrott, Pat McGeehan, June Haver, Jack Owens, Danny Thomas, Mary Hickox, Jack Moyles, Vic Livoti, Jack Webb, Macdonald Carey, Dennis Day, Stephen McNally, Alice Drake, Jane Wyatt, Loretta Young, J. Carroll Marsh, and Frank Lovejoy. Many of these actors appeared first in the radio program and were brought back to star in original half-hour television productions when *The Hour* became a television show. Other actors, such as Jack Nicholson, appeared in episodes of the television series before they became Hollywood stars. In "The Challenge" Nicholson played a young man who decides to become a priest for reasons that shift from him looking for a challenge to accepting the happiness that he feels from his new vocation.[78]

Quite fittingly in July 1950 Noonan was elected assistant secretary and treasurer at the third national convention of the National Catholic Broadcasters (part of the International Catholic Association for Radio and Television or Unda—wave in latin). A first for the Franciscans, Noonan's elevation in this organization began a tradition in which those who worked on *The Hour of St. Francis* became part of this group.[79] The show also consistently won awards. In 1951 *The Hour* took top prize in its category at the fifteenth American Exhibition of Education Radio Programs sponsored by an institute at Ohio State University that specialized in radio and television. The program won that particular award at least three times in the 1950s. The radio series became a fixture at similar award banquets and built the foundation for a television production company.[80]

In 1950 Henriques came to help produce *The Hour of St. Francis*; by 1951, because Noonan had to step away from the program due to illness, Henriques came in to direct the radio productions. During his first year as director, he increased the number of stations playing the show to five hundred and, according to Holtsnider, "he also introduced the taping of programs, which made it easier for distributing them not only to radio stations, but also to schools, retreat houses, and other groups who wished to use them. By September 1951 . . . there were more than 1000 outlets for 'The Hour.'"

That same year *The Hour of St. Francis* took a leap and filmed a live program for television. On March 21, 1951, *The Hour* aired its first television program, an adaptation from a radio script based on a Leo Tolstoy story. The

78. "The Challenge," *The Hour of St. Francis* (television program), in file "Television Presentations," box 1, *The Hour of St. Francis*, Franciscan Communications.
79. Holtsnider, 6.
80. Ibid., 6–7.

episode was called "Michael Has Company for Coffee" and featured Wallace Ford and Lloyd Corrigan. Ford, a British-born actor, enjoyed a long career on Broadway and Hollywood and appeared in John Ford Westerns during the 1950s as one of Ford's most consistently featured character actors. Corrigan also enjoyed a long career in movies and was perhaps most famous in the 1950s for his role as the millionaire Arthur Manleder in the *Boston Blackie* films. In this episode of *The Hour*, Ford played a cobbler who, as in Tolstoy's story, turns to reading the Bible following a string of personal tragedies. He discovers God in the small acts of kindness he begins to perform as a result of reading the Gospels. Corrigan's character is one of the souls the cobbler befriends, sharing coffee on a cold day. The episode ends with the cobbler realizing that he has found God in his life through his own actions. But however successful this first episode was, aspirations for producing a television series stalled as financing and production facilities fell through. By 1955 Henriques had seen enough. Disappointed by the lack of support he received from his community, he resigned as director of *The Hour* and signed up to serve as a chaplain in the US Air Force. After his stint in military service, he enrolled at Oxford University, earned a degree in journalism, and then returned to the Santa Barbara Province, becoming the editor of *The Way/Catholic Viewpoints* magazine.[81]

Henriques's departure placed the program in limbo until Noonan returned to the position he originally held, but only for a brief time. During the mid- to late 1950s *The Hour of St. Francis* continued to produce radio episodes as new friars were brought in and tried for positions for which none, for the most part, had any training. Holtsnider became Noonan's main assistant and began to amass practical experience producing episodes for the radio show while he sifted through the backlog of episodes cataloged by another friar, the immensely capable Father Kenan Osborne, OFM. Osborne's catalog yielded a valuable source of income for *The Hour*—by organizing past radio episodes according to their topics, he enabled his colleagues to sell thousands of recordings to Catholic educators for catechetical instruction. Thus the expanse of radio episodes—more than four hundred during the first years of Holtsnider's tenure—grew into a source of Catholic media for many parishes throughout the United States.

Within its first decade *The Hour of St. Francis* grew from Pudlowski's initial idea to become a national and international program under Noonan. According to a newsletter that *The Hour* published each year, by 1956 the program had more than three hundred scripts in circulation "on every problem of human existence." The organization distributed hundreds of "scripts and peace prayers . . . each week and increased its radio distribution from the

---

81. Ibid., 7.

original station in the Midwest to 600 around the world." Outlets for the program expanded as well, into "veterans' hospitals, Army bases, colleges and universities . . . retreat houses, study clubs, parish family organizations, CYO [Catholic Youth Organization] units, and societies for retarded [sic] children." Each newsletter announced new radio stations that carried *The Hour*'s programs and quite frequently listed awards the radio program won. The success of radio productions again suggested a move into television, but the difficulty of financing the episodes remained.[82]

Noonan's health problems forced him to return to the Serra Retreat in Malibu in 1960, but he continued to help his successor, Holtsnider, at the production studio in Los Angeles. Holtsnider remembers that "almost immediately [I] discontinued production of the radio programs and plunged into the production of half-hour TV shows, based on the same idea as the radio programs." While the distribution of the radio programs continued, producing the television episodes absorbed every molecule of energy and fund-raising acumen of the friars. The first series of the program used the familiar title, *The Hour of St. Francis*, but subsequent series were released as *Search* and *The Church in the Modern World*. Holtsnider recalls that one of the short films even made the cover of *TV Guide*. With Holtsnider, Noonan, and Cronin directing as well as writing, editing, and doing generally anything else that needed to be done, the productions moved ahead with impressive speed. Among the most exotic locations where this team shot was the massive estate of William Randolph Hearst, called San Simeon. Noonan was friends with Hearst's heirs and received permission to shoot interior scenes of a film about St. Thomas More inside Hearst Castle. Up to that point, no other film crew had been allowed access to the estate.[83]

As film production developed, the contributions required to sustain the more costly production increased as well. A National Franciscan Radio Committee helped coordinate financial efforts through a $1 per capita tax each year on membership of the Third Order. The first installment of this tax brought in nearly $20,000. The total fluctuated from year to year depending on contributions from people outside the order and from the members' own ability to sustain giving. For example, in 1957 and 1958 the financial report of *The Hour of St. Francis* showed that contributions from the First Order and Third Order for television and radio productions totaled $33,955.91, with expenses totaling $36,041. Both income and expenses had increased by almost thirty percent from the previous year, and *The Hour* had amassed

---

82. For a cross-section of newsletters and other material related to the promotion of *The Hour of St. Francis* on both radio and television, see folder "Newsletters," box 1, *The Hour of St. Francis*, Franciscan Communications.
83. Holtsnider, 10–11.

almost $12,000 in cash assets from selling tapes of the radio show. In short, pushing to make films for television would bring *The Hour* to the brink of financial insolvency.[84]

The *Franciscan Herald and Forum* ran a series of articles on *The Hour of St. Francis* television films, celebrating that the production team completed "twenty-six dramatic films and gained an audience of 100,000 people in the United States and Canada" within four years. *The Hour* also won a competition at the American Film Festival in 1961 for an episode titled "The Third Devil," which took a sardonic look at materialism by imagining how the Devil, who made wealth an end itself, might attract people to hell to stabilize his economic problems there. In 1962 an animation feature, *Mary of Nazareth*, won a Golden Eagle award from the Council on International Non-Theatrical Events (CINE), "thereby becoming eligible to represent the United States in film festivals abroad." No other Franciscan outfit was producing films of the quality that emerged from the Holtsnider team.[85]

St. Anthony Messenger also spent space promoting the success of the half-hour television show, noting that "170 stations broadcast the 26 films of the first two series . . . viewed by more than 100 million Americans of all faiths . . . and seen by thousands . . . in schools, at various meetings, or on retreats."[86] *The Hour of St. Francis* television program covered topics similar to the radio show, among them choosing the priesthood, depictions of St. Francis, the trials of alcoholism, marriage, gambling, and communism. The team made episodes that could have been taken directly from the exchanges printed in *St. Anthony Messenger*, such as the television episode called "House Divided" about a marriage of a couple from different Churches "who think they have the answer to differences in religion when they promise to avoid discussing the subject. The birth of a child shows them that the question mark in their marriage is permanent."[87] An episode entitled "Keeto Begay, Navajo Boy," sounded like work chronicled in *Padre's Trail*; filmed in color to capture the Red Hills of Arizona and using an "all-Indian cast," the show sought to document "the struggles of a people torn between progress and devotion to age-old ways."[88]

The *Franciscan Herald and Forum* constituted the leading periodical of the Third Order; therefore, as a chief promoter of *The Hour of St. Francis* and

84. Ibid., 13; *The Hour of St. Francis* financial statements for 1956–57 and 1957–58, in file 3, "Financial Statements," box 1, *The Hour of St. Francis*, Franciscan Communications.

85. "The Hour of St. Francis," *Franciscan Herald and Forum* 44 (January 1965): 4–5.

86. Jeremy Harrington, "Television: The Men of the Hour," *St. Anthony Messenger* 73 (September 1965): 22.

87. "House Divided," *The Hour of St. Francis* (television program), in file "Promotional Material," box 1, *The Hour of St. Francis*, Franciscan Communications.

88. "The Hour in Navajoland," *Franciscan Herald and Forum*, 44 (May 1965), 135.

its team, the magazine made a special effort to clarify the intellectual dimensions of the radio and film productions. "While remaining entirely Catholic in philosophy," the magazine editorialized, "[*The Hour*] avoided controversial topics which could not be handled adequately in its 15 minute radio and half-hour television format. It steered clear of propagandizing. Through stories that are incisive, problem-solving, conscience-probing, wholesome and substantial, it has attracted a large following among non-Catholics as well as those of the Faith."[89] Holtsnider and his colleagues at *The Hour* hoped that the good will generated by their films and the positive publicity they received in Franciscan periodicals would help generate funding for their most ambitious scheme: building a movie studio.

In a prospectus sent to potential donors, the leaders of *The Hour of St. Francis* laid the groundwork for constructing what they imagined would be the best Catholic film studio in the world. Up to that point, the staff made films in the auditorium of St. Joseph's High School, an old Catholic school in Los Angeles that was ultimately condemned. Holtsnider and others wanted a production studio in order to get serious about film production. The appeal for funding began by framing the need for a Franciscan film studio to counter the darkness of American society: "The bland acceptance of lower moral standards, the indifference to corruption of principle, the step by step elimination of long-standing traditions and institutions are undermining our culture." *The Hour* hoped to appeal to the idea that media done right would make society better. "In 1946," the letter read, "THE HOUR OF ST. FRANCIS launched a series of dramatic 15 minute radio shows to help counteract the bad fare in entertainment, and to bring something constructive and positive into the homes of its listeners." Reflecting on both the popularity of the radio program and significant influence and reach of television, *The Hour* staff intended to provide "good theater, top production, and leading Hollywood stars [to make] dramas which appeal to everybody." The pitch was simple: fund morally wholesome programming that had access to America's Hollywood stars.[90]

And the pitch met with success. Father Edward Henriques, brother of Father Kenneth Henriques, helped Holtsnider raise $125,000 from the Raskob Foundation as the seed money for the project. Noonan, Holtsnider, and the firm of Quinn and Associates raised another $125,000 to complete the building. By the spring of 1964 the Franciscan Communications Center (FC) completed construction and officially opened with a five hundred–guest ceremony on February 10, 1965. Walter O'Keefe presided as master of ceremonies; Edward Fischer, professor of communications at the University of Notre

---

89. "The Hour of St. Francis," *Franciscan Herald and Forum* 44 (January 1965): 6.

90. Appeal to funders, n.d., in file 3, "Financial Statements," box 1, *The Hour of St. Francis*, Franciscan Communications.

Dame, delivered the keynote; and Cronin, by then the provincial of the Santa Barbara Province, was the guest of honor. Declared the first Catholic professional motion picture and television studio in the world, the new building welcomed Cardinal James Francis McIntyre, who presided over the dedication ceremony on February 14, 1965. The building had seven thousand square feet of studio floor space with 21.5-foot ceilings, a soundproof stage, 2,500 square feet of office space, and another 2,500 square feet of technical production facilities that included an art studio, script room, and makeup and dressing room.[91]

The group that gathered around *The Hour of St. Francis* were conscious of the special opportunity they had and conscientious about the work they wanted to produce. The first major project they launched was a film appreciation series in 1965, pitched as a "war on gobbledegook." This project was the first major creative endeavor undertaken in the new studio. Featured in *Variety* for undertaking "a public service that the motion picture industry should perform for its own betterment," the Franciscans joined forces with Edward Fischer, of the University of Notre Dame and the film critic for the Catholic magazine *Ave Maria*. Fischer's inclusion in this project had special significance because of his reputation as a film critic who sought to reform the traditionally prudish approach American Catholic officials had taken toward movies. For instance, in a review of Fischer's popular book, *The Screen Arts*, a critic writing for *Kirkus* described it as "a book on TV and films issued by a Catholic press [that would be] of particular interest to high school and college students, parents and teachers, at a time when the church is exercising censorship in regard to certain areas of the screen arts. This establishes a standard—a guide to appreciation—a measuring stick of taste for proper enjoyment of the film media. He contends that the moral problem here relates more to time-wasting and to saturating oneself with inartistic fare than with isolated offensive sequences flashed on the screen."[92] In other words, Fischer and his Franciscan partners sought to improve the reputation of Catholic movie criticism through the medium itself.[93]

However, by the 1960s the Vatican encouraged marshaling the power of mass communication to engage the faithful who were, when not in Church, the audience for electronic media. Yet the work of the people attached to FC

---

91. Holtsnider, "History of the Hour," 14. See also "Hour of St. Francis: War on Gobbledegook," *Airtime* 7 (Autumn 1964): 38–40; Frank Scully, "The Hour of St. Francis," *Catholic Digest* (October 1961), in file 5, "Pamphlets, Brochures, *Airtime Magazine*," The Hour Collection; "The Hour of St. Francis Television," in file "Television Presentations," The Hour Collection.

92. https://www.kirkusreviews.com/book-reviews/edward-fischer-3/the-screen-arts-2//.

93. "The 'Hour' in *Variety*," *Franciscan Herald and Forum* 44 (June 1965): 194–95; "Hour of St. Francis," *Airtime* 7 (Autumn 1964): 38–40.

had irony at its core: while expressly attempting to make good (meaning high-quality) films, the organization also wanted to make and at times was requested to make good (meaning pious) films. For example, they made at least two films at the behest of Citizens for Decent Literature (CDL), an organization that took over when the Legion of Decency no longer had relevance or power. Though it was not an overtly censoring body like the Legion, the CDL aggressively policed media for works that it deemed harmful and assumed their findings should apply to all so-called decent Americans. While FC did not become an agent of the CDL, it did hope to "show people what goes into making a film worthwhile."[94] In retrospect Holtsnider acknowledged that while *The Hour of St. Francis* "did several films for them [CDL], the [studio] eventually broke with them because of philosophical differences." "They were extremely conservative," Holtsnider added, "and 'The Hour' preferred to work on more liberal materials, with a social consciousness." Meanwhile other partnerships with outside groups included the Franciscan Missionary Union for the Cincinnati province.[95]

So even though FC did not necessarily share a common ideology with the commercial film industry, it certainly shared a common understanding of technique and finances. In 1965 large-circulation Franciscan magazines reported on *The Hour of St. Francis* and the amount of work and time the staff devoted to making films. The publicity was well deserved but also specific to the cause of raising awareness and raising funds for the new production studio. Throughout its life *The Hour* received most of its financing from annual donations from tertiaries. Whereas Fischer's film appreciation series seemed intended to educate Catholic audiences, the articles about it seemed written to inform the Franciscans who sponsored its production. When asked about the significance of "How to See a Film," assistant producer and scriptwriter Father Simon Scanlon declared it "the most important thing the Hour has done." In 1965 thirteen full-time staff members were producing, writing, filming, editing, promoting, and distributing the films; but the core, as Harrington noted in his 1965 profile of *The Hour* in *St. Anthony Messenger*, comprised Holtsnider, Scanlan, Vaughn, and Emery Tang, OFM.[96]

Harrington's article on the Franciscans behind *The Hour of St. Francis* came during a significant shift in religious media production. For over thirty years the FCC had required radio (and eventually television) stations to broad-

---

94. "Birds of Many Feathers," *Franciscan Herald and Forum* 44 (August 1965): 231–32.

95. Holtsnider, 15.

96. Scanlon quoted in Harrington, "Television," 24. See also *Franciscan Communications: Fortieth Anniversary*, in file 5, "Pamphlets, Brochures, *Airtime Magazine*," The Hour Collection.

cast public-interest programs, including religious shows such as *The Hour of St. Francis*. Most of the time, noncommercial broadcasts aired outside prime time, when advertising revenue was relatively low; thus religious shows aired on Sunday mornings in the so-called TV ghetto. But Holtsnider explained to Harrington that even this non–prime time allowed programs to reach far more people than he and his fellow priests could address by preaching solely in churches. Television, the tertiaries could see, was a good investment in evangelism. However, Holtsnider admitted that "chances are extremely remote" that *The Hour* or any other FC production might consistently compete with commercial broadcasts over the long term. So following the FCC's 1960 ruling that local stations could begin to sell airtime and still receive public interest credit, the media calculus changed. Not only would the work of FC compete with commercial productions, but other religious groups could also raise money to buy prime spots for their programs.[97]

Underlying Harrington's essay on *The Hour of St. Francis* was a combination of hope and resignation. Holtsnider appealed to readers by asking them to write letters of support for shows produced by the Franciscans and to become part of a larger movement of Catholics "to help show that the Church is 'not opposed to the arts but really the patron and mother.'" That strategy sounded different from the one the Catholic Church had used throughout most of film and television history. A new strategy of positive reinforcement and more generally informed appreciation began to hold sway. However, the rise of religious groups with lucrative media budgets that used television (especially) to raise money, not merely to convey messages, created a major challenge. Support for *The Hour* continued to come from the lay Franciscans of the Third Order as well as some one-time gifts from foundations. Such fundraising allowed FC to produce films for $20,000 rather than the more typical $100,000 budget a commercial company might have.[98]

In a way the nexus of financial constraints and creative talent inspired FC to make productions that were both avant-garde and a bit sentimental. The production team often debated how to strike a balance between the obvious artistic potential of their craft and the equally obvious proselytizing impulses that characterized much religious media. The history of *The Hour of St. Francis* looked similar to the history of most religious programming—sometimes brilliant and able to stand on its own dramatic merits, other times more overtly preachy in ways that did not appeal to folks sitting in their living rooms.[99] By the mid-1960s the financial model for making films was failing. "Half hour dramatic films were extremely expensive to produce," said Holtsnider, "and

---

97. Harrington, "Television," 28.
98. Karl Holtsnider, quoted in ibid., 29.
99. Ibid., 30.

the traditional source of funding, the Third Order, was not keeping pace with fiscal need."[100] It was due to this impasse that Holstnider and his colleagues conceived their most innovative project to date: TeleKETICS, an alternative to thirty-minute television episodes and a play on the traditional cathechetics used by the Catholic Church to educate the laity in doctrine. Beginning in 1969, TeleKETICS became a way for Franciscans to construct a fifteen-minute film and a kit of educational material that, according to Wintz, "helped spark the current revolution in religious education."[101] "Encapsulate the gospel message in story form," Holstnider explained; "the stories need not be long. Ten or fifteen minutes were plenty . . . and shorter films allowed plenty of time to prepare the audience before the film, show the film, and then plumb its symbols and hidden meanings at length." Yet again the Franciscan community pledged to support this initiative with the hope that it would sustain itself after a few years. According to Holstnider these shorter films on the sacraments—for example, Baptism, Eucharist, Confirmation, and Penance—did more "sales the first year alone than the entire catalog of over 50 half hour films produced by FC."[102]

With TeleKETICS, Holstnider and FC thought they found a way to circumvent the religious television–money axis. They produced dramatically shorter versions of these films, called TeleSPOTS, as well as short episodes for radio, called AudioSPOTS. These "commercials for God" ran as public service commercials on major stations and networks. The production quality remained high, and the topics were timely and relevant. Their length also enabled stations to run them during the day, when many listeners and viewers would be tuned in.

A single AudioSPOT might therefore be heard by twenty million people. In another article about FC in *St. Anthony Messenger*, Wintz described a thirty-second radio exchange that people driving home one evening might hear on an AudioSPOT:

> "What is a nigger?" asks a male interviewer. "Water," answers a bubbly little girl in ignorant bliss. "What is a Polack . . . a Chink . . . a Dago?" the interviewer asks separately. The girl gives the innocent and corresponding replies: "Ice cream . . . rabbit . . . birdie." Finally the interviewer inquires, "What is love?" and surprisingly on target the girl says, "A kiss!" and then adds, "Did I do good?" "You were perfect," he says, and they kiss . . . as an announcer concludes, "Love makes all things new again."[103]

---

100. Holstnider, 15.
101. Jack Wintz, OFM, "TeleSPOTS: Marketing the Message," *St. Anthony Messenger* 81 (September 1973): 23.
102. Ibid., 19.
103. Wintz, "TeleSPOTS," 19.

The creator of the radio episodes was Father Ed Wrobleski, a Paulist priest working with the Franciscans who garnered a remarkable following and recognition in awards from advertising organizations and media colleagues. "What I am trying to do," said Wrobleski, "is use contemporary tools of communication to restate the basic and primary commandment—love"—a sentiment that reflected the general approach of FC in their short works.[104]

AudioSPOTS were also distributed as a series, such as *Sounds of Love*, which included a sixty-second spot called "Aw, What's the Use" that portrayed the thankless moments of everyday life—a man losing confidence in himself, a child getting "bubble gum all over the dog," and a housewife reeling from "the housework, the kids, the dinner. Who notices and who cares?" The spot concluded with the announcer saying: "The sounds of love don't just happen, you have to make them." Similar radio moments were made for thirty-second spots, and both kinds of spots won multiple awards.[105] According to Wintz, from 1968 to 1973 FC made at least eight different AudioSPOTS and TeleSPOTS that were then "released to 3,400 radio and 650 TV stations in the United States, not to mention stations in Canada and remote points like the Philippines and Australia, and armed forces stations around the world."[106]

One of the writers for the TeleSPOTS was Darlene Hartman. In his informal history of FC, Holtsnider explained how Hartman discovered she had written an especially effective spot. One of Hartman's neighbors had told her that she had just caught "the best thing . . . [she'd]ever seen on television." The neighbor had watched a commercial in which a middle-class woman "walking toward a church and looking in a rather condescending way to several ethnic persons" enters the church. A voice-over says "If you don't find God here"—with a close-up of the people the woman passed—"you probably won't find Him in there," referring to the church. Hartman excitedly replied to her neighbor, "I wrote that spot."[107]

Yet TeleSPOTS illustrated the predicament that Franciscan Communications was in. Artistically, the TeleSPOTS were inventive; financially, they were challenged. The idea behind them was simple: develop short parables to fill space that commercial stations could give as part of their public service obligation. Father Tony Scannel, a Capuchin Franciscan, came to work at FC in

104. Wintz, "TeleSPOTS," 19; see also Joseph J. La Barbera, "Love Commercials: New Non-Commercial Product," *Hollywood Studio Magazine* 5 (December 1970), in file "Patents (TeleSPOTS, AudioSPOTS, StoryScope)," Franciscan Communications.

105. "Aw, What's The Use?" *Audiospot*, series 1, #1; and "AUDIOSPOTS Receive Awards," file "AudioSPOTS, TeleSPOTS, Storyscape," box 1, *The Hour of St. Francis*, Franciscan Communications.

106. Wintz, "TeleSPOTS," 19.

107. Holtsnider, "History of the Hour," 16.

1970, at the apex of its relevance in American media. In a talk about his history with FC, he explained that the group hoped the stories they produced would start conversations, pushing people beyond the program they watched into reflecting on the way their lives resonated with deeper religious meaning. "Begin with life experiences, with stories," Scannel said, "and lead to faith discovery, to the continual way God is revealing Godself in human life."[108]

Bruce Baker, a professional filmmaker living in Los Angeles, made the first TeleSPOT series. Nick and Tony Frangakis directed fifteen-minute films for FC. And Emery Tang, OFM, was one of the chief promoters of the TeleSPOTS and the shorter films. Tang helped shape FC by traveling to radio and television stations to speak about these spots to as many groups as would hear him. He even made famous appearances on talk shows hosted by Mike Douglas and Merv Griffin. Tang had been the principal of St. Mary's High School in Stockton, California, but his presence was requested by the staff of *The Hour of St. Francis*.[109] For an article on the FC's noncommercial products in *Hollywood Studio Magazine*, Tang explained that the TeleSPOTS and AudioSPOTS avoided moralizing in favor of prodding people to consider the small things that ordinary people can do that could ultimately make a big difference in their lives. "Most important," Tang related, "the trick is to get the viewer to make up his own mind, stimulated by a pointed presentation of a day-to-day episode at home, on the street, at work, at play. Large issues like communism, poverty, unemployment, pollution, while important and irksome, are usually TOO large for the ordinary person." Instead, the TeleSPOTS and AudioSPOTS prodded viewers to consider paying more attention to their families and less attention to women as sex objects. "The beauty of it is that you can actually get people thinking and listening to what's being said about justice, peace, love, generosity, loyalty. And we'll all admit," Tang added, "that it's the lack of these things that has created some of the nightmares of our time."[110]

Holtsnider explained that the sacramental films produced for TeleKET-ICS in 1968 sold better than all the half-hour films *The Hour of St. Francis* had made in its history. Building on this success FC produced *Images of Faith* for the United States Catholic Conference (now the United States Conference of Catholic Bishops, or USCCB). This project was a multimedia program that replaced an older program called *Know Your Faith*. FC produced three volumes of *Images of Faith* and even increased the staff at the studio to accom-

---

108. Anthony Scannel, OFM Cap, "Presentation, International Study Commission on Media, Religion and Culture," May 2, 1998, http://www.waccnorthamerica.org/mrcproject/english/scannel.htm.

109. Holtsnider, "History of the Hour," 15.

110. Emery Tang, OFM, quoted in La Barbera, "Love Commercials."

modate the increased output. While these kits were sold to schools, churches, and other groups, the short films were given to stations for free to broadcast. The point, of course, was that neither side in the deal made any money. Even this possibility changed when television stations were no longer compelled to offer public service time to any group. Scannel explained that this fact, along with the reality that video was replacing film, made the economics of producing high-quality films a disproportionately expensive proposition. Holtsnider put it bluntly: "FC has always been in broadcasting but it was always public service broadcasting. The Hour of St. Francis programs, at first on radio, later on TV were given away. TeleSPOTS and AudioSPOTS were given away." The Lilly Foundation had provided over $400,000 to FC to make and distribute films for religious education—a significant aspect of the foundation's mission—but without revenue-generating products, FC was at the mercy of the commercial market.[111]

FC did not find a model that would make money. It did, as Wintz argued, "mirror the modern revolution in religious education, which has, in turn, mirrored the deeper theological revolution." "Its films not only reflect the thinking of Vatican II," Wintz observed, "but seemed destined as pacesetters for the future." FC created films for the USCCB and the different campaigns it launched as part of a more forthright focus on social justice. The catalog amassed by FC lists dozens of films, videos, programs, and even printed material covering a spectrum of spiritual needs: from resources on Scripture, the sacraments, Christian witness, prayer, and holidays to materials for retreats, families, parishes, communities, children, and teens. Wintz noted, though, that even if Franciscan Communications (the name officially registered in 1981 with the FCC) weathered the competitive religious media market, it still dealt with the paradox of religious education. Wintz editorialized that the work of Holtsnider and Scannel and others had "come a long way from the Baltimore Catechism"; but like the Baltimore Catechism, of which "many began to make an idol . . . assuming it to be the sole model and example of how revelation worked," media—radio, television, and film—was also in danger of "carrying the whole burden of education."[112]

Franciscan Communications—FC— remained a viable media production outlet for the Franciscans until 1994, when the operation and its catalog were sold to St. Anthony Messenger Press. Looking back on what FC accomplished, Scannel viewed the fate of the enterprise as part of the larger trends affecting religious programming in general: "It proved very difficult for a church of 200 independent and autonomous bishops to agree on any national vision for communications, except in very general terms and with little

---

111. Scannel, presentation; Holtsnider, "History of the Hour," 21, 25.
112. Wintz, "TeleSPOTS," 24.

prophetic vision and commitment." "The only religious broadcasters who have been successful in gathering sizable audiences and sustained support," Scannel observed, "have been independents, men or women who were their own church, so to speak, or Mother Angelica who is like a church unto herself as well."[113]

Scannel's comment offers something more than simply an observation on the type of religious media that seems to succeed. The period that followed the rise and then stagnation of FC was characterized by ideological battles over the legacy of the 1960s. Consideration of questions involving the laity, ecumenism, the Mass, and the Church's declarations on the fate of humanity became issues for political movements and campaigns. The rise of culture wars in the United States favored the kind of personality-driven and issue-oriented religious media of figures such as Mother Angelica. Even though she was one of many prominent religious personalities of the culture wars, she had the distinction of being one of the few Catholics and one of two Franciscans to enjoy such prominence, as the next chapter discusses.

---

113. Scannel, presentation.

Chapter 5:
The Culture Wars With Mother Angelica and Father Richard

I f Franciscan media hoped to reach a wide audience, the period from the 1980s to the 2010s has posed a stiff challenge. Rather than unity under a television antennae, this period has been characterized by audience segmentation and ideological demographics. In an age of fracture, cultural standards that once gave shape to what Andrew Hartman calls "normative America" were contested by groups often marginalized in a version of American life that they want to change, if not reject.[1] Sociologist James Davison Hunter introduced the term "culture wars" into the American lexicon with his 1991 book describing the stakes of this conflict over traditions in the United States. Hunter argued that American society had forgotten how to speak a common moral language, a fact that matters when issues concerning the body—abortion, pornography, homosexuality, euthanasia, AIDS—dominate public discussions.[2] Professional pundit and 1992 presidential candidate Pat Buchanan made "culture wars" a household term: "There is a religious war going [on] in this country," he declared at the 1992 Republican National Convention. "It is a cultural war, as critical to the kind of nation we shall be as the Cold War itself. For this war is for the soul of America."[3] The idea of the culture wars resounded during the 1990s as real wars faded from the American landscape and the effects of revolutions waged in the 1960s and 1970s finally took hold.[4]

Franciscan media made particular contributions to the culture wars. One aspect that made the history of Franciscan media significant was the light it shed on the relationship between the laity and the Church. At its most dynamic, such insight provided evidence of new ways to confess, of alternative theologies for women, and of media itself. In the post–Vatican II period, the work of Mother Angelica and Father Richard Rohr—two Franciscans with very

---

1. Andrew Hartman, *A War for the Soul of America: A History of the Culture Wars* (Chicago: University of Chicago Press, 2015), 1–7.

2. James Davidson Hunter, *Culture Wars: The Struggle to Control the Family, Art, Education, Law, and Politics* (New York: Basic Books, 1991), xi.

3. Hartman, *A War for the Soul of America*, 1.

4. James Davison Hunter, *Culture Wars: The Struggle to Control the Family, Art, Education, Law, and Politics in America* (New York: Basic Books, 1992), xi.

different agendas, audiences, and theological visions—has shown how spiritual nourishment for the laity can exist almost completely apart from traditional Catholic leadership structures. If the culture wars have illustrated the development of a culture separate from a more traditional America, then Mother Angelica and Father Richard Rohr have built spheres of spirituality that exist in tension with (if not often separate from) traditional Catholic institutions. Neither Mother Angelica nor Rohr have renounced their Franciscanism, because both have found the image of Francis as a revolutionary within the Church to reflect their identities. To understand their roles in Franciscan media requires getting a sense of the contexts in which they crafted their identities.

Writing for *Christianity Today* in 1995, John Kennedy points to an impulse common among conservative Christian media: "This vision for redeeming the wasteland for the cause of Christ has resulted in around-the-clock televised Christianity worldwide. Although Christian broadcasters have succeeded in spectacular fashion in bringing Christian programming to a global audience, troubling questions remain as to whether television as a medium has watered down the gospel message, whether it is effective in reaching nonbelievers, and whether Christian programs service an almost exclusively Christian audience." Success measured in ratings has become far more important than determining whether media are making the world a better place. Kennedy reminds readers that in 1960 Pat Robertson founded the Christian Broadcasting Network (CBN), and by 1995 he established himself as among the most powerful individuals in the United States, with his network boasting "annual revenues totaling $189 million and outreach in 60 countries." His flagship program, *The 700 Club*, first aired in 1966 and by 1995 had 2.2 million viewers daily. The format of this show, which still airs today, became the standard for televangelists: it features a live studio audience of 150 people and is divided into two half-hour segments, including thirty minutes of news from a so-called biblical perspective, as well as features and ministry profiles. The key to the network's success, though, is the constancy with which viewers call CBN for counseling (1.78 million called in 1994) and for fund-raising. Robertson raised so much money in the early decades that he was able to transform the format of his programming by introducing entertainment through his Family Channel, which was, by his admission, not preachy. The irony was that he could fund high-quality productions that resembled the work pioneered by *The Hour of St. Francis* and FC. Not surprisingly Robertson hoped that his new channel would successfully compete with secular cable and network channels.[5]

Other religious networks emerged around the same time, including Trinity Broadcasting Network (TBN), which by the 1990s was the biggest Protes-

---

5. John W. Kennedy, "Redeeming the Wasteland?," *Christianity Today*, October 2, 1995, 92–94.

tant network in the United States. Launched in 1973, TBN reached twenty-seven million American homes by 1978. Like CBN this network has also received a big boost by couching religious issues as part of the culture wars and addressing topics such as homosexuals in the military, religious schools, and religious liberty. Other denominational networks include the Faith and Values Channel (F&V) and the American Christian Television System (ACTS), broadcasting more mainline Protestant programming, though neither has been as successful as their evangelical competitors.

MOTHER ANGELICA

But the largest religious network throughout the 1990s was run not by a male evangelical Protestant, but by a Franciscan nun named Mother Angelica, founder of the Eternal Word Television Network (EWTN). Kennedy calls Mother Angelica an "improbable television superstar," in part because the centerpiece of her network was originally *Mother Angelica Live*, an hour-long show taped before a studio audience on Tuesday and Wednesday evenings.[6] She hosted the show in a habit that framed her face—a style that most viewers had not seen since the days before Vatican II. Yet EWTN, begun in 1981 "from a converted garage," reached thirty-eight million homes by Kennedy's article in 1995 and pulled in $13 million in viewer contributions. Devotions to Mary became an especially big draw for the network—a feature that viewers in forty-two countries could watch all day, every day. Kennedy observes, "One moment [Mother Angelica] is cackling in comic monologue, the next she is deadly serious about the wicked state of the world. Indeed, the talk is often apocalyptic."[7] She told Kennedy: "I don't try to be funny. It just comes out that way. I have Muslims, agnostics, and atheists listening to see what in God's name I'm going to say next."[8] While it is true that Mother Angelica's monologue and dialogue with the audience could seem unscripted, her ideological position was always quite clear. She emphatically pushed a line consonant with other critics and naysayers of reforms following Vatican II. Her conservatism became, somewhat like that of other culture warriors, a response to the social upheavals in the 1960s.

Mother Angelica had a compelling personal story that played a role in her appeal to audiences. She was born Rita Antoinette Rizo in Canton, Ohio, and grew up during the Great Depression in a broken home with her mother. It has become part of her personal lore that when she was young, she suffered

---

6. *Mother Angelica Live* originally aired from 1983 to 2002. Classic episodes are still rebroadcast on EWTN as of this writing, and episodes can also be found online.

7. Kennedy, "Redeeming the Wasteland?," 99.

8. Mother Angelica, quoted in ibid., 99.

from an abdominal disorder that appeared incurable until she visited Rhonda Wise, "a mystic and stigmatic who claimed to receive regular visions of Jesus and Saint Thérèse of Lisieux [the Little Flower], who had a reputation for working miraculous cures." Following Wise's instructions, the young Rizo said a Little Flower novena and on the ninth day was cured. The price for this miracle was her promise to devote her life to the Blessed Virgin. At nineteen years old she left home and entered the order of the Franciscan Nuns of the Most Blessed Sacrament, later called the Poor Clares of Perpetual Adoration— an order that Pope Pius IX made a pontifical institute that would "answer only to the Holy See."[9]

This order of Poor Clares wears a traditional habit with a Franciscan cord and is part of the Second Order of St. Francis of Assisi, which means, as they state, "the Nuns consecrate their entire lives to Adoration of Our Lord Jesus Christ in the Most Blessed Sacrament, solemnly exposed in the Monstrance in their Monastery Chapel."[10] The order founded its first American monastery in the Diocese of Cleveland in 1925, and these were the sisters who welcomed Rizo. She professed her vows in Cleveland, taking the name Mary Angelica of the Annunciation, PCPA, but Alabama was where she made her mark.

In her rise to prominence, Mother Angelica developed two characteristics that were both her greatest strengths and her greatest liabilities—speaking and generating revenue. To understand how these things affected Mother Angelica as a leader in media, note the paradox near the beginning of her career. She became the abbess of an order of cloistered nuns in the city of Birmingham, Alabama, in early 1961. She had her sisters build the monastery of Our Lady of Angels and almost immediately asked Catholic officials for permission to change the order's name from the Franciscan Nuns of the Most Blessed Sacrament to the Poor Clares of the Holy Eucharist. Mother Angelica's arrival in Alabama and her development of her order coincided with the revolution unleashed by Vatican II. Raymond Arroyo, an EWTN anchor and the author of the best biography of Mother Angelica to date, explains that we might consider the abbess as something of a creature of that revolution, for it both gave her the room she desired to build a distinct Catholic calling and produced movements she fought for most of her life.[11]

From the beginning she caught the spirit of renewal projected by Vatican II and sought to infect her order with evangelizing action. Calling Mother Angelica's proposed changes "progressive and mildly feminist," Arroyo quotes one of the abbess's early articles on renewing religious life: "Rules that control

9. Michael O. Garvey, "Anchorwoman," *Commonweal*, November 18, 2005, 22–23.

10. http://www.thepoorclares.com/history.html.

11. Raymond Arroyo, *Mother Angelica: The Remarkable Story of a Nun, Her Nerve, and Network of Miracles* (New York: Doubleday, 2005).

standing, sitting, and walking tend to create an appearance of affection. What we need is religious who are truly human, fully women, and imbued with the realization that unless the love of God shines forth from them and enhances their human personality they have failed in the duty of bring Christ to the world." Whether enacting changes in the Church or fighting them, Mother Angelica committed herself to sharing her views with as many people as possible and raising the necessary funds to do so.[12]

By the early 1970s Mother Angelica had grown into a local favorite among Christian groups in Birmingham. She reportedly gave talks three or four evenings a week and began taping short lectures for broadcast by WBRC in central Alabama. The popularity of her engagements both inside and outside the monastery developed into a cottage industry. She expanded her observations and lectures into longer booklets and manuscripts; the first one, entitled *Journey into Prayer*, was published by the sisters themselves. Ever mindful of controlling the content and the reach of her words, Mother Angelica decided to dive into the publishing business. The boldness of this action captured the almost incomprehensible faith Mother Angelica had in herself, her order, and, as she liked to claim, in God. Arroyo explains that despite opposition from the nuns of her order and the fact that they had only $200 in their bank account, the abbess "impulsively picked out a printing press, a cutter, a stapler, which collectively cost fourteen thousand dollars." Banks rejected the nuns' applications for loans, so she determined to raise the money she needed privately through fund-raising and obtained a $10,000 loan signed for by Albert Moore, a regular volunteer at the monastery. In short order the nuns were able to produce upwards of three thousand books a day.[13]

Book publishing had served many religious orders well throughout the twentieth century. Franciscans' success extended well into the 1990s before the age of the Internet cut into book culture. And much like other Franciscan media outlets, Mother Angelica diversified into radio and television. Though she had given lectures and talks for both radio and television programs, she had not by the late 1970s controlled her own electronic media. That changed on a trip to Chicago when, as Arroyo relates, Mother Angelica spied "Channel 38's satellite equipment on the rooftop. Mother stared at it for a long moment. Without breaking her glance, she spoke to Sister Joseph: 'Boy, it don't take much to reach the masses, you know.'"[14] Epiphany or not, over the next two years Mother Angelica launched herself into the world of television ministry. With great shrewdness she began producing tapes of her meditations about the Gospels, ruminations about the Apostles, and talks relating

---

12. Mother Angelica, quoted in ibid., 113.
13. Arroyo, *Mother Angelica*, 129–30.
14. Mother Angelica, quoted in ibid., 136.

contemporary life to the lives of the saints. These tapes began airing on Robertson's CBN at his invitation, because he saw in Mother Angelica's reflections a way for CBN to appeal to Catholics.[15]

Mother Angelica saw what CBN had developed into, and she imagined that she too might cultivate her audience into a media empire. In a speech to a group in Clearwater, Florida, in July 1978, Mother Angelica laid out in one sentence the imperative that drove her creative genius: "For too long," she said to four thousand enthusiastic supporters in the audience, "the TV tube has been in the hands of the enemy."[16] Over the next decade the identity of that enemy would shift in her eyes to include those who programmed other Catholic television programs; the Catholic bishops in the United States, who either paid no attention to her or took an active interest in opposing her; and large swaths of American society which, she believed, stood in moral peril for failing to accept her interpretation of the Gospels. By the end of 1980 Mother Angelica and surprisingly few associates founded EWTN as a nonprofit civil corporation (with no formal association with the Catholic Church) and began its first year "more than a million dollars in debt and facing operating expenses of $1.5 million a year," according to Arroyo. He says Mother Angelica characterized her financial gamble as part of a much larger project—"a theology of risk." She admitted to the *New York Times*: "Most people think we're a little touched in the head."[17] But with this bold and risky move, the abbess of Our Lady of Angels had founded the first Roman Catholic cable television network with a mission that in many ways was a culmination of Franciscan media. "We're after the man in the pew, the woman who is suffering from heartache, the child who is lonely," Mother Angelica declared. " I'm hoping we can teach without teaching, enlighten the heart and relax the body."[18]

The same year that EWTN launched, the United States Catholic Conference (now the United States Conference of Catholic Bishops, or USCCB) sponsored its own network, the Catholic Telecommunications Network of America (CTNA). The American bishops hoped that this for-profit venture would link all dioceses in the United States and provide programming for schools, parishes, and even phone services.[19] Although both Mother Angelica and the bishops attempted to avoid direct competition (EWTN even broad-

---

15. Arroyo, *Mother Angelica*, 141.

16. Mother Angelica, quoted in ibid., 142.

17. Albin Krebs and Robert McG. Thomas, "Notes on People: A New Cable-TV Network with a Difference," *New York Times*, August 15, 1981, 15

18. Arroyo, *Mother Angelica*, 151, 153.

19. "Catholics in US Plan Satellite TV Network," *New York Times*, November 15, 1981, 59.

cast an hour of programming from the CTNA), they grew suspicious of each other fairly quickly. When both networks launched, Mother Angelica observed, "Whoever has the media will have the Church."[20] She was determined, though, that her network—rather than the one officially sanctioned by the American bishops—would win over Catholics. She turned out to be correct. In the summer of 1983 EWTN made the strategically smart move of featuring its greatest asset, Mother Angelica, by producing her own live show. For the next twenty years the format of the show did not change. Arroyo provides an apt description of the show's appeal: "Slouching on the brown sofa each week, her braced legs crossed at the ankle, Mother was like no one else on television. She coughed when her Asthma acted up, chomped on lozenges, unleashed explosive sneezes that drew tears from her eyes, and regularly collapsed in fits of laughter. This purposively unvarnished approached endeared her to the audience. In the gaffes and imperfections they saw themselves." The show's strength, like much of other Franciscan media, came from its approachability. People felt comfortable relating the messiness of their lives to the spiritual guidance of, in this case, a grandmotherly nun. "Applying the spiritual balm to the wounds of the common man," Arroyo observes, "her program tackled drug addition, alcoholism, the pain of divorce, and loneliness." The litany of daily afflictions that Mother Angelica addressed had not changed much from those answered in the pages of *St. Anthony Messenger* by Father Fulgence Meyer. But when Mother Angelica spoke to a caller about marital problems, she was talking to an audience spread across 220 cable systems and two million homes. In 1985 EWTN was rated as one of the fastest growing cable networks in the United States.[21]

The US Catholic bishops could not compete with Mother Angelica's reach and popularity. Evidence of the imbalance grew more pronounced once EWTN moved to a twenty-four–hour format and Pope John Paul II announced a visit to the United States in 1987. No other network could approach the kind of coverage that EWTN provided of this historic visit. CTNA acknowledged the power of Mother Angelica's media empire when it asked EWTN to partner with the bishops for the pope's visit. During John Paul II's ten-day trip through the United States, an estimated seven hundred cable systems and twenty million homes picked up EWTN. The effect on Mother Angelica's network was profound and long-lasting. In the years to come, Mother Angelica brokered and then ended a relationship with the bishops, both on her terms; built a multi-million–dollar radio network called WEWN with funding from a Dutch billionaire named Piet Derksen; and by 1998 claimed, according to the IRS, $49 million in assets and an annual

---

20. Arroyo, *Mother Angelica*, 192.
21. Ibid., 194.

income (from contributions) of $19 million for her media empire.[22] Not surprisingly such power courted controversy.

In the summer of 1994, prolific writer and professor Raymond Schroth, SJ, reported in the *National Catholic Reporter* that he spent nearly two weeks trying to watch as much of EWTN as he could. Considering what surveys have revealed about religious television, especially the repetition of programming compounded by the constancy of messages, Schroth viewed a legitimate sample of EWTN. Researchers have concluded that individual ministries can raise exponentially more money through television than what might be possible through churches or parishes, though the actual size of audiences for these religious networks is fairly small.[23] However, Mother Angelica had the distinction of serving the single largest denomination in the United States and providing an ideologically consistent product. Robert Wuthnow, the well-regarded Princeton sociologist of religion, suggests that many of those who watch religious programming do so as much to receive news about contemporary affairs as to receive religious instruction.[24]

Schroth's contentions regarding Mother Angelica's influence can be summarized in two points. First, he said, "anyone who watches EWTN will have to conclude that Catholicism is a Disneyland of pseudo-miracles, with a piety that exalts Mary over Jesus, more determined to squelch the Spirit than to allow him or her to speak." And second, Mother Angelica is an expert culture warrior. In describing her call-in show taped before a live audience, Schroth reported, Mother Angelica could get three thousand calls in twenty minutes. Ostensibly answering questions on live TV allowed her to pronounce on the evils of liberalism and the liberal Church, while she praised miracles and championed a certain kind of religious conservatism. "There is an apparent logic to EWTN's method," Schroth observed. "With the collapse of traditional structures, grammar schools and high schools run by religious orders that once taught basic Christian doctrine, American Catholics are religiously illiterate. EWTN fills that hole with the Baltimore Catechism, or rather their selective version of 1940s Catholicism which they imagine will restore their lost world."[25]

Schroth provided an analysis of the EWTN approach. At base, he wrote, EWTN was declaring with confidence that we are "a world headed for destruction, an apocalyptic moment, which only the intervention of the Blessed Virgin Mary can prevent." Such devotion to Mary is part of a particular view of

---

22. Ibid., 281.
23. Stewart Hoover, "The Religious Television Audience: A Matter of Significance, or Size?," *Review of Religious Research* 29, no. 2 (December 1987): 149.
24. Robert Wuthnow, "The Social Significance of Religious Television," *Review of Religious Research* 29, no. 2 (December 1987): 128.
25. Raymond A. Schroth, SJ, "Angelica, EWTN Push Disneyland Church," *National Catholic Reporter*, July 15, 1994, 12–13.

Catholicism, he said, that finds it a faith "of bizarre miracles, apparitions and evil spirits." Perhaps most importantly for cultivating committed viewers, EWTN promoted the idea that "this is a world of absolute certainty, a certainty we share by doing what we're told." Yet EWTN's conservatism came with a twist, for while most of the hosts pledged fidelity to the Church, they also disagreed, quite vociferously, with theologians who have studied and interpreted the Church. Such conservatism contributes to a culture war by purporting that "the greatest sin—sometimes it seems the only social evil—is abortion." Moreover EWTN has embraced the kind of retrograde Catholicism that celebrates families with lots of kids, proclaiming that the traditional Mass has "been unaffected by Vatican II," and generally feels proud that "neither Mother nor her priest cohorts have kept up with Catholic biblical scholarship in the 20th century." But of course like other culture warriors, they viewed their ignorance as a badge of resistance against changes that would only bring ruin to the institutions upon which civilization and salvation rested.[26]

Schroth emphasized that the "overwhelming tone of so many of the EWTN mini-courses is that the viewers are idiots, incapable of absorbing anything deeper or more complex than the religious training they first received when they were children."[27] An example of the kind of battle that Mother Angelica clearly joined was her constant denunciation of feminism. She called all women she disagreed with feminists and saw the Catholic Church as an institution that by right had to be dominated by men,[28] despite the fact that she was one of the most powerful people in the US Church.

Ironically Mother Angelica was not faithful to her own admonitions. On November 12, 1997, she criticized a pastoral letter on the Eucharist from Cardinal Roger Mahoney, the archbishop of Los Angeles.[29] Mahoney's mistake, according to Mother Angelica, was his inadequate attention and devotion to transubstantiation. She went so far as to claim that as she understood the letter, the cardinal "did not believe in the real presence of Christ in the Eucharist." James Martin, SJ, reported on this situation for *America*, writing: "It's not every day that you see an archbishop accused of heresy on television." But of course that was a key point in this situation. Although Mahoney asked for Mother Angelica to be disciplined by the Holy See, his hope for ecclesiastical punishment met with her populist defiance. As Martin observed: "It is indeed ironic that someone with such a professed love for the church—

---

26. Ibid., 12–13.

27. Ibid., 13.

28. For one notorious, but not extraordinary, example of Mother Angelica's approach, see "Enemies," *Mother Angelica Live*, February 1, 1994, YouTube video posted by EWTN, accessed July 13, 2017, http://www.youtube.com/watch?v=MckZdHAAXPE.

29. James Martin, "Cardinal Mahony and Mother Angelica," *America*, March 7, 1998, 3.

especially for the magisterium—could issue a call for disobedience to the archbishop of a major metropolitan see." But because her authority had been built almost exclusively through her media empire, she demonstrated the power of personality that was, though vastly multiplied by television, akin to that of those didactic editors of Franciscan magazines throughout the postwar era.[30]

Mother Angelica was also quite clearly the successor to the nation's most popular Catholic to grace television, Bishop Fulton Sheen. But even at the height of his popularity during the Cold War, Sheen could not have imagined what a global media empire might do. Mother Angelica built herself into a singular Catholic presence, flourishing while many other attempts by many religious institutions, including the US bishops, failed. A. G. Gancarski, writing in *The American Conservative*, declares that Mother Angelica "was empowered to represent the spiritual concerns of that great Silent Majority of traditionalist Catholics and moved to privilege discussions of doctrinal values and advancement of Catechism over the 'social justice' fare liberals in the Church preferred."[31] Mother Angelica played a role, then, in the culture wars that came to define American politics during the 1990s and offered an alternative to an era that was also defined by Cardinal Joseph Bernardin of Chicago—an American Catholic Church, she believed, that related too closely to the peace movement, economic justice efforts, and other liberal movements. So while Mother Angelica might have developed her media persona in contrast to liberal bishops, her popularity grew as American society grew increasingly interested in pitting religious liberals against religious conservatives. In short, Mother Angelica was both shaped by the era and made it her own.[32] In fact her approach and audience were much like those of other successful televangelists, such as Robertson and Jerry Falwell, though not as expressly political.

Of course Gancarski's interpretation of Mother Angelica accords closely with the official story told by Raymond Arroyo and other supporters of the abbess. But even Arroyo makes clear in his book that so much of the money required to build EWTN came from a relatively small group of Americans and Europeans, who paid for a message they wanted Catholics to hear. Like all empires, Mother Angelica's infrastructure relied on material wealth to rise above competing voices in what has been an ideological engagement. There is no denying the popular appeal she has engendered for her message or the substantial support she and her mission continue to receive from the Catholic laity. Yet it is equally significant to consider that the large amount of money

---

30. Ibid., 3–4.

31. A. G. Gancarski, "Cable's Catechism," *The American Conservative*, January 2002, 25.

32. For context on the culture wars and Catholics, see Andrew L. Pieper, "Loyalty Lost: Catholics, Liberals, and the Culture Wars," *Journal of Media and Religion* 12 (2013): 145–47, 151–57.

EWTN has received has been devoted to producing a Catholic network that established itself outside official Catholic Church approval.

Most people do not know Mother Angelica as the abbess of a media empire. They know her as the television nun who relates directly to them and, in her folksy way, often provides profound counsel. In a 1987 book called *Mother Angelica's Answers, Not Promises*, she and her coauthor capture the sense of the experience that made *Mother Angelica Live* so popular on television. In an introduction that she undoubtedly wrote, Mother Angelica relates: "The calls come from every section of country, from as many men as women, from people of every conceivable faith and every walk of life." She calls them her "EWTN family," and the callers find her approachable, she says, perhaps because she is a woman. "The questions are rarely easy," Mother Angelica observes. "A little boy may want to know why his father died. A wife may want to know how to forgive a husband who abused their child. A lot of questions have to do with the burden of loneliness." The book's organization reflects the scope of the questions she receives—her faithful need help understanding their personal relationship to God; they need assistance negotiating the problems of love and pain; and they want to learn how to deal with illness and death. A remarkable aspect of Mother Angelica's show was how it confirms that the concerns of contemporary American society are strikingly similar to those in the letters and essays published in Franciscan periodicals for over a hundred years. Simply put, Mother Angelica feeds an audience hungry for spiritual nourishment.[33]

In a chapter on suffering, Mother Angelica's brand of folk theology can be seen clearly: "We don't need a Ph.D. to know that God exists," she explains. "But we do need a brand of spiritual smarts, and that is what we are going to work on now." She asserts that most people don't think about God "until something really jolts us. Usually it's a tragedy." The inevitable next step is to feel sorry for ourselves and wonder why bad things happen to us. But "if you look to the world to answer the question of why we suffer," Mother Angelica observes, "you will come up empty-handed. The world cannot tell you why we suffer. This is why most of us are content to stew about in self-pity or punch our fists through walls or bend our neighbor's ear all day long about this ailment or that. As a group, we don't handle suffering very well." One is not likely to find a better counterpoint to the attitude driving self-help books and twelve-step programs. "The positive thinkers who try to cheer us out of our depression, who tell us we're okay when we're not, lead us very badly astray," she argues. "Accepting our trials and pain and suffering with grace is the hardest thing in life," Mother Angelica counsels. And

---

33. Mother Angelica, with Christine Allison, *Mother Angelica's Answers Not Promises* (New York: Simon and Schuster, 1987), 14–15, 20.

while her advice tends to default to "God wills all things," she also invites her audience to wrestle with their faith: "Knowing that God is with you every moment and bringing good out of it all takes a constant infusion of Faith, Hope, and Love. Following in Jesus's Footsteps is not easy; it's the hardest path you can take. But that path leads to holiness. And holiness leads to God. And this is why—as difficult and confounding and demanding as it is—we must muster our courage in suffering."[34]

Mother Angelica died on Easter Sunday, March 27, 2016 at the age of 92. Writing in the *Washington Post*, Raymond Arroyo reminded readers: "she was the only woman in the history of broadcast television who had founded and led a cable network as chief executive and show host for 20 years. Her Eternal Word Television Network became the largest religious media empire on the planet, bringing a message of hope to 260 million households in more than 100 countries. The EWTN radio network broadcasts on more than 300 affiliates in the United States and a stand-alone Sirius channel."[35] In an age of near-permanence through social media, Mother Angelica will continue to be part of Catholic culture through youtube videos of her show and replays on the network she created. Her legacy, though, has perhaps only begun to be understood. Raymond Schroth wondered in a brief essay on Mother Angelica in May 2016 whether ETWN "wants to be considered real journalism or the mouthpiece of the *National Catholic Register*—which it owns—and the Knights of Columbus who support them, a sort of Catholic Fox News." Schroth further wondered whether "the bishops, the Catholic universities with strong media, theology and social justice programs [might] put their heads together" and produce an alternative to EWTN.[36] His two insights provide the prevailing view of Mother Angelica at the time of her death—she never wanted to engage changes in the Catholic Church but, instead, sought to provide faithful supporters a sense of meaning if they joined a fight to make the church a place that never really existed in twentieth-century America.

FATHER RICHARD ROHR

In a way Mother Angelica represents the culmination of Franciscan media because she fully understood and capitalized on her ability to shape culture

---

34. Ibid., 72–74.

35. Raymond Arroyo, "How Mother Angelica fought through painful illness to become a female broadcasting titan," *Washington Post*, March 29, 2016, https://www. washingtonpost.com/news/acts-of-faith/wp/2016/03/29/how-mother-angelica-fought-through-pain-to-become-a-female-broadcasting-titan/?utm_term=.042f92f838de.

36. Raymond A. Schroth, "Can Catholic TV move beyond Mother Angelica's legacy?" *National Catholic Reporter*, May 20, 2016, https://www.ncronline.org/news/media/can-catholic-tv-move-beyond-mother-angelicas-legacy?_ga=2.198526447. 1546251853.1507430247-186898903.1487383708.

in her image of Christianity. An alternative to her model of spiritual engagement has been Father Richard Rohr, a Franciscan priest who has attracted a great deal of attention with his outreach through personal reflection, self-realization, and Christian discernment. In a 1994 essay that corresponded with the publication of Rohr's book *The Quest for the Grail*, Michael Farrell—a former priest, Irishman, award-winning novelist, and former editor at the *National Catholic Reporter*—discussed Rohr's ideas regarding the need for a reconstructed Church. "I believe we are living at a time when the quest is *not* real," Rohr declared. "Our people are unsure of the goal, insecure in their search for meaningful patterns and even unconvinced of any divine origins. It is a major crisis of meaning for the West, and at the deepest level it is a loss of hope."[37] Perhaps not surprisingly Rohr has made a dramatic appeal that sounds similar to Mother Angelica's appeal, though his interpretation of how to understand and overcome society's collective spiritual crisis is different in some fundamental ways.

Rohr grew up in Topeka, Kansas. He joined the Franciscans and was ordained in 1970 just as the effects of Vatican II were sparking a full-fledged debate. Rohr taught at Roger Bacon High School in Cincinnati, Ohio, and embarked on a project to tape Scripture talks through St. Anthony Messenger Press in 1971. The venture transformed both the press and Rohr, remaking the press into a more fully formed multimedia enterprise, and launching Rohr on the path to media stardom. That year he also had a charismatic experience that led him to found the lay Catholic community of families called the New Jerusalem Community outside Cincinnati. Rohr's recordings during this period marked his growth as a charismatic leader. "The tapes reflect what I was trying to do," he explained, "relationships and sexuality, everything about social psychology and group dynamics, the enneagram." According to Farrell, by the mid-1990s Rohr's talks on the enneagram sold thousands of tapes.[38] In a sense he was addressing issues similar to those Mother Angelica addressed, but with vastly different language and approach.

The enneagram, Rohr explained, "is a tool for discernment and a gift of the Spirit which can help transform lives, lead people to God, and release the great giftedness in us."[39] While not exclusively Christian, the enneagram has a heritage like many modern ideas that was passed from the desert fathers (those third-century Christians who lived primarily in Egypt as hermits and

---

37. Michael J. Farrell, "Richard Rohr Is Forever Searching for Elusive Meaning," *National Catholic Reporter*, December 2, 1994, 18.

38. Ibid., 19.

39. Rohr quoted in "The Enneagram (Any-a-gram)," Safe Harbor Christian Counseling, accessed July 13, 2017, http://www.safeharbor1.com/documents/Enneagram-Personality-Type-Indicator.pdf.

mystics) to Jesuits in Europe and then to South American priests. The enneagram is made up of nine points or styles that correlate to nine basic sins of
human nature, from anger to lust to envy. For Rohr the enneagram helps
people "name their illusions" and thereby enables them to increase their sense
of being outside themselves, moving closer to others and ultimately to God.[40]

The popularity of his message moved Rohr onto the speaker circuit, as
he began to give lectures and run retreats all over the United States. During
the 1980s he grew more involved in third-world social justice issues and began
to explore how best to merge his concern for the self with his concern for collective injustices. That period led him to move away from public engagements
and retreat to Gethsemane Abbey in Kentucky, made famous by Thomas
Merton and his celebrated book, *The Seven Storey Mountain*. Rohr further
built on his retreat experience by moving to Albuquerque, New Mexico,
where he founded the Center for Action and Contemplation. His book *The
Quest for the Grail* emerged out of retreats he offered for men at his south-
western home.[41]

However, Rohr's unorthodox approach to spirituality has also had detrac-
tors and critics. Stephanie Block, writing in 1996 for the conservative, traditionalist Catholic publication *The Wanderer*, argued: "It is apparent that the
Center for Action and Contemplation has become a magnet for the dissenting
elements of the Catholic Church, particularly in Albuquerque." She reported
that parishioners of nearby Holy Rosary parish objected to the center's publication *Radical Grace* being made available on Church property because it is
"a distortion of Scripture, an affront to doctrine, and a perversion of their
Catholic call to holiness." "They referred specifically," she noted, "to the
enneagram, to the We Are Church referendum, and to the teaching that Scripture does not condemn homosexuality."[42] In the *New Oxford Review* in 2006,
Reverend Bryce Sibley, the pastor of St. Joseph Catholic Church in Parks,
Louisiana, took issue with Rohr's approach by criticizing the theological evi-
dence Rohr uses in written work and popular retreats. "After reading [Rohr's
"Men Matters: A Quest for the True Self" a keynote address delivered in the
fall of 1994 in cities across the United States based on his book *Adam's
Return* (1994)], going through a few of his other writings, and then listening
to his presentation," Sibley concluded, "I have come to believe that Fr.
Richard Rohr adheres to some very questionable, if not dangerous beliefs.
Although most of what he says and writes may appear harmless to most

40. "Dismantling Our Trances," *National Catholic Reporter*, February 7, 2007, 10.
41. Farrell, "Richard Rohr," 19.
42. Stephanie Block, "The Center for Action and Contemplation," *The Wanderer*,
May 22, 1996, reprinted at CatholicCulture.org, accessed July 13, 2017, http://
www.catholicculture.org/culture/library/view.cfm?recnum=655.

people, the discerning Catholic reader will notice that underneath the surface lie ideas and opinions, some of them fundamental to Rohr's message, that reside outside of the realm of orthodox Catholic teaching."[43] Sibley took exception to Rohr's characterization of God as something other than "father." "He [Rohr] writes . . . that we must 'find public ways to recognize, honor, and name the feminine nature of God.'"[44] To Sibley such a notion "runs into the problem of Divine Revelation: Christ has definitely revealed God as Father. To say that God could just as easily be called 'Mother' is in direct contradiction to Divine Revelation."[45]

However, if one takes a longer view of Rohr's work, one also finds that Rohr has directed his message to men because he hopes that recovering a certain kind of spirituality might offset what he sees as the heart-numbing rationalism of the present age. "Because we have lost the great mythic universe, we find ourselves in a post-Christian era dominated by rationalism, with its desire to understand and control," Rohr says. "So we lack a mythic language that is nature-based or mystery-filled. Mythic language is always pointing outward and upward." Where Mother Angelica preached self-fulfillment through devotion to the Church as she idealized it, Rohr offers self-discovery through a broad contemplative tradition that often offends his more conservative Catholic brothers and sisters. Another area where he and Mother Angelica depart, ironically, concerns women religious—Rohr is an outspoken champion of them. "Many of the most heroic things [in the contemporary Church] have been done by women," he says. "In the Catholic Church, the clergy are at least 20 years behind the nuns. And behind the rest of the church, too." So Rohr too offers pointed criticism for the contemporary Church, but the focus of his criticism includes the type of parish priests and seminarians celebrated by Mother Angelica.[46]

Underlying their different approaches, though, is a fundamental similarity: "What most characterizes modern America is deconstruction," Rohr argues. "Everything is undercut, devalued, debunked, dismissed. It's a very cynical worldview, and for most people under 35 that's the only world they've ever known." Rohr argues that the 1960s accelerated or punctuated the deconstruction of thought and belief that had become characteristic of modernity. Thus perception turned toward postmodernity as the loss of belief in myth became dominant. In this way Rohr finds problems with feminism and

---

43. Bryce Andrew Sibley, "The Fr. Richard Rohr Phenomenon," *New Oxford Review* 73, no. 3 (March 2006), https://www.catholicculture.org/culture/library/view.cfm?recnum=6819.
44. Ibid., quoting Richard Rohr.
45. Sibley, "Rohr Phenomenon."
46. Farrell, "Richard Rohr," 20.

New Age spirituality. He contends that whether liberal or conservative, "both ideologies lend themselves to the private ego. It is just a matter of temperamental preferences and different disguises."[47]

In an interview with Catherine Walsh for *America* in 1995, Rohr contextualized his views on the culture wars within the Church: "We had to go through the last 25 to 30 years. Vatican II was a necessary opening. As Father Leonard Foley [an editor at *St. Anthony Messenger*] used to say, we've got to realize it wasn't the church that changed first; it was the culture that changed. And the church has been trying to keep in dialogue with this Western culture." Out of his concern for the future relevance of the Church, Rohr said he launched a project of reconstruction to counter the social and spiritual deconstruction he believed ruled the moment. At the Center for Action and Contemplation, the founding mantra is a response to the destructive aspects of modernity: "You cannot build on death. You can only build on life. We must be sustained by a sense of what we are for and not just what we are against." Through seminars, classes, retreats, and electronic media, Rohr said, he hopes to make the center a site for reconstruction. Where Mother Angelica found the source problems in the abandonment of an idealized Catholic culture, Rohr asks for a culture to be constructed of ideals. "Our people are dying from a lack of vision, from a lack of transcendent meaning to name their souls and their struggles," he said in his interview with Walsh. "What good is inclusive language if no one is even listening to the message."[48]

Rohr has maintained a remarkable travel schedule and writing routine for most of his adult life. Starting in 1973 he began marketing cassette tapes of his talks, graduated to speaking to groups at gatherings all over the world, and more recently engaged the multitudes through webcasts. His latest project is called a Living School for Action and Contemplation, which is based online as well as at the center. In 2013, at age seventy-one, Rohr told Jamie Mason of the *National Catholic Reporter*, "After 42 years of itinerant ministry, I had to accept that I shouldn't take myself so seriously and that I do not need to save the world." Rohr said he intends to teach in New Mexico, rather than leave a "carbon footprint" around the world, and uses the Web to connect with and encourage people to participate in this curriculum. "I talk about so many different subjects, from the Enneagram to social justice to sexuality. Sometimes I feel like I'm jack-of-all-trades and master of none!" Rohr admitted to Mason. "That's not false humility. I really had to ask myself, why do people trust me? I think because my gift is to synthesize different fields: philosophy, theology, sociology, anthropology, psychology. I'm not an expert in

47. Ibid., 21.
48. Richard Rohr, quoted in Catherine Walsh, "Perspective," *America*, March 25, 1995, 7.

any of them, but I've done my homework in terms of reading the people who are experts. And as I read, the lights start going off about how things connect to one another. All of these disciplines have contributed to, what I discovered, are seven underlying themes that have developed over my career and my ongoing contemplation."[49] Those themes explain Rohr's concept for the Living School: involving the students in their own journey toward a deeper realization of their spiritual core. The approach entails a methodology (Scripture validated by experience), foundation (be not afraid of God, but ground oneself in God), frame (by reason of the Incarnation of Christ, there is no truthful distinction between sacred and profane), ecumenical (everything belongs), transformation (the "separate self" is the problem), process (trials in life, from darkness to death, teach those willing to be transformed), and goal (divine union, not private perfection, is the goal of all religion).[50]

Rohr's approach has attracted attention and support from America's spiritual luminaries, including Oprah Winfrey. Oprah's media empire is the photographic negative of Mother Angelica's EWTN. As the high priestess of American consumer spirituality, Oprah is as much about the postreligious, consumption-oriented contemporary historical moment as Mother Angelica's empire is about reclaiming an idealized religious past. Kathryn Lofton, a scholar of the postreligious age, contends: "In order for us to understand contemporary American women and their discontents, in order for us to access the ways public religion has melded to consumer compulsion, Oprah is our optimal guide."[51]

With that characterization in mind, it is interesting that Oprah featured Rohr on an episode of her eponymous show titled "SuperSoul Sunday."[52] Rohr's efforts to engage men's spirituality and push people to look beyond themselves—to be something other than consumers—does not on its face recommend him to Oprah's audience. Yet the fact that the host and her audience were frequently searching for ways to make modernity and religious traditions compatible probably led them to Rohr and his thoughts. In Rohr's episode Oprah and the Franciscan priest spoke about "letting go" of one's selfish disposition to find what he told Oprah is a "true self." Rohr and Oprah spoke at the picturesque Santa Barbara Mission, discussing the role that beauty plays in the chapel and grounds of the mission. The Franciscan ideal of finding God

---

49. Richard Rohr, quoted in Jamie Mason, "Richard Rohr on the Living School and Getting Off the Road," *National Catholic Reporter*, January 16, 2013, https://www.ncronline.org/blogs/grace-margins/richard-rohr-living-school-and-getting-road.

50. See "Lineage and Themes," Center for Action and Contemplation, accessed July 13, 2017, https://cac.org/living-school/program-details/lineage-and-themes.

51. Kathryn Lofton, *Oprah: The Gospel of an Icon* (Berkeley: University of California Press, 2011), 12.

52. http://www.supersoul.tv/tag/richard-rohr.

in the environment and the ordinary as well as among the formal and institutional allowed Rohr to remind the audience that he speaks from a particular religious tradition but also addresses an audience who might benefit from considering that perspective.

As of this writing Rohr has now stopped traveling as much and has moved his energy into developing the Living School for Action and Contemplation. He continues to engage thousands of people every year, mainly through his school. In its first year, more than 1,500 people requested applications, almost 700 submitted applications, and the center staff anticipates enrolling 150 to 180 new students each year for a two-year program. The demographic characteristics of the applicants also suggest Rohr's broad appeal: a minority of applicants (thirty-five percent) are Catholic, with an age range of twenty-five to ninety years, covering a spectrum of professions and interests.[53] When asked about the purpose of the Rohr Institute (the unofficial name of this endeavor), Matt Sholler, associate director of the Living School explained: "We start with experiential, not the didactic. There will be a healthy amount of academic-minded curriculum, but what will make the school distinctive is how we incorporate lived experience. How we build our experiential practices into the curriculum is the most challenging and creative opportunity for us in developing the school."[54]

Rohr has woven reflections on St. Francis throughout his published work, writing directly about the saint very early in his career. In 1981 as a regular contributor to *Sojourners*, a politically radical Christian magazine founded by evangelical preacher and pacifist Jim Wallis, Rohr wrote an essay entitled "A Life Pure and Simple: Reflections of St. Francis of Assisi," in which he mused upon Franciscanism:

> Franciscan spirituality has never been an abstraction. It is grounded in Jesus' specific instructions to his disciples and not in theology. It is not easily able to move into ideology or to hide behind denominational screens into which we have projected our own metaphysics. Francis' living gospel was just that: It was lifestyle pure and simple. It was the incarnation continuing in space and time. It was the presence of the Spirit taken absolutely seriously. It was being Jesus more than simply worshiping him. At its best, Franciscanism is not words or even ethics. It is flesh—naked flesh—unable to deny its limitations, unable to cover its wounds. He called it poverty.[55]

---

53. Jamie Mason, "Rohr's Living School: Taking the Loneliness Out of the Spiritual Journey," *National Catholic Reporter* (February 4, 2013), http://ncronline.org/blogs/grace-margins/rohrs-living-school-taking-loneliness-out-spiritual-journey.

54. Matt Sholler, quoted in ibid.

55. Richard Rohr, "A Life Pure and Simple: Reflections on St. Francis of Assisi," reprinted in Richard Rohr, *Near Occasions of Grace* (New York: Orbis, 1993), 81.

Rohr has declared his relationship to Franciscanism as grounded in "alternative Franciscan orthodoxy" in which he practices "contemplation and self-emptying [and] expressing [himself] in radical compassion, particularly for the socially marginalized."[56]

That commitment has led him to take positions consistent with Franciscan compassion but at odds with institutional Church doctrine, such as when Rohr has reached out publically to gays and lesbians. In October 2000 Rohr wrote a public letter supporting the members of SoulForce, a national non-profit that, as their website states, works through nonviolent means to oppose and stop the religious and political oppression of LGBTQ people. Rohr's letter is an extraordinarily succinct and incisive interpretation of Jesus' ethic of love, applied to a group of people who are in fact Christians, as Rohr observed in his letter: "Jesus came to draw us all into union with God, whom he called his Father. How sad if the public image of our church continues to be a group of people that judge first, exclude easily, and use theological arguments to cover basic 'political' stances of power, image, and management of constituency. These seem to be things that Jesus cared about very little." Rohr compared the group to the abolitionist Christians of the nineteenth century and the civil rights movement of the twentieth century, suggesting that their belief is no different from the beliefs of those in the institutional Church—only that they believe without the support of the institutional Church. SoulForce proclaims the Gospels, Rohr contended, while the Church trips over them.[57]

Rohr's endorsement of SoulForce has sparked a good deal of criticism. In his 2006 article Sibley contended that "since homosexual activity is the ultimate denial of sexual difference, Rohr's support of homosexual-advocacy groups such as SoulForce (and thus his implicit support of homosexual activity) is a radical contradiction of the apparent importance he places on sexual difference in his presentation on 'male spirituality.'" Sibley continued his critique by quoting parts of the *Catechism of the Catholic Church* that expressly denounce homosexuality, thereby attempting to demonstrate Rohr's violation of basic Catholic teaching. Sibley concluded: "Though he claimed at his conference [on male spirituality] to sit in the 'larger Christian and Catholic tradition,' he fails to demonstrate how referring to God as Mother, encouraging homosexual advocacy, denying the spiritual reality of Original Sin, denying the necessity of the Cross for

---

56. Richard Rohr, quoted in "Richard Rohr, OFM," Center for Action and Contemplation, accessed July 13, 2017, https://cac.org/richard-rohr/richard-rohr-ofm.

57. Richard Rohr, "Fr. Richard Rohr's Letter of Endorsement" (October 8, 2000), SoulForce, accessed July 13, 2017, http://www.archives.soulforce.org/2000/10/08/fr-richard-rohrs-letter-of-endorsement/.

redemption, and promoting pagan rituals resides within the Catholic or even Christian tradition."[58]

In his 2014 book *Eager to Love: The Alternative Way of St. Francis*, Rohr returns to a topic that might please supporters and critics alike. In it he fuses his contemplative Christian mysticism to the countercultural implications of Franciscanism.[59] Dana Greene of the *National Catholic Reporter* praised Rohr's book for reclaiming "the mysticism inherent in the Franciscan legacy and . . . [offering] it as an alternative to the hierarchical, patriarchal, and authoritarian Christianity that he suggests has primary responsibility for so much of contemporary agnosticism in the West." Greene noted that the book is not a systematic treatment of any aspect of St. Francis (libraries are full of those) but is rather a book full of riffs on the challenge that Rohr believes Francis represents. "My emphasis in the book," Rohr told *America*'s Sean Salai, "is on what flowed from him, what was validated by him and then toward the end of the book I look at the source: Francis himself." Rohr explained that he wanted to "get beyond what I call birdbath Franciscanism, this very soft romantic notion of Francis as a statue in the garden that has no social message whatsoever, but just a pious pretty message [rather than] the radical flow that came from his message." Greene observed that Rohr's book holds up the Franciscan tradition as "prophetic rather than priestly. It offers a third way of heterodoxy, one between traditional orthodoxy and heresy."[60]

Rohr is the author of over thirty books; and while he often writes at the edges of official Catholic teaching and has chosen positions at odds with some in the Church, he is also a conservative of a particular kind. He argues in *Eager to Love*: "Franciscanism . . . is not an iconoclastic dismissal of traditional Christian images, history, or culture, but a positive choosing of the deep, shining, and enduring divine images that are hidden beneath the too-easy formu-

---

58. Sibley, "Rohr Phenomenon." See also Stephanie Block, "Coloring Outside the Lines," *The Wanderer*, May 22, 1997, reprinted at CatholicCulture.org, accessed July 13, 2017, https://www.catholicculture.org/culture/library/view.cfm?recnum=649; "The Roaring Modernism of Fr. Richard Rohr," *Novus Ordo Watch*, March 20, 2014, accessed July 13, 2017, http://www.novusordowatch.org/wire/richard-rohr-modernism.htm; Martin Barillas, "Controversial Priest to Lecture in New Orleans with Blessing of Local Catholic Bishop," *Spero News*, March 29, 2011, accessed July 13, 2017, http://www.speroforum.com/a/51193/Controversial-priest-to-lecture-in-New-Orleans-with-blessing-of-local-Catholic-bishop#.V6t46xSqfS0; Dan Burke, "Can I Trust Fr. Richard Rohr?," Spiritual Direction.com, http://www.spiritualdirection.com/2014/09/05/can-trust-fr-richard-rohr.

59. Richard Rohr, *Eager to Love: The Alternative Way of Francis of Assisi* (Cincinnati, OH: Franciscan Media, 2014).

60. Dana Greene, "Seize the Franciscan Moment, Rohr Advises," *National Catholic Reporter*, July 23, 2014, 19; Sean Salai, "Eager to Love: Author Q&A with Father Richard Rohr, OFM," *America*, August 6, 2014, accessed July 13, 2017, http://americamagazine.org/content/all-things/eager-love-author-qa-father-richard-rohr-ofm.

las." As in much of his work, Rohr in *Eager to Love* is attracted to ancient ideas that seem to speak to a basic essence in humanity. "Both Jesus and Francis did not let the old get in the way of the new," he says, "but like all religious geniuses, revealed what the old was saying all along."[61]

Mother Angelica and Father Richard Rohr are more than merely Catholic exponents of the American culture wars. They have represented ways that Americans understand and practice faith, and they have exposed aspects of the contemporary landscape of spirituality that have existed for generations but could not be acted upon easily until the advent of new media. They represent the collective us, even if we don't identify with their specific movements or practices, because they are a product of our time. Historian Joseph Chinnici, in an essay about the postconciliar culture wars, concludes that the conflicts we witness in such figures as Mother Angelica and Richard Rohr "indicate once again the close alliance between political culture and church life. As in society itself, factions would play off of each other; each side claiming abstractions and gravitating toward dichotomous centers of power. . . . The middle would disappear. Catholic communal identity as a diversity within unity, a dynamic field full of contrary but not contradictory tensions, would recede."[62] It is folly to imagine that a singular Catholic identity has ever existed, but what Franciscan media demonstrates is the long conversation Catholics have had about what their admittedly complicated identity might be. It is a media almost as messy as life itself.

61. Rohr, *Eager to Love*, xix–xx.
62. Joseph P. Chinnici, "An Historian's Creed and the Emergence of Postconciliar Culture Wars," *The Catholic Historical Review* 94, no. 2 (April 2008): 243.

Conclusion:
Life as a Mess

The elevation of a pope who took the name Francis was clearly a cause for happy reflection, if not outright celebration, among Franciscans. However, the election of Pope Francis in 2013 bookended an era of crisis that began with disclosures of clergy sexual abuse cases against children. The public airing of sexual abuse cases involving clergy of all Catholic orders, including Franciscans, created a crisis that demanded a new kind of Francis. Yet even before the election of this pope, Franciscan media demonstrated a resolve to show a radical empathy in a troubled time.

THE CLERGY SEXUAL ABUSE CRISIS

The clergy sexual abuse crisis received significant coverage in Franciscan media, as it did in secular media, in 2002 when a scandal involving the Boston archdiocese broke in a series of articles published by the *Boston Globe*. Yet before that case, *St. Anthony Messenger* ran a series of award-winning articles in the 1990s about Catholic priests who had abused children. One of the most significant articles about clergy sexual abuse appeared in the February 1994 issue of *St. Anthony Messenger*. In June 1993 the US Catholic bishops had at last officially acknowledged their responsibility to do something about sexual abuse. The bishops formed an ad hoc committee on sexual abuse and began discussing policies that bishops could use with their dioceses. John Bookser Feister, a regular contributor to *St. Anthony Messenger*, wrote a blockbuster piece about this admission—but chose not to focus on the ambiguous actions taken by the bishops and instead discussed the historical mess that the American Catholic Church found itself in. For his efforts Feister won a first-place prize from the Catholic Press Association.

Feister provided insight difficult to come by anywhere else in the Catholic press. He explained:

> Over five months, I visited two of the nation's leading treatment centers and interviewed their directors, talked with several victims and a victim's sister, had informal chats with a national and a local journalist who have been accused—wrongly they feel—of 'Catholic bashing' for publicizing abuse accusations. I had a series of interviews with a priest who had been in treatment for abusing teens. I reported a case of abuse to a religious

superior and heard him weep. The more I learned, the more aware I became of the enormity of this problem.

Feister's piece contained two bombshells. First, he wrote dispassionately about a priest in his late thirties who admitted to having abused teenage boys since he was a teenager himself. Second, Feister disclosed that he himself "was an adolescent victim of sexual abuse by a religious brother. It was his superior who wept when I called." It had taken Feister fifteen years to recognize that he had been abused, and relating that experience personalized what might otherwise had been a clinical reporting of official Church deliberations.[1]

The subject of the article was ostensibly the Servants of the Paraclete, an order established in 1947 by Father Gerald Fitzgerald to deal with problem priests, including those who sexually abused minors. Feister interviewed Liam Hoare, sP, who at the time was the servant general of the society, which numbered thirty-nine men. Hoare, an Irish priest with a degree in clinical psychology, met with Feister at Via Coeli monastery in Jemez Springs, New Mexico, where hundreds of priests had been sent for a variety of illnesses. However, in 1992 the Servants were named in a multi-million–dollar lawsuit brought by twenty-five victims named in the case against Father James Porter. Porter had spent time in Jemez Springs because he had abused children in parishes in Massachusetts and then was sent to a halfway house in Minnesota associated with the Servants of the Paraclete in the late 1960s, after which he continued to prey on children in Minnesota until he was forced from the priesthood. His indictment in 1992 exposed the Servants to public scrutiny for the first time, forcing the order to pay out thousands of dollars to Porter's victims. In what some might characterize as an odd admission, Feister reported that the Servants claimed "no wrongdoing but only ignorance about a disorder no one understood."[2]

Feister's examination of the Servants of the Paraclete in his *St. Anthony Messenger* articles raised an obvious question: what did the Catholic Church think it was doing with abuser priests? In a shorter essay that focused exclusively on one abuser priest, entitled "'Please Don't Hate Me': The Story of Father John Doe," Feister provided insight that, he explained, "at minimum [would give] readers a chance to understand better this illness." Like Porter, Doe [not his real name] was admitted to Jemez Springs for treatment, and like Porter, he was released to a diocese so he could continue to work—just not as an active priest. Among the most important and difficult sections of this piece was Doe's

---

1. John Bookser Feister, "How the Church Is Confronting Clergy Sexual Abuse," *St. Anthony Messenger* 101 (February 1994): 29.

2. Ibid., 29–32; see also Tom Roberts, "Bishops Were Warned of Abusive Priests," *National Catholic Reporter*, March 30, 2009.

account of knowing what he had done, as quoted by Feister. "Over 25 years, says Father Doe, he suffered the illusion that his shameful compulsion would go away: 'Maybe if I become a priest this will go away, I told myself. It certainly has to go away. I can remember growing up thinking that by the time I'm 16 it will be gone. By the time I'm 18 I won't do this anymore. By the time I'm 21 I won't be thinking of doing this. By the time I'm ordained I'll stop being this way. I really believed that.'" Feister let Doe's story stand as a testament to the slow disclosing of a reality that, while not exclusive to the Catholic Church, had profound implications for its future relationship with the laity. Feister ended the article with a stark warning: "I recently had a conversation with a victim who blew the whistle on a priest who had sexually abused more than 60 boys in the 1960s and 1970s. Although the abuser is now in jail, this victim says he fears other abusers who received treatment are still functioning as priests. Whether he is right or wrong, he points to an enormous credibility problem that our bishops continue to face. We are clearly closer to the beginning of this story than to the end."[3]

Feister was correct—the story had just begun. In 2002 and 2003 Franciscan periodicals and websites provided extraordinary coverage of the scandal that shook the Catholic Church again. The case that led the bishops to act more decisively was the scandal surrounding Father John Geoghan in Boston who, as Feister reported, had been "known as a pedophile by his superiors since 1984 [and] had access to children until he was defrocked in 1998." Unlike previous coverage of the sexual abuse crisis, the articles in 2002 and 2003 focused far more on the role and exasperation of the laity. Feister wrote in an editorial: "If you sit in the pews on Sunday, you're less likely to feel patient with priests and bishops on this one. Yes, we love our Church and pray for it to thrive. No, we will not put up with child endangerment."[4] In that same issue of *St. Anthony Messenger*, Pat McCloskey answered a reader who asked, in light of this crisis, "Why shouldn't I seek out another Church?" That question allowed McCloskey to speak to a question that shaped the *Messenger*'s general position: "Some decisions by Catholic leaders were based on . . . earlier, erroneous information," McCloskey explained. "Other decisions were simply a refusal to admit the seriousness of what was happening, a refusal to admit that there was a clear pattern of deviant behavior that needed to be confronted effectively. The rights of victims should have been the Church's primary concern but all too often were not."[5]

---

3. Feister, "Church Is Confronting," 31, 33, 35.
4. John Bookser Feister, "Clergy Sexual Abuse: Put Children First," *St. Anthony Messenger* 109 (May 2002): 23.
5. Anonymous, letter, and Pat McCloskey, OFM, response, Ask a Franciscan, *St. Anthony Messenger* 109 (May 2002): 46–47.

What developed over the course of a year in the pages of a few Franciscan periodicals was a forum on the obligation the Catholic Church had to its followers and the role of the laity in defining that relationship. Susan Hines-Brigger reported in *St. Anthony Messenger* in 2003 that as a journalist for Catholic periodicals she had taken it as her duty to keep her readers "accurately informed." The officials she spoke to about the crisis in the Church seemed to suggest that Catholic media needed to mediate that relationship and—as Seán O'Malley, OFM Cap, now cardinal-archbishop of Boston, told her—to "correct the false impression being given by the secular press." Franciscan media chose to emphasize the interests of its readers—the laity—more than the officials issuing reports and being sued for crimes.[6]

The letters to *St. Anthony Messenger* illustrate the urgency behind that decision. In June 2002 readers wrote in to express their dismay regarding an article encouraging vocations. The choice of articles contained some irony—the *Messenger*'s mission in its early years was to raise money and prayers to support poor boys studying for the priesthood. In 2002 one reader wrote, "Why should I encourage my sons to become priests? Right now, I am ashamed to even be Catholic."[7] Another wrote: "In light of recent news, you probably are not surprised that people like myself are not taking your editorial to heart."[8] Consistently throughout letters like these, readers of the *Messenger* described their sense of "betrayal" and "abuse," their sense of "feeling used" by the Church; they asked officials to treat the laity with more respect and to recognize their "wisdom and common sense" on pastoral issues.[9]

In June 2003 *St. Anthony Messenger* ran an issue almost completely devoted to the sexual abuse scandal. What stood out about the issue were the subjects of the articles—almost all were people or groups outside the official structure of the Church. McCloskey's article, "Honesty Comes Before Healing," framed the articles and began with a quote from the US bishops' 2002 *Charter for the Protection of Children and Young People*: "The Church in the United States is experiencing a crisis without precedent in our times." While accurate in many ways, coverage by the *Messenger* suggested this acknowledgment was quite late in coming. McCloskey explained that although the magazine had published many special issues over the years (and had consistently been the highest-circulation Franciscan periodical in the United States), "none

---

6. Susan Hines-Brigger, "Cracking the Code: Sex-Abuse Norms 101," *St. Anthony Messenger* 110 (February 2003): 39.

7. K.J. Abbott, "Discourages Church Vocations," Letters to the editor, "From Our Readers," *St. Anthony Messenger* 110 (June 2002): 4.

8. Kevin McGrane, "Feels Used, Abused, Betrayed," Letters to the editor, "From Our Readers," *St. Anthony Messenger* 110 (June 2002): 4.

9. Letters to the editor, "From Our Readers," *St. Anthony Messenger* 110 (August 2002): 3–4.

[were] about a scandal that has enraged so many Catholics and caused some people to question why they remain Catholic." With that understanding, the magazine's staff unsurprisingly noted that the articles were all written by them (not by Church officials) and that the subjects included victims of sexual abuse, parents of abused children, members of Voice of the Faithful (a lay organization that gained force in Boston in the wake of the scandals there), and a counselor who worked with people who had been sexually abused.[10]

Jack Wintz, long-time editor and writer at the magazine, wrote the editorial for the issue. He remarked pointedly that the cover art for the issue was intended to send a message. Pictured on the cover was a broken church being cradled in caring hands. The staff intended the image to suggest concretely the Franciscan contribution to healing. "The image of the broken church," Wintz offered, "takes us directly back to that day in the early 13th century when Francis of Assisi, searching desperately to find his mission in life . . . heard these challenging words: 'Francis, repair my house which, as you see, is falling completely into ruin.'" In case there was any ambiguity in that message, Wintz continued: "The clergy sex-abuse scandal has revealed a faulty tendency in our hierarchal system, namely, the unequal distribution of respect." Indeed, listening to the laity had been an earmark of Franciscan media for a long time, especially *St. Anthony Messenger*.[11]

In letters to the magazine, readers praised the tone and focus of the issue. One wrote, "God Bless the Press. . . . Thank you for your courageous special issue."[12] Another wrote: "Jack Wintz . . . asks 'How can we begin the work of reconciliation?' You have already started with this most wonderful issue."[13] The staff received letters of praise from priests, bishops, and the community of health care providers who worked with sexual abuse victims. Some wrote to exclaim their displeasure with articles that featured the Voice of the Faithful, and others wondered if liberals in the Church would use the crisis as an opportunity to push their agendas. The culture wars both inside and outside the Catholic Church continued, but *St. Anthony Messenger* largely abstained from acknowledging such conflicts in light of what it clearly saw as a much more fundamental issue.[14]

---

10. Pat McCloskey, "Honesty Comes Before Healing," *St. Anthony Messenger* 111 (June 2003): 12–13.

11. Jack Wintz, "Rebuilding Our Structures and Our Hearts," *St. Anthony Messenger* 111 (June 2003): 57.

12. Nora E. Johnson, "God Bless the Press," Letters to the editor, "From Our Readers," *St. Anthony Messenger* 111 (August 2003): 3.

13. Corinne Roberts, "Reconcilliation Is Under Way," Letters to the editor, "From Our Readers," *St. Anthony Messenger* 111 (August 2003): 3.

14. Letters to the editor, "From Our Readers," *St. Anthony Messenger* 111 (August 2003): 3–5.

St. Anthony Messenger opened a window that helped people see the complicated and charged public crisis of the Church. *The Cord*, a journal for more formal and academic discussions about Franciscanism, offered Franciscan priests an opportunity to discuss the child sexual abuse crisis within the mission of an ancient Church and within the context of a longer and at times darker history. The tone taken by *The Cord* bordered on defensiveness, though. Opening the March/April 2003 issue with a guest editorial, Canice Connors argued: "Perhaps a complementary consideration might be not to allow our fervor for reform and integral response to victims to mute the telling of the stories of those friars who passaged through the thorns of conversion and are witnesses to the liberating power of grace. If we do not celebrate their soul-wrenching change do we not contribute to the heresy that recovery is impossible?"[15] But what recovery did Connors think was possible? Others writers suggested answers. Lawrence Jagfeld, OFM, wondered if the callousness of society and the Church had desensitized his community to feel for perpetrators and victims alike. "I believe we need to work at removing the calluses so that we can feel the pain. Perhaps we would find ourselves being evangelized by the pain of our brothers and sisters."[16] In the end the writers featured in this issue of *The Cord* wanted to tell their fellow Franciscans that while most of them had nothing to do with this crisis, nor would they have much officially to do with its resolution, they had to remember that their Church had survived grave crises in the past (a reference again to St. Francis) and that in the midst of their contemporary crisis they needed to remind themselves, as Tom Washburn argued, "that this situation is scandalous precisely because it is *not* what we believe."[17]

The Franciscan who best captured the complicated meaning of the crisis also contributed to this issue of *The Cord*—but he offered more than an academic explanation of how Franciscans understood the child sexual abuse by priests. Joseph Chinnici, OFM, wrote about the sexual abuse crisis as both a Church historian and the leader of the California province of the Friars Minor. Unlike almost anybody else who wrote about child sexual abuse in the Church, Chinnici viewed the crimes in both contemporary time and historical time, for he had direct responsibility over decisions that affected the lives of abusers and the abused. In his subsequent book *When Values Collide: The Catholic Church, Sexual Abuse, and the Challenges of Leadership*, Chinnici argued: "The violent intensity of the crisis has all but obscured any substantial

15. Canice Connors, OFM Conv, guest editorial, *The Cord* 53 (March/April 2003): 49–50.

16. Lawrence Jagfeld, OFM, "'Thick Skin' and the Franciscan Charism: A Paradox," *The Cord* 53 (March/April 2003): 56.

17. Tom Washburn, OFM, "Reflection on the Scandal from Francis of Assisi," *The Cord* 53 (March/April 2003): 84.

theological reflection on the impact of the crisis on the life of faith and the spirituality of the believer." His hope was to "find a way forward," to work toward finding "something we can learn from history that will strengthen our faith and help give a stronger witness to society." In June 1988 the Franciscan Friars of the Province of Santa Barbara had elected Chinnici to the top position of leadership as provincial minister. Forty-three years old, Chinnici had been a professor of history for twelve years and with his election began a term that would end in 1997. He came to lead his province just as the original sexual abuse crisis became public. Thus he offered his account as someone in leadership, and his experience was that of someone who had to make decisions "to purify the Church of abusive activity and to bridge the differences between colliding systems and values in the clerical and lay worlds." Out of his particular experience, he said, he hoped to provide insight into "the much deeper and more institutional challenge to create mediating structures of reciprocal exchange where the failures of relational power could be confronted and its positive energies released." Getting beyond the crisis of scandal and pain and betrayal entailed simultaneously creating and dismantling.[18]

The case that propelled action at Chinnici's province was the discovery at St. Anthony Seminary, the minor seminary in Santa Barbara, that a friar in the early 1960s had preyed on more than one boy from a local family. Later more accusations followed, eventually implicating eleven friars in the abuse of at least thirty-four seminarians from the 1960s through the 1980s. Chinnici's actions, he explained to readers, unfolded both within the larger national context of the Catholic Church in America and within the very specific and personal context of his community of friars and families around Santa Barbara. The intersection of the national and local, the institutional and personal, tested Chinnici's resolve as both a father to his flock and a member of society thick with laws and policies. "The facts were clear enough," he wrote, "and could not be denied. Uncertainty and a sense of being overwhelmed joined hands with a resolute firmness to do what was necessary to help others and redress wrongs." Chinnici said he found some solace in a psalm: "Behold you are pleased with sincerity of heart, and in my inmost being you teach me wisdom." Ultimately, his mission became rebuilding trust with a community that had been his Church.[19]

---

18. Joseph P. Chinnici, *When Values Collide: The Catholic Church, Sexual Abuse, and the Challenges of Leadership* (Marynoll, NY: Orbis Books, 2010), 7–11. See also the documents assembled at BishopAccountability.org, especially *John Roe 4 v. Does 1 through 100, in camera* application to amend complaint to identify fictitious defendants, Santa Barbara County (CA) Superior Court, case no. 1156450 (filed August 27, 2004), accessed July 13, 2017, http://www.bishop-accountability.org/complaints/2004_08_27_John_Roe_4_v_Does_Santa_Barbara.htm#Connolly.

19. Chinnici, *When Values Collide*, 34.

Reviewers of Chinnici's book commented on the special qualities Franciscans brought to the crisis and the ways Chinnici attempted to rely upon them. At times it was St. Bonaventure's emphasis on the primacy of love that helped Chinnici; at other times it took the ability of Franciscans to work with both the people of Santa Barbara as well as the hierarchy of the Church. But ultimately, as Jeff Scheeler, OFM, wrote in *St. Anthony Messenger*, the Franciscan spiritual tradition helped Chinnici remember "that the human condition in its glory and its sin is a place where God can be found." If Franciscan media had helped friars meet people where they lived, Chinnici's account provided a heartbreaking example of the hurt and horror of those lives and the limitations of Franciscans to comprehend fully what the lives of the laity were truly like.[20]

POPE FRANCIS

A radical need for empathy inspired Pope Francis to choose his name. "Right away, with regard to the poor, I thought of St. Francis of Assisi," the new pope explained, and "then I thought of war. Francis loved peace, and this is how the name came to me." In an article about Pope Francis's election for *St. Anthony Messenger*, Christopher Heffron observed that the new pope is a realist: "he recognized that the Catholic Church is made up of 'virtues and sins' and urged people to focus on the 'truth, goodness and beauty' that live on." "Healing and progress are attainable," Heffron editorialized, "but only when there is harmony among the faithful."[21]

McCloskey, the long-time writer and editor at *St. Anthony Messenger*, wrote that in choosing the name Francis, the pope "set the bar high for himself and, by extension, for the Catholic Church." The decision reminded the world that St. Francis was a teacher who, as the new pope explained, was a "man of poverty, the man of peace, the man who loves and protects creation . . . with which we don't have such a good relationship." McCloskey noted approvingly that the pope chose to live in Rome—as he did in his home country of Argentina—in simple lodgings, closer to the people to whom he ministers. The humility of the new pope defines his identity and that of his papacy, it seems. On July 25, 2013, Pope Francis told an audience at Copacabana Beach to "Put on Christ. . . . Place your trust in him and you will never be disappointed! You see how faith accomplishes a revolution in us, one which can call Copernican, because it removes us from the center and restores it to

---

20. Jeff Scheeler, OFM, review of *When Values Collide*, by Joseph P. Chinnici, *St. Anthony Messenger* 118 (November 2010): 51. See also Thomas J. Shelley, "Rebuilding Trust," *America*, November 29, 2010, 28–29.

21. Christopher Heffron, "From Argentina to the World," *St. Anthony Messenger* 121 (May 2013): 31–32.

God; faith immerses us in his love and gives security, strength, and hope." McCloskey adds: "Francis of Assisi would heartily agree."[22]

Father Richard Rohr has enthusiastically championed the new pope as well. In one interview Rohr declared: "I have to pinch myself every day to believe that I've lived to see such a pope!" The pope reflects the radical potential of the traditional Church that Rohr appreciates: "It gives the rest of us who are trying to preach the gospel just a validation from home base, from the center of our church."[23] In *Eager to Love* Rohr heaped praise on Pope Francis for showing "us that the Franciscan vision is possible at every level and in every age. Not only did he take the name of Francis; but he seems so eager to proclaim both the 'foolishness' and the wisdom of the Gospel to every level of society. He has the passion, love, and urgency of Francis himself, and has moved the papacy from the palace to the streets."[24]

The fact that the Catholic Church has its first Pope Francis at a time of crisis in its relationship to the laity has, at the very least, illuminated the Franciscan sense of empathy. Throughout the order's attempt to evangelize through its media, it has demonstrated empathy with those who try to live as Catholics in America. Mass media are not a perfect reflection of their patrons, just as Franciscans cannot be a perfect reflection of God's will. Yet in Franciscan media we find echoes of the founder of the order. In a 2015 article in the *New York Review of Books* Gary Wills wrote pointedly that the new pope chose the name Francis to send a message both to his Church and to the people who ostensibly run it—namely, that God is with the laity. Wills noted that because St. Francis and his *fraticelli* (little brethren) were "trailblazers" by preaching the Gospel to lay persons, "bishops sent their priests to learn from these non-priests how to speak to the people." In his "closeness to the laity," Wills observed, Pope Francis "earns the name he has chosen. He tells bishops and priests to get out of their palaces and rectories, to go to 'the periphery,' where they can get 'the smell of the sheep.'" Franciscans have consistently dwelled in that periphery, ministering to people and reaching them by whatever means necessary, including those who read, listen to, and watch Franciscan media.[25]

---

22. Pope Francis quoted in, Pat McCloskey, "Pope Francis: The Name Fits," *St. Anthony Messenger* 121 (October 2013): 40–43.

23. Salai, "Eager to Love."

24. Rohr, *Eager to Love*, 265.

25. Gary Wills, "Why the Pope Chose Francis," *NYR Daily*, June 4, 2015, http://www.nybooks.com/daily/2015/06/04/why-name-pope-francis.

Acknowledgements

This book began as part of project sponsored by the American Academy of Franciscan History shepherded by Jeffrey Burns and Father Joseph Chinnici. I am grateful for the confidence and encouragement throughout the writing of this book. In his role as editor of this project, Jeff Burns has been tremendously helpful; I am happy to call him a friend.

To those who reviewed my project at various stages, I thank especially Father Jack Clark Robinson, provincial minister of Our Lady of Guadalupe Province in New Mexico, Father David Endres, editor of *U.S. Catholic Historian*, and James McCartin of Fordham. All gave their time to my project in different ways, though whatever flaws remain are solely mine. I also thank my colleagues at IUPUI and the Center for the Study of Religion and American Culture, especially its director, Philip Goff.

In the course of researching Franciscan media, I received much help from librarians at the Catholic Theological Union and archivists and scholars at two provinces in particular—Santa Barbara Province in California, and St. John the Baptist Province in Cincinnati. The men and women who run these places were generous with their time when I asked a slew of questions related to Franciscan media. Such research trips can be quite lonely, but I was fortunate to have wonderfully engaging hosts. Among the best was Karl Holtsnider, a former Franciscan priest who worked diligently and expertly for years producing episodes of *The Hour of St. Francis*. Karl and his wife welcomed me to their home in Los Angeles, fed me, and introduced me to other members of Franciscan Communications. Karl also shared with me his unpublished history of FC, which I am grateful to be able to use in this book with his permission.

I began this book as a professor at Marian University (I am now at IUPUI), and thank the librarians for helping me use the collection of journals maintained at the library. But I also relied on the good will and counsel of Marian's women religious. The group of women I came to know and admire are part of long, extraordinary history of leadership made good by compassion. I want to thank them all, with particular gratitude toward Sr. Norma Rocklage, OSF, Sr. Janice Scheidler, OSF, and Sr. Monica Zore, OSF, for the time and guidance they gave me.

No book I have written has been completed without the love and support of my family. I thank my wife Shenan for finding humor as well as significance in the stuff I write and for being an unconditional source of love and support.

I am also happy that our daughter Devon has a curiosity about how history happens and how I write about it—she keeps me on my toes!

I grew up in the New York Archdiocese, finding the church to be a strong and positive presence in my life, mostly because I saw Catholicism through the work of my mother Alice. Like so many of the women whom I encountered doing research for this book, she had a complex relationship to the church. From attending Catholic school to running the religious education program in our parish, she has seen the church as both a profound source for the good and an institution that too often falls short of expectations. However, when I think about being Catholic, I have my mother as an example of the values and ethics of a church that promises to care for all people. She has been the most consistent model of empathy and grace to my sisters and me. I thank her for that and dedicate this book to her.

Bibliography

Archival Resources

Franciscan Communications Collection, Santa Barbara Province Archives, Santa Barbara, CA
Franciscan Media Library, St. John the Baptist Province, Cincinnati, Ohio
Fulgence Meyers Papers, Provincial Archives of St. John the Baptist, Cincinnati, Ohio
Thomas Merton Papers, Thomas Merton Center, Bellermine University

Official Catholic Church Documents

Rerum Novarum (On Capital and Labor), Pope Leo XIII, May 15, 1891
Testem Benevolente Nostrae (Concerning New Opinions, Virtue, Nature and Grace, with Regard to Americanism), Pope Leo XII, January 22, 1899
Vigilanti cura (Papal Letter on the Motion Picture), Pope Pius XI, June 29, 1936.
Miranda Prorsus (On the Communication Fields: Movies, Television, and Radio), Pope Pius XII, August 8, 1957
Humanae Vitae (On the Regulation of Human Births), Pope Paul VI, July 25, 1968
"Renewal of the Religious Life," Pope Paul VI, June 29, 1971

Unpublished Material

Jeffrey M. Burns, "Simon Scanlon, *The Way*, and Race," (unpublished paper, American Catholic Historical Association Meeting, January 8, 2016, Atlanta, GA).
Karl Holtsnider, "History of the Hour of St. Francis and Franciscan Communications" (unpublished manuscript, 2012).
Jack Clark Robinson, "Structural History of the Franciscan Family in the United States, 1840–2000" (unpublished manuscript, 2013).

Periodicals

The Anthonian, 1927–present
The Cord, 1950–2010
Friar, 1954–1973
The View: A Catholic View on the News, 1952–1963
Padre: A Franciscan Monthly of General Catholic Interest, 1950–1973
The Way (*The Western Tertiary, The Way: Catholic Viewpoints, Way of St. Francis, The Way of St. Francis*), 1938–present
Immaculata, 1950–present
Padres' Trail (*The Franciscan Missions of the Southwest, Traveling the Padres' Trail*), 1913–1984

Franciscan Message, 1947–1974
The Lamp, 1903–1974
Franciscan Herald and Forum, 1940–1986
Franciscan Herald (Messenger of the Holy Childhood Church and School), 1895–1940
Third Order Forum, 1921–1940
St. Anthony Messenger, 1892–present
Communications and the Franciscan Message: Reports of the Fortieth and Forty-First Meeting of the Franciscan Educational Conference, Washington, D.C., 1959.

Radio and Televison Shows

The Rosary Hour
The Padre's Hour
The Ave Maria Hour
The Hour of St. Francis

Personal Communications

Interview, Jeremy Harrington, February 8, 2016
Interview, Daniel Kroger,
Interview, Patrick McCloskey
Email, Jude Lutsyk, December 14, 2015

Books and Dissertations

Alexander, Charles C. *Here the Country Lies: Nationalism and the Arts in Twentieth Century America* (Bloomington: Indiana University Press, 1980).

Allen, Frederick Lewis. *Only Yesterday: An Informal History of the 1920s* (New York: Harper and Row, 1931).

Allitt, Patrick. *Catholic Intellectuals and Conservative Politics in America, 1950–1985* (Ithaca, NY: Cornell University Press, 1993).

Angelica Mother (with Christine Allison). *Mother Angelica's Answers Not Promises* (Simon and Schuster, 1987).

Arroyo, Raymond. *Mother Angelica: The Remarkable Story of a Nun, Her Nerve, and Network of Miracles* (New York: Doubleday, 2005).

Black, Gregory D. *The Catholic Crusade Against Movies, 1940–1975* (Cambridge: Cambridge University Press, 1997).

Burns, Jeffrey M. *Disturbing the Peace: History of the Christian Family Movement, 1949–1974* (South Bend, IL: University of Notre Dame Press, 1999).

Buscino, Thomas. *A Nation Forged in War: How World War II Taught Americans to Get Along* (Knoxville: University of Tennesse Press, 2010).

Cadegan, Uda. *All Good Books Are Catholic Books: Print Culture, Censorship, and Modernity in Twentieth Century America* (Ithaca, NY: Cornell University Press, 2013).

Chinnici, Joseph P. *When Values Collide: The Catholic Church, Sexual Abuse, and the Challenges of Leadership* (Marynoll, NY: Orbis Books, 2010).

Coben, Stanely. *Rebellion Against Victorianism: The Impulse for Cultural Change in 1920s America* (New York: Oxford University Press, 1991).

Cotkin, George. *William James: Public Philosopher* (Urbana, IL: University of Illinois Press, 1989).

———. *Morality's Muddy Waters: Ethical Quandaries in Modern America* (Philadelphia: University of Pennsylvania Press, 2010).

Couvares, Francis G., ed. *Movie Censorship and American Culture* (Washington: Smithsonian Institution Press, 1996).

Cummings, Kathleen Sprows. *New Women of the Old Faith: Gender and American Catholicism in the Progressive Era* (Chapel Hill: University of North Carolina Press, 2009).

Diggins, John Patrick. *Up From Communism* (New York: Columbia University Press, 1975).

Dolan, Jay, P. *The American Catholic Experience: A History from Colonial Times to the Present* (New York: Doubleday, 1985).

Dumenil, Lynn. *The Modern Temper: American Culture and Society in the 1920s* (New York: Hill and Wang, 1995).

Ebel, Jonathan H. *G.I. Messiahs: Soldiering, War, and American Civil Religion* (New Haven, CT: Yale University Press, 2015).

Engelhardt, Tom. *The End of Victory Culture: Cold War America and the Disillusioning of a Generation* (New York: Basic Books, 1995).

Farrell, James J. *The Spirit of the Sixites: Making Postwar Radicalism* (New York: Routledge, 1997).

Fass, Paula. *The Damned and the Beautiful: American Youth in the 1920s* (New York: Oxford University Press, 1977).

Francis, Mother Mary. *A Right to Be Merry* (New York: Sheed and Ward, 1956).

Gunn, T. Jeremy. *Spiritual Weapons: The Cold War and the Forging of an American National Religion* (Westport, CT: Praeger, 2009).

Haberski, Raymond J., Jr. *It's Only a Movie: Films and Critics in American Culture* (Lexington, KY: University Press of Kentucky, 2001).

———. *Freedom to Offend: How New York Remade Movie Culture* (Lexington, KY: University Press of Kentucky, 2007).

———. *God and War: American Civil Religion Since 1945* (New Brunswick: Rutgers University Press, 2012).

Hajkowski, Stanislaw. "The Cultural Transition and the Attitudes of Polish Immigrant Families Towards Divorce and Parental Authority in the United States, 1931–1940" (Ph.D. Dissertation, The Catholic University of America, 2010).

Halsey, William M. *The Survival of American Innocence: Catholicism in an Era of Disillusionment, 1920–1940* (South Bend, IN: University of Notre Dame Press, 1980).

Hartman, Andrew. *A War for the Soul of America: A History of the Culture Wars* (Chicago: University of Chicago Press, 2015).

Henold, Mary J. *Catholic and Feminist: The Surprising History of the American Catholic Feminist Movement* (Chapel Hill: University of North Carolina Press, 2008).

Hunter, James Davison. *Culture Wars: The Struggle to Control the Family, Art, Education, Law, and Politics in America* (New York: Basic Book, 1992).

Inglis, Fred. *The Cruel Peace: Everyday Life in the Cold War* (New York: Basic Books, 1991).

Jewett, Andrew. *Science, Democracy, and the American University: From the Civil War to the Cold War* (Cambridge: Cambridge University Press, 2014).

Kenny, Michael. *No God Next Door: Red Rule in Mexico and Our Responsibility* (New York: William J. Hirten, Co., 1935).

Lofton, Kathryn. *Oprah: The Gospel of an Icon* (Berkeley: University of California Press, 2011).

Massa, Mark. *Catholics and American Cutlure: Fulton Sheen, Dorothy Day, and the Notre Dame Football Team* (New York: Crossroad Publishing, 1999).

Massaro, Thomas J. and Thomas A. Shannon. *Catholic Perspectives on Peace and War* (Oxford: Sheed and Ward, 2003).

Meyer, Fulgence. *Youth's Pathfinder: Heart to Heart Chats with Catholic Young Men and Women* (Cincinnati, OH: St. Francis Book Shop, 1927).

McCarraher, Eugene. *Christian Critics: Religion and the Impasse in Modern American Social Thought* (Ithaca, NY: Cornell University Press, 2000).

McGreevy, John T. *Catholicism and American Freedom: A History* (New York: Norton, 2003).

McLaughlin, Mary L. *A Study of the National Catholic Office of Motion Pictures* (Ph.D. diss., Communication Arts, University of Wisconsin–Madison, 1974).

Miller, Stephen P. *The Age of Evangelicalism: America's Born-Again Years* (New York: Oxford University Press, 2014).

Orsi, Robert, A. *Thank You, St. Jude: Women's Devotion to the Patron Saint of Hopeless Causes* (New Haven, CT: Yale University Press, 1996).

O'Toole, James, M., ed. *Habits of Devotion: Religious Practice in Twentieth Century America* (Ithaca, NY: Cornell University Press, 2004).

Rodgers, Daniel T., *Atlantic Crossings: Social Politics in the Progressive Age* (Cambridge: Harvard University Press, 1998)

———. *The Age of Fracture* (Boston: Belknap Press of Harvard University Press, 2011).

Rohr, Richard. *Near Occasions of Grace* (New York: Orbis, 1993).

———. *Eager to Love: The Alternative Way of Francis of Assisi* (Cincinnati: Franciscan Media, 2014).

Roohan, James E. *American Catholics and the Social Question, 1865–1900* (New York: Arno Press, 1976).

Schrecker, Ellen. *Many Are the Crimes: McCarthyism in America* (New York: Little, Brown & Company, 1998).

Sehat, David. *The Myth of American Religious Freedom* Updated Edition (New York: Oxford University Press, 2015).

Stevens, Jason, W. *God-Fearing and Free: A Spiritual History of America's Cold War* (Cambridge: Harvard University Press, 2010).

Sudlow, Brian. *Catholic Literature and Secularism in France and England, 1800–1914* (Manchester: Manchester University Press, 2011).

Sullivan, Rebecca. *Visual Habits: Nuns, Feminism, and American Postwar Popular Culture* (Toronto: University of Toronto Press, 2005).

Sutton, Matthew Avery. *Aimee Semple McPherson and the Resurrection of Christian America* (Cambridge: Harvard University Press, 2009).

Vecsey, Christopher. *On the Padre's Trail* (Notre Dame, IN: University of Notre Dame Press, 1996).

Walsh, Frank. *Sin and Censorship: The Catholic Church and the Motion Picture Industry* (New Haven, CT: Yale University Press, 1996).

White, Joseph M. *"Peace and Good" in America: A History of the Holy Name Province Order of Franciscan Minors, 1850s to the Present* (New York: Holy Name Province, 2004).

Wittern-Keller, Laura and Raymond J. Haberski, Jr. *The Miracle Case: Film Censorship and the Supreme Court* (Lawrence KS: University Press of Kansas, 2008)

Wuthnow, Robert. *The Restructuring of American Religion: Society and Faith Since World War II* (Princeton: Princeton University Press, 1988)

Articles and Essays

Burns, Jeffrey, M. "Catholic Laywomen in the Culture of American Catholicism in the 1950s," *US Catholic Historian* 5, nos. 3&4 (Summer/Fall 1986), 385–400.

———. "John O'Connor and the 'New Age' of Catholic Journalism, 1960-1967," *US Catholic Historian* 25 (Summer 2007), 109–26.

Chinnici, Joseph P. "Virgil Michel and the Tradition of the Affective Prayer," *Worship* 62 (May 1988), 225–236.

———. "An Historian's Creed and the Emergence of the Postconciliar Culture Wars," *The Catholic Historical Review* 94, no. 2 (April 2008), 219–44.

Ciepley, David. "The Thirties to the Fifties: Totalitarianism and the Second American Enlightenment," in Charles Matthews and Christopher McKnight Nichols, eds. *Prophecies of Godlessness: Predictions of America's Imminent Secularization from the Puritans to the Present Day* (New York: Oxford University Press, 2008).

Ellis, John Tracy. "American Catholics and the Intellectual Life," *Thought* 30 (1955), 351–88.

Enochs, Ross. "The Franciscan Mission to the Navajos: Mission Method and Indigenous Religion, 1898–1940," *The Catholic Historical Review*, 92, no. 1 (January 2006), 46–73.

Fore, William F. "The Unknown History of Televangelism," *Media Development* 54, no. 1 (2007), 45–48.

Goff, Philip K. "'We Have Heard the Joyful Sound': Charles E. Fuller's Radio Broadcast and the Rise of Modern Evangelicalism," *Religion and American Culture: A Journal of Interpretation* 9 (Winter 1999), 67–96.

Hoover, Stewart M. "The Religious Television Audience: A Matter of Significance, or Size?" *Review of Religious Research* 29, no. 2 (December 1987), 135–151.

———. "The Culturalist Turn in Scholarship on Media and Relgion," *Journal of Media and Religion*, 1, no. 1 (2002), 25–36.

Hogue, Kellie Jean. "A Saint of Their Own: Native Petitions Supporting the Canonization of Kateri Tekakwitha, 1884–1885," *US Catholic Historian*, 32 (Summer 2014), 25–44.

Hurley, Daniel. "St. Anthony Messenger: 100 Years of Good News," *St. Anthony Messenger*, 100 (June 1992), 10–18.

Murray, John Courtney. "Literature and Censorship," *Books on Trial*, (June-July 1956), 665–77.

Osborne, Catherine R. "From Sputnik to Spaceship Earth: American Catholics and the Space Age," *Religion and American Culture: A Journal of Interpretation* 25 (Summer 2015), 218–263.

Orsi, Robert, A. "US Catholics Between Memory and Modernity: How Catholics Are American," in R. Scott Appleby and Kathleen Sprows Cummings, eds. *Catholics and the American Century: Recasting Narratives of US History* (Ithaca, NY: Cornell University Press, 2012), 11–42.

Piper, Andrew L. "Loyalty Lost: Catholics, Liberals, and the Culture Wars," *Journal of Media and Religion* 12 (2013), 144–164.

Poche, Justin D. "Catholic Like Me: The Conversions of John Howard Griffin," *US Catholic Historian*, 32 (Spring 2014), 117–42.

Schneider, Mary L. "American Sisters and the Roots of Change: The 1950s," *US Catholic Historian* 7 (Winter 1988), 55–72.

Sibley, Bryce Andrew. "The Fr. Richard Rohr Phenomenon," *New Oxford Review* 73, no. 3 (March 2006), 21–28.

Stamm, Michael. "Broadcasting Mainline Protestantism: The Chicago Sunday Evening Club and the Evolution of Audience Expectations from Radio to Television," *Religion and American Culture: A Journal of Interpretation* 22, no. 2 (Summer 2002), 233–64.

Tentler, Leslie Woodcock. "Souls and Bodies: The Birth Control Controversy and the Collapse of Confession," in Michael J. Lacy and Francis Oakley, eds., *Crisis of Authority in Catholic Modernity* (New York: Oxford University Press, 2011), 295–315.

Winsboro, Irvin D.S. and Michael Epple. "Religion, Culture, and the Cold War: Bishop Fulton J. Sheen and America's Anti-Communist Crusade in the 1950s," *The Historian* 71, no. 2 (Summer 2009), 209–233.

Wuthnow, Robert. "The Social Significance of Religious Television," *Review of Religious Research* 29, no. 2 (December 1987), 125–134.

Websites

Bishop Accountability (Documenting the Abuse Crisis in the Roman Catholic Church) http://www.bishop-accountability.org

The Cord Index: http://cord.sbu.edu

Franciscan Media (formerly St. Anthony Messenger Press and Franciscan Communications) http://info.franciscanmedia.org

Holy Name Province: https://hnp.org

The Hour of St. Francis (radio): https://www.oldtimeradiodownloads.com/drama/the-hour-of-saint-francis

Mission of the Immaculata: http://missionimmaculata.com

Mother Angelica Programs: https://www.youtube.com/channel/UCGuE-HIL1uGoq5b3kJw6DoGw

National Fraternity of the Secular Franciscan Order, USA: http://www.nafraformation.org

Richard Rohr and the Center for Action and Contemplation: https://cac.org/richard-rohr/richard-rohr-ofm/

The Rosary Hour Talks (in English): http://www.rosaryhour.com/program_talks.html

Index